Sport, Identity and Ethnicity

Ethnic Identities Series

ISSN: 1354-3628

General Editors:
Shirley Ardener, *Director, Centre for Cross-Cultural Research on Women, University of Oxford*

Tamara Dragadze, *School of Slavonic and East European Studies, University of London*

Jonathan Webber, *Institute of Social and Cultural Anthropology, University of Oxford*

Book previously published in the Series

Sharon Macdonald (ed.), *Inside European Identities: Ethnography in Western Europe*

Joanne Eicher (ed.), *Dress and Ethnicity*

Sport, Identity and Ethnicity

Edited by
Jeremy MacClancy

First published in 1996 by
Berg
Editorial offices:
150 Cowley Road, Oxford, OX4 1JJ, UK
13950 Park Center Road, Herndon, VA 22071, USA

Berg is the imprint of Oxford International Publishers Ltd.

Library of Congress Cataloging-in-Publication Data

A catalogue record for this book is available from the Library of Congress.

QV
706
.5
S665

British Library Cataloguing-in-Publication Data

A catalogue record for this book is available from the British Library.

ISBN 1 85973 140 6 (Cloth)
       1 85973 145 7 (Paper)

Printed in the United Kingdom by WBC Book Manufacturers,
Mid-Glamorgan.

Contents

Preface

This volume brings together some recent ethnographic studies of sport and identity. My original reason for deciding to collate a book on the topic was my growing realization, while doing fieldwork on contested, modern notions of identity in the Basqueland, that it had been neglected. The Basques I was living among were busy revitalizing traditional sports, adapting imported ones, and inventing others, such as races of large, multi-man go-karts down steep urban hills. To my neighbours and friends, these games were an important, invigorating way of expressing their ethnic identity. If I wished to study whom the locals thought they were I had to learn about these sports and what exactly they meant to them. Yet I found, to my surprise, that few other anthropologists had written on the theme.

Once back at the Institute of Social Anthropology, Oxford University, I mentioned the idea of running a seminar series on 'Sport, Identity and Ethnicity' to Shirley Ardener. She agreed enthusiastically and the series was made part of the 'Identity and Ethnicity' seminar which she, Jonathan Webber and Tamara Dragadze have been running at the Institute for several years. The seminars were particularly well attended and were even discussed in the sports pages of *The Times*. More people offered to give papers than could be accommodated. As guest convenor of the seminar series and as editor of this book I was forced to be selective. Yet I would like to thank all those who offered to speak for whom we could not find space, and those who did speak but whose papers we have not been able to include.

I am grateful, above all, to Shirley Ardener for her constant support throughout this project, especially during the final stages of producing this volume. I also wish to extend my thanks to our seminar audience and all the contributors to this book. Bob McIntyre 'page-made' the text with exemplary efficiency. Kathyrn Earle and Sara Everett of Berg Publishers ensured I never overshot their deadlines by too great a margin. But if readers do manage to find any errors, inaccuracies or significant omissions, they should not blame any of the above, rather

Jeremy MacClancy
Oxford Brookes University

Notes on Contributors

Jeremy MacClancy is a senior lecturer in social anthropology at Oxford Brookes University. He has done major fieldwork in island Melanesia and northern Spain (supported by an ESRC fellowship). He is the author of *To Kill a Bird with Two Stones. A history of Vanuatu*, Vila 1980, and *Consuming Culture*, Chapmans 1992. His forthcoming books include *Popularizing Anthropology*, co-edited with Christian McDonaugh, Routledge 1996, and *The Decline of Carlism: Anthropology and History in Northern Spain, 1939-1989.*

Peter Parkes teaches social anthropology at the University of Kent at Canterbury. He has previously taught at the Universities of Heidelberg, Belfast and London. He has carried out extended fieldwork in northern Pakistan since the early 1970s. He has published widely on the ethnography of the area, about which he made an award-winning programme, *Kalasha Rites of Spring*, for Granada Television. His forthcoming book is *Kalasha Society*, Oxford University Press.

Lidia D. Sciama has lectured on Italian literature at Cambridgeshire College of Arts and Teaching and has been a visiting lecturer in social anthropology and comparative literature at Mount Holyoke College. She has carried out major fieldwork on the Venetian island of Burano. She has published articles in *Women and Space*, *The Yearbook of Agricultural Cooperation for 1981-1982*, *The Incorporated Wife*, *Dress and Gender*, and *International Journal of Moral and Social Studies*.

Martin Stokes is a lecturer of social anthropology and ethnomusicology at Queen's University, Belfast. He is the author of *The Arabesk Debate: music and musicians in modern Turkey*, Oxford University Press 1992, and editor of *Ethnicity, Identity and Sport*, Berg 1994.

Ossie Stuart is a research fellow at the Social Policy Research Unit, University of York. He has carried out major fieldwork in African on African soccer and in Britain on Afro-Caribbean cricket. He has worked as a consultant on sport for the BBC World Service. He has published extensively in academic sports journals, as well as contributing chapters to *Disabling Barriers, Enabling Environments, Reflections. Views of Black Disabled People on their lives and community care*, and *Ethnicity, Culture and Politics*, edited by T.O.Ranger.

Pnina Werbner is a senior lecturer in social anthropology at Keele University and Research Administrator of the International Centre for Contemporary Cultural Research at the Universities of Manchester and Keele. Her publications include *The Migration Process: Capital, Gifts and Offerings among British Pakistanis*, Berg 1990, *Black and Ethnic Leaderships in Britain: The Cultural Dimensions of Political Action*, co-edited with Muhammad Anwar, Routledge 1991, and *Economy and Culture in Pakistan: Migrants and Cities in a Muslim Society*, co-edited with Hastings Donnan. Her forthcoming book, *Diaspora and Millennium: Islam, Identity, Politics and the Aesthetics of the Religious Imagination* is on the poetics and politics of identity among British Pakistanis. She is currently the director of a major research project funded by the ESRC on 'South Asian Popular Culture: Gender, Generation and Identity'.

1

Sport, Identity and Ethnicity

Jeremy MacClancy

Until fairly recently most sociologists, and social historians and many anthropologists have neglected sport as a potentially fruitful object of study. According to the feminist sociologist of sport, Jennifer Hargreaves (1994: 6), this neglect was partly due to the fact that mainstream ideas about sports are concerned with the physical body, which was viewed as 'natural' and 'unchangeable'; hence it was thought there was nothing deserving of analysis. A further reason for this neglect was the influence of the popular belief that sports have 'a life of their own', one essentially separate from 'important' aspects of the social world such as work, politics, and economics. On this lay view, sports are intrinsically innocent and liberating; enjoyable to pursue but not profitable to study.

Given the continuing prevalence of these prejudices against the academic investigation of sport as an integral part of social and cultural life, it is necessary to justify the printing of this collection. In the first place, it is easy to point out that those who regard sport as merely an entertaining adjunct to the 'real business' of modern collective life – the fate of post-industrial economies, political strife, the state of public morals – ignore the daily evidence of their newspapers and television screens. For organized sport is not just an extremely popular pursuit involving many millions of people everyday (sometimes simultaneously, such as live transmission of Olympic events), it is now both very big business and a major arena for the disputes of politicians, and has long been considered a vehicle of ethics, whether of moral decay or promotion.

The economic importance, in our world, of sport is simply too patent to avoid; it is an integral part of the third largest industry on the globe (leisure and tourism is only outranked on the monetary scales by oil and cars). Leaders of countries vie with one another for the highly profitable privilege of staging the Olympics in their nation-state. The machinations of football-club owning entrepreneurs warrant front-page headlines in even the quality press.

Patent : obvious

These days most of those who argue that 'politics should be kept out of sport' realize that the argument has already been lost; President Nixon used table tennis as a key diplomatic ploy in his opening negotiations with the Chinese Government. The visit of a British cricket team captained by Mike Gatting led to such large, and sometimes violent, demonstrations that the tour had to be cancelled. Two Central American countries very nearly went to war over one soccer match while a pair of African states actually did get to the stage of armed hostilities because of a game between their respective national teams. Try imagining what the Olympics would be like without any political posturing by blocs of countries or by individuals (e.g. the 'Black Power' salute made by two African-Americans on receiving their medals in 1968). It would be a very different event from the one which we are now used to.

Examples of sport as moral activity are legion and easy to list. Sylvester Stallone's *Rocky III*, in which the American protagonist beat his Soviet opposite number, was meant to be seen as the 'good' boxing his way to triumph over the 'evil'. English public schoolboys used to be told that a good teamsman displayed the right kind of character, especially for positions of responsibility in the colonial service (Kirk-Greene 1989). Similarly it was believed that those colonized subjects who learnt how to 'play up, play up, and play the game' were well on the way to becoming the sort of persons upon whom expatriate whites might be able to rely.

My catalogue of examples could continue but I hope the point is already sufficiently well made. For social scientists, the study of sport is not some tangential topic, to be pursued occasionally as an intellectual form of light relief from 'the real stuff' of economics, politics, and public morality. Sport is a central activity in our societies, one embodying social values, and, as such, as deserving of systematic investigation as any other. Sport might be fun. That does not mean it should be disregarded by academics.

Sport and Identity

Sports, as the imperialist example mentioned above suggests, help to define moral and political community. They are vehicles of identity, providing people with a sense of difference and a way of classifying themselves and others, whether latitudinally or hierarchically. The most extreme example here is those adult football fans who so identify with 'their' team that they name their children after all the leading eleven players of its pack. (For an early example of the role of football in British

village life, see Frankenberg 1990 (1957).) Less dramatic examples
include those members of the middle classes who join expensive golf
and tennis clubs for what they term 'social reasons', i.e. they pay their
annual subscription fees not so much out of a love of the particular sport
but because they wish to spend part of their leisure time with people they
consider their peers – perhaps in pursuit of their own Joan Hunter Donnes
– and because they wish to be known and seen as members of a certain
peer group. (On the role of sports in the delineation of class barriers in
Britain, see Lowerson 1993.) A more classical anthropological example
might come from Afghanistan where, in the traditional game of *buzkashi*,
tens of men on horseback compete for the possession of a calf carcass
(Azoy 1982). *Buzkashi*, which commemorates the past equestrian culture
of the area (on which the most glorious periods of Afghan history are
based), provides the most dramatic sanctioned opportunity for the
expression of the local version of masculine values: courage; strength;
and dominance. It also serves as a metaphor for otherwise
unacknowledged aspects of experience, for the chaotic, uninhibited and
uncontrollable competition which 'lurks below the apparently co-
operative surface'. As an Afghan diplomat told Azoy, 'If you wish to
understand this country, go to a *buzkashi*.'

Sport may not be just a marker of one's already established social
identity but a means by which to create a new social identity for oneself
as well. In the industrialized-urban societies that emerged in Britain
during the last century, spectatorship at team sports become an important
means for the male offspring of rural emigrants from different areas to
forge a communal identity. Once firmly established, these sporting clubs
provided their members with an inter-generational, sub-cultural marker
of identity (Goldhurst 1987: ix). For the same formal reasons of creating
a new social identity for themselves, some upwardly mobile British
people have their children attend pony lessons and maybe even learn to
ride to hounds themselves; some urban-dwelling Basque nationalists,
as a way of demonstrating their commitment to the cause, learn marked
'traditional' rural sports such as competitive stone-lifting, stone-carrying,
and wood-chopping; in the Melanesian islands of Vanuatu, youths may
take pride in the fact that the football teams they assemble create new
forms of association which cut across traditional divides.

These sport-based identities are not necessarily exclusive (the Gaelic
Athletic Association is an obvious exception), for people may have
multiple identities either simultaneously, seasonally or consecutively. A
man, for instance, may enjoy in different contexts the identity that comes
from being a fly-half in a rugby club, a committed follower of a football

team, a member of the second string in a cross-country running team, and a noted dartsplayer in his local pub. Schoolboys may find their position in the informal ranking of their classmates changing over the months as the scholastic sports calendar makes its annual progress from football or rugby to hockey to cricket. Members of the British social elites may mark their year in terms of sporting events – Epsom Derby, Royal Ascot, Wimbledon, Henley Regatta, the 'Glorious Twelfth', Cowes Regatta, and the annual winter ball of the local hunt. A woman may chose to be a sprinter as an adolescent, take up golf in early middle-age, and then turn to bowls as her strength declines. The creative possibilities by which people, via different sports, can play with their identity is only limited by the number of sports available to them at any one time within their lived space. In other words, sports are ways of fabricating in a potentially complex manner a space for oneself in their social world.

In this sense, what is important about a particular sport is not so much its content, but the category supplied by its creation. This taxonomic function of sport should not be understood in some static, structuralist manner as though people differentiated themselves according to the rigidities of a culturally constructed template located somewhere deep in the unconscious. Sport does not merely 'reveal' underlying social values, it is a major mode of their expression. Sport is not a 'reflection' of some postulated essence of society, but an integral part of society and one, moreover, which may be used as a means of *reflecting on* society. Turkish wrestling, as Stokes' chapter in this volume shows, is systematically used in the construction of 'a moral education of almost chivalric notions of contest and display'. Yet, as he observes, wrestling may at the same time serve as 'a repository of subversive knowledges, as a recognition that all is not what it seems, that strength is not moral purity, that deceit and guile are necessary parts of social life, that one frequently has to cope with losing face, that compromise is sometimes better than contest'. In the movement between these two poles, a bout of wrestling may become a way for Turks to explore their own cultural construction of male relationships and to expose 'the deceits and inconsistencies of a pervasive masculinist ideology'. On this reading, Turkish wrestling becomes something good to think with.

Any particular sport is not intrinsically associated with a particular set of meanings or social values. What it is meant to represent is not laid down like some commandment etched in stone. Rather, a sport is an embodied practice in which meanings are generated, and whose representation and interpretation are open to negotiation and contest. A performance of *capoeira*, the African-American martial art, may be viewed by a naive audience as primarily a spectacular form of sport because of the pair of players' impressive acrobatic movements and because of the ever-present potential for violence. But to aficionados it would be seen as a skilful weaving of body, musical, and verbal play and would be judged in those terms (Lewis 1992: 214). When Liverpool comes top of the league at the end of the football season, Southerners may see the event as simply one of the best team winning the competition but Liverpudlians can interpret it as yet further evidence of the unity and solidarity expressed in an assertively masculinist mode for which their city-home is famed. Until fairly recently, certain Liverpudlians would also have seen the victory in religious terms: as, indirectly, the triumph of a Catholic club over their local Protestant rivals, Everton (Cohen 1994: 119–120).

Sports and sporting events cannot be comprehended without reference to relations of power: who attempts to control how a sport is to be organized and played, and by whom; how it is to be represented; how it is to be interpreted. Among the ancient Aztecs, for instance, it was the nobility and warrior classes who developed a particularly elaborate, highly-regulated, and competitive version of the ballgame played throughout much of Mesoamerica. These Aztec elites used their variant of the game as a major means of resolving conflict within and between polities. For a period, local rulers had ritual human sacrifice performed during the game, partly to reaffirm publicly their power, partly to demonstrate the deadly prerogatives of their status (Scarborough and Wilcox 1991). To turn to Afghanistan once again, the staging of a *buzkashi* has to be sponsored, usually by a local leader. If the game turns out well, he enhances his regional reputation over that of his political competitors. At least up until the Soviet invasion, the supreme leaders of the country – the government – sponsored their own form of the game, *qarajai*. As though to demonstrate the government's degree of authority and control, *qarajai* is a much more formalized version of the sport, with authorized umpires, well-defined boundaries, and players grouped into teams. Unlike the original, wilder type of *buzkashi*, which often ends in disputes over who exactly has won, the rule-governed nature of *qarajai* ensures there is rarely doubt over who the victors are. In this way, the government demonstrates its command: by gathering together the best horsemen and having them play a controlled, memorable game which redounds to its credit (Azoy 1982).

Parkes (in this volume) demonstrates the play of comparable political processes in the development of Pakistani polo: the formalization and appropriation of a traditionally localized game by a national elite for their own self-aggrandizing purposes. One key difference, however, between *buzkashi* and polo is the transformation of the latter because of the interest sport-hungry British officers took in the game. These colonials, protagonists in an imperial world system, took the sport home, where they laid down an extended set of rules; polo-playing elite Pakistanis then imposed this 'civilized' version on the indigenous game. The latest stage in this evolutionary process is the creation of a post-modern variant, the annual Shandur Tournament. The premier tourist attraction of Pakistan, its performance is simultaneously graced by the presence of the country's highest officials and watched – thanks to satellite television – by villagers in the remotest areas of the Himalayan foothills. A second key difference was the nature of support for the players. In *buzkashi* there is no necessary link, of kinship or alliance, between the players and the audience. In the feudal principalities of northern Pakistan, which existed until the early 1970s, however, polo players, though members of a knightly nobility, were interrelated by ties of foster allegiance with the pedestrian population of their districts. Thus the competitive performance of polo by the powerful played out wider coalitions, transcending estate and locality, enabling the lowliest spectator to identify with the sporting fortunes of 'his prince' and quasi-kin. As Parkes points out, the perpetual internecine struggles between princes for rulership of these petty states meant that 'the coalitional identification of spectators and players on the polo-ground signified far more than mystified fanship, for these factions were ever ready to erupt in violent support of their princely pretenders to the throne'.

The most extreme example of coalitional identification through sport, however, occurred in the Eastern wing of the later Roman Empire. Horsemen in the chariot races were grouped into either the 'blues' or the 'greens'. As Gibbon described, in a famous passage on this troubled period, these sporting sides developed into strong and irreconcilable factions, support for which sharply divided families and friends. The two factions grew so powerful that any candidate for public office had to seek actively the support of either one. Justinian, Eastern emperor from 527 to 565, patronized the 'blues' and chose to overlook the disorder they created. 'Insolent with royal favour, the "blues" affected to strike terror by Hun-like long hair, close sleeves and ample garments, a lofty step and a sonorous voice' (Gibbon 1966: 308). At night in Constantinople they assembled as armed bands, dedicated to the violent assault and rape of 'greens' and innocent persons. Those prefects, counts and governors who dared to punish their crimes were their especial targets. In 532 at the festival of the ides of January, thousands of 'greens' disturbed the

Internecine: mutually destructive.

beginning of the races by appealing to Justinian for justice. Failing to win him over, they rioted. Street-battles between factional mobs left much of the city in flames or ruins. They were only stopped when war-hardened troops of Justinian slew 30,000 'greens'. Their leaders were executed, their palaces razed, and their fortunes confiscated. The hippodrome was closed for several years. On its reopening, the disorders revived. They continued to afflict the Eastern Empire throughout Justinian's reign (Gibbon 1966: 309–13).

Proponents of different sports commonly try to boost their popularity by lauding them as instruments of social harmony, as means of self-expression, or as vehicles for satisfying both individual and collective needs. But these promoters of organized forms of the physically active life are frequently forced to acknowledge that sports may also give rise to conflict. As Sciama (in this volume) shows in her study of the evolution of the Venetian regatta, early forms of this annual event were intended by the legislators of the city to be celebrations of community and to augment amity among all its members. But by the fourteenth century, the authorities chose to suppress the regatta, because it encouraged fierce competition between different quarters of the city. Instead of fomenting peace among the potentially turbulent populace, it kept alive division. Today, in many Western countries, certain sub-groups may reject organized sports simply because they are too strongly associated with the workethic. For instance, in north London today, 'membership of street-gangs is almost incompatible with the acquiescence to authority that representing school teams implies' (Fleming 1991: 51). They reject the sense of control organized sport represents.

A new sport may be introduced into a particular culture for the sake of increasing social consonance but the actual results may be quite different, the novel form of entertainment merely providing a new arena in which old rivalries may be expressed. The advent of baseball among the Pueblo Indians of Cochiti, New Mexico, led to the aligning of opposed families in two different teams and fights between mothers of players on opposing sides. In order to restore peace, the village council decided to prohibit the game (Fox 1961).

Sports, in sum, may be used to fulfil a plethora of functions: to define more sharply the already established boundaries of moral and political communities; to assist in the creation of new social identities; to give physical expression to certain social values and to act as a means of reflecting on those values; to serve as potentially contested space by opposed groups. As the chapters in this book demonstrate, sports are vehicles and embodiments of meaning, whose status and interpretation

plethora : superabundance

is continually open to negotiation and subject to conflict.

In this context I do not feel any need to enter into or to discuss the debates about the definition of sport versus games and ritual (e.g. Lévi-Strauss 1966; Caillois 1969; Guttmann 1978; Blanchard and Cheska 1985), for the definition itself of sport is part of the social processes which the contributors examine. Taurine aficionados might well be outraged to find a chapter about what they consider to be the 'art' of bullfighting in a book on sport. Spanish opponents of the practice, however, would see that as a form of special pleading to defend an already indefensible activity. Militant anti-anglers (discussed in my chapter on the practice) argue that angling should not be seen as merely a pleasant pastime but as a cruel pursuit on a par with foxhunting and harecoursing. They contend that the definition of this practice should be changed from innocent entertainment to bloodsport. Far from being a quiet activity for gentle weekenders, angling has become an increasingly contested practice whose very identity is now in question. Sciama, in her chapter on the evolution of Venetian regatta, shows how a primarily ritual event has, over the years, developed a strong sporting aspect. Applying a rigid pair of definitions differentiating ritual from sport would be totally inappropriate and positively misleading here.

One thing that *is* clear is that sports need not necessarily contain any competitive element. The example of the Melanesians – introduced to football by missionaries – who would play the game for days until both sides had come to a draw is already well-known. Native Americans would play lacrosse for days at a time, ending the game only when they had achieved a tie. The log races of the Amazonian Xavante are performed in a similar spirit. The logs are carried by two teams, representing the oppositions which they believe constitute the universe. But if one log is much heavier than the other, some carriers of the lighter one transfer to the weighter in order to spread the burden and ensure both reach the finishing post at the same time. The aim of the event is to emphasize that the antitheses of Xavante cosmology need not tear the world apart. 'If one is careful, oppositions can be controlled, they can complement each other and create equilibrium and harmony. And what better symbol of equilibrium than two teams that exert themselves to the utmost and finish in a dead heat?' (Maybury-Lewis 1992: 153).

Sport, Ethnicity and the Nation-state

From its beginning, the term ethnicity has been one concerned with opposition, on the nature of difference between antagonistic groups (Chapman 1993). One of the most common contemporary forms of collective identification, many of its actualizations successfully act as foci for collective sentiment and loyalty, and as remarkably powerful means of mustering large groups of people for particular social ends. Thanks to the unending series of bloody conflicts fought in the name of ethnic sovereignty, reports of which daily fill our newspapers, the word itself has become part of common parlance. The 'rise of the ethnic' has been so pervasive that it feels at times as though every person is meant to 'belong' to some ethnicity, almost every one of which is implicitly supposed to have the right to have or to campaign for its own nation-state, almost on the lines of that old slogan, 'A People, A Nation, A State'.

It is easy to state that, for a certain people, sport has contributed to their sense of ethnicity (or nation) and to their sense of community. But it is important to be exact here, and to ask, whose ethnicity (or nation)? Whose community? And during what time period? (Jarvie and Walker 1994). For instance, within the modern spaces all Westerners inhabit, different fractions within a diasporic ethnic group may express their understanding of 'their' identity in different ways in different contexts. As Pnina Werbner shows (in this volume), among contemporary British Pakistanis, dominant male elders strive to legitimate their leadership of their community by stressing an ascetic variant of Islamic morality. In contrast to their seniors' upholding of a spiritual, self-denying ethic, young British Pakistani men try to empower themselves by drawing at times on their South Asian, non-Islamic roots. Rather than fall in line with the religiously based solemnity of their fathers' generation, they celebrate a culture of fun by, among other activities, playing cricket.

Thanks to the work of Hobsbawm and Ranger (1983), studies of the culture of ethnonationalist movements have tended to concentrate on the 'invention of tradition', as though their ideologues were more concerned with their image of the past than with their vision of the future. In some areas, it is true, the ethnic revival has led to the revitalization of local games (such as lacrosse among native Americans (Vennum 1994) and the celebration of the Highland Games in Scotland (Jarvie 1991b)) and their positive revaluation by ethnic players. But, contrary to many of the studies spawned by Hobsbawm and Ranger's influential work, the leaders of many ethnonationalist movements have in fact stressed simultaneously both the distinctively traditional *and* the distinctively modern aspects

foci : adjust ; Cause to converge ; concentrate

of their culture. In this sense, they have a far less ossified conception of culture than many of their academic commentators give them credit for. In my chapter (in this volume) on the roles of Basque football within the nationalist community, I attempt to demonstrate the part played by Athletic Bilbao, the leading Basque team, in the construction of a nationalist community and the way that its particular style of play (fieriness and long passes) came to be seen as something peculiarly Basque. By lauding both the Basque language (the only remaining non-Indo-European one in the continent) and Basque football, nationalists could proclaim themselves and their fellows to be, at one and the same time, a very ancient people and a very up-to-date one. In this way, their evolving nationalist culture was constituted partly by practices which were deeply rooted and absolutely distinctive, and partly by ones which, while having been transformed into something their very own, were directly comparable with the latest activities of the most developed nations.

A somewhat similar process of 'naturalization' of an imported sport occurred in the Trobriands with the introduction of cricket (as memorably portrayed in Gerry Leach's film *Trobriand Cricket* (Powell 1952; Leach 1975; Weiner 1977)) and in postwar Japan with the arrival there of baseball (Whiting 1977). In Japan players of the game there, whether indigenous or American, have to observe what Whiting calls 'the Samurai Code of Conduct for Baseball' – a generally recognized, though unwritten set of rules derived ultimately from the medieval warrior ethic of *bushido*. The 'Code' stresses such values as unwavering loyalty, extreme self-discipline, great simplicity, discretion, modesty, acceptance of hierarchy, unquestioning obedience, and subjection of oneself for the sake of harmony among the team. The most popular sport in the country, baseball, though imported from the United States, is, as played in Japan, something both internationally recognized and characteristically Japanese.

Sports may be used as a resource by which the powerful attempt to dominate others. The forgers of the Soviet state were well aware of its potential. To them, sport was a tool for socializing the population into the newly established system of values. It could encourage compliance and co-operation in both work and politics, and be used as a way to combat 'unhealthy, deviant, anti-social behaviour' such as drunkenness, delinquency, prostitution, religiosity, and intellectual dissidence. Also, if deployed skilfully, it could unite wider sections of the population than any other social activity, transcending differences of nationality, sex, age, social position, geographical location, and political attitudes. 'It has proved to be of utility by reason of its inherent qualities of being easily understood and enjoyed, being capable of generating mass enthusiasm . . . It has had an advantage over literature, theatre and other forms of cultural expression in being more readily comprehensible to the mass public . . . It has had the advantage over political meetings and parades by being less demanding in intellect and patience' (Riordan 1977: 8, 397–8; 1991). (On the exploitation of sport by the Chinese government see Brownell 1995). Stoddart contends that at the turn of the century, cricket was a major bulwark against social and political change in the English-speaking Caribbean: 'In Barbados and the other colonies, until 1914 at least, the colonial elites established a cultural primacy through cricket as much as through economic power and political position' (1988: 253). The Sandinista government of Nicaragua (Wagner 1988) tried hard to promote sport because its leaders believed that people playing together in self-organized teams in locally created leagues would instill a collective mentality (and also because they believed a fit population would be better able to defend itself). But accepting the thesis that sports may be used strategically by elites in their bid to establish hegemony does not mean that we have at the same time to concur with the stark, and rather simple-minded view that these strategies usually succeed in a blanket fashion. The processes involved are more complex.

Where sport is already a vital part of popular culture and hence harbours the potential of being an integral component of the undercurrents which fuel discord, it becomes for the forces of the state neither easy to penetrate nor to manipulate. While certain regimes may deploy sport as a way to manipulate the masses into conformity with the social order, the dominated may skilfully exploit the organization of these games for their own ends, in their attempt to resist control and to assert their own values. (For a Gramscian analysis of the relations between sport, power and culture in Britain, see Hargreaves 1986). Thus in cases where the state and civil society are in profound conflict, the cultural domain of sport becomes an increasingly politicized terrain, control of which is highly contested. Following this logic, the British state has created for itself a dilemma in its governance of contemporary Northern Ireland (Sugden and Bairner 1993). Though the British state is ideologically committed to and statutorily responsible for the promotion of sport, the fulfilment of that commitment will provide further opportunity for sectarian differentiation. Sport can divide as much as it may unite.

Stuart (in this volume) demonstrates this divisive potential of sport in his analysis of a strike by African footballers against their colonial

bulwark : rampart ; any form of defence

would-be controllers. He argues against those historians of Africa who have seen the introduction of soccer to colonized populations as a diversionary tactic to delay modernization. While the game may have at times exacerbated a certain degree of division among the African urban population of Bulawayo, Southern Rhodesia (now Zimbabwe), it also played a crucial role in the independent, indigenous construction of a modern African urban identity. White settlers had promoted soccer as a way to occupy what they regarded as the indolent young males who had moved into town. But soccer, far from distracting youths from the necessity for political struggle, itself became an arena for political contest between the colonizers and the colonized. By successfully striking against the white controllers of their soccer league, the players established an autonomous space in urban life for themselves and other indigenes, one from which they could build. Instead of hindering progress, the creation and running of football clubs provided black townspeople with a stable focal point within the otherwise rapidly evolving city.

The ability of sport to assist in the creation of a sense of identity also occurs at the level of the nation-state, particularly perhaps for subject countries within imperial regimes and for newly independent states within the developing world eager to transcend traditional ethnic affiliations. Some of the smaller states within the Warsaw Pact, such as Hungary and Czechoslovakia, sometimes had to turn to the exploitation of sport as the only viable means of asserting a degree of national independence from the USSR. As Sugden and Bairner (1993: 126) observe, the superpower strategy of associating sports success with national pride has benefited, in a rather unexpected manner, those developing states (such as Cuba, Kenya, and Ethiopia) who find it far cheaper to procure athletic prowess than military might, economic development, or scientific eminence. Just because they cannot afford a large standing army does not mean that their man or woman will not be the first past the post.

The almost super-nationalistic competitive nature of sport is, of course, best exemplified by the Olympic Games, an institution without parallel in kind or scope in this century; it has more member-countries than the United Nations and wins a television audience of almost half the world's population (MacAloon 1981). Originally conceived of by its turn-of-the-century reviver, the Baron Pierre de Coubertin, as a world-wide athletic festival, the Olympics have since been transformed into a deeply politicized arena where states vie with one another through the medium of sport. Hitler tried to exploit it as a showpiece setting to demonstrate Aryan supremacy. The superpowers treated it as yet another stage for their Cold War conflict, competing for the premier position on the tally of medals or simply refusing to attend when the Games are hosted by their rival. Blocs of developing nations take advantage of its importance to press one or other of their own claims. Most notoriously of all perhaps, Palestinian gunmen used this extremely publicized setting as the site for one of their attacks on the Israeli state.

Any account, with pretensions to roundness, of the relations between sport, identity, ethnicity, and the nation-state, would have to discuss the role of the media and it is our regret that we were unable to include a chapter focusing on this aspect within this collection. For in the modern world much of the importance of sport as a social phenomenon comes from its broadcasting on the radio or television. Indeed the current level of popularity and of participation rates of certain sports (such as snooker and wrestling in Britain) is today almost entirely due to their repeated exposure on television. Sports might be spectacles but spectators are now massively outnumbered by their listening and viewing public. Many sports only exist in their present form thanks to the media companies which help to fund their performance. For instance, the rules of American football have been changed to suit the pattern of television scheduling. Without the benefits, both direct and indirect, of radio or television, football, baseball or basketball clubs could not pay the prices they do for players, national teams would be of much less significance, and the Olympics would be a much, much smaller event. Barnett (1990: 131) argues that one effect of the American television networks' broadcasting of the Olympics was, almost single-handedly, the transformation of the Games from an idealistic celebrations of athletics into its present state as 'an orgy of telegenic profiteering'.

Sports are so attractive to television companies and networks because they are a cheaper way of filling airtime than specially made programmes. The resulting high level of exposure of sports on television plus the concomitant professionalization of many sports has led to the increasing annexation of these activities by the leisure and entertainment industries. One consequence of this has been the conversion of many high level spectator sports from primarily local communal resources into a form of commercialized recreation (Goldhurst 1987). This transformation of the breadth and nature of the sports-viewing public, who may now watch a plethora of foreign games relayed direct by satellite, has its own effects on popular nationalism and national stereotypes. Sports journalists and commentators present the style of the German or the Brazilian football teams as 'evidence' of their respective national character. Wimbledon is promoted as 'proof' of the historical continuities of British life (Arbena

1988: 3; Blain, Boyle and O'Donnell 1993). As I learnt, while doing fieldwork in a northern Spanish village, the broadcasted and illegal, activities of English football fans abroad come easily to be regarded as a telling commentary on the contemporary state of the nation. And when some fans turned up in the provincial capital for a European Cup qualifier, the public theatrical antics of the more drunken among them provided local journalists with an easy symbol for the decline of British society.

At the same time, this televisual globalization of local practices has added a further dimension to the multiple identities individuals can create for themselves; I may play croquet, attend the games of my local football team, and learn to become an aficionado of sumo in Japan by watching assiduously the fights on late-night shows. While the invention of new technologies has given some people the opportunity to make their own 'programmes', in many countries the media are still strictly controlled by the government. (The recent banning of satellite dishes by the Iranian authorities is simply the most stark example of this form of censorship.) In these situations, exactly which games are broadcast, when, where, and how is a question of political disposition, and one which deserves further investigation.

Gender and Identity

Sports may also be used to underline or contest the current gender divisions of a particular culture (Guttmann 1991). The sorts of questions relevant here are: why do women participate in particular sports? Why don't they participate in certain other ones? How do they construct and transform them? What meanings and values do different sports hold for them? What is the counter-hegemonic significance that some women may attach to certain sports? What visions may women have about alternatives (Hargreaves 1994: 12)?

Sports feminists may reveal some of the more unexpected ways in which sports are already constructed in order to benefit men. For instance, men run the marathon faster than women. But if its length is doubled it is women, thanks to their greater reserves of fat, who come in first. Males might shine at tasks which require relatively short bursts of high energy but women, it seems, are naturally better endurance athletes than men. The only Briton to have swum the English Channel three times without stopping is a woman. At one stage women held the 24-hour cycling endurance record and the best performance for the Three

Peaks race of Ben Nevis, Scafell Pike and Snowdon. They are also more likely than men to finish the London Marathon.

Sports feminists may also demonstrate the ways by which the mass media trivialize, marginalize and sexualize women's sports. A male runner may be 'a powerhouse athlete who looks as though he could give piggy-backs to elephants', but his female team-mate may well be described as a 'national treasure who in the flesh is far slighter and prettier than on camera and her legs are a knockout.' A trio of sports academics at Nottingham University found that 58% of published photographs of women athletes were passive and taken after the event, emphasizing sexuality and emotions, while 76% of pictures of men were action shots. Sportsmen were referred to as men, sportswomen as girls, more attention being drawn to their personality, sexuality and attractiveness (Dobson 1995).

Sports, as embodied practices, are one of the arenas within which the social struggle for control of the physical body occurs. This is a conflict over what constitutes the differences and similarities between male and female bodies, the nature of their physique, what they are capable of, and what, or in what ways, they should be allowed to exercise. By the turn of the century in England, the campaign for the improvement of female education had led to a significantly increased degree of participation by women (predominantly middle-class ones) in a few particular sports, such as hockey and tennis. The majority of other physically energetic activities were regarded as totally inappropriate for these 'vulnerable' and 'emotional' creatures. Those women who tried to form cricket or football teams were scoffed at while fathers refused to allow their daughters to appear scantily clad in athletic events or swimming competitions. Cycling became popular but the sight of speeding women controlling their own mobility was too much for some of their contemporaries who wrote sharply critical comments on the practice to the press. Thus, for members of the suppressed gender, hockey and tennis were the only socially acceptable ways of challenging the existing social mores. They were a rare means by which women of that time could be physically active, strive for excellence, and compete openly (McCrone 1988; Holt 1989).

In my chapter on female bull-fighting I argue that previous anthropological accounts of the practice have misrepresented its nature because their authors appear to have listened only to male aficionados about what constitutes a 'proper' bullfight. Accepting all too readily the locally dominant view, they have either ignored the long history of female bullfighters or treated it dismissively as a chronicle of substandard comic performers. In fact, on the evidence available, it seems that even more women would have entered the ring than actually did if they had not been so frequently banned from doing so by the authorities, who were concerned to maintain a dominant drawing of the line between the genders. The example of female bullfighters shows that over the last two centuries in Spain some women have always been ready to contest this ideological restriction. Challenging an otherwise exclusively male prerogative, they have been prepared to demonstrate publicly their ability to domineer over a large and potentially very dangerous beast. This example suggests that anthropologists of Spain have tended to stress dichotomy when discussing gender difference instead of investigating diversity. And perhaps the reason why they did so, at least during the Franquist regime, was that they spent their time talking with dominant male villagers, the very ones who would have been most concerned to see reproduced the traditionalist binary conception of gender differences propagated by the dictator's departments. The anthropological implication of all this is that local conceptions of masculine and feminine identities cannot be adequately comprehended without taking into account the relationship between local and national ideologies.

Many male sports are represented as epitomes of markedly masculine activity, to be strictly understood in a heterosexual mode. Many spectators and viewers are still uncomfortable at the sight of muddy, muscular footballers embracing and kissing after one of them has scored a goal. In this cultural domain, open expressions of male homosexuality are tabu. As the gay athlete Brian Pronger argues, the pronounced unmasculine behaviour of gay athletes gives the lie to the conventional interpretation of *mens sana in corpore sano* and threatens to blunt the competitive edge coaches try to instill in their charges. Thus the great erotic potential of many aspects of sport are firmly suppressed, 'the body contact of football, rugby, hockey, boxing and water-polo; the practice of gymnastic routines, springboard diving and figure skating; the attention coaches lavish on their athletes; the exposure of naked sportsmen in locker rooms and showers' (Pronger 1990: 9). In reaction to this repression, some gay sportsmen organize their own communal events. Though some participants in these activities are keen to copy the orthodox athletic sensibilities of mainstream sport, many are highly resistant to the idea of imitating the style of their heterosexual peers and prefer to exploit the camp dimensions of these events. For instance at gay swim meets in north America, pink flamingo relays have become a common feature: suitably dressed-up pairs compete down the lanes, the front man swimming with his arms, the other holding on to his legs and kicking with his own. At the International Gay Games, many men emphasize their ironic relation to conventional sports by wearing strings of costume pearls over their traditional athletic outfits (ibid.) Gay athletes, by creating their own events and even their own sorts of competitive activities, attempt to challenge the binary division of gender identities that is hegemonically embodied in many sports. Instead of reinforcing a narrowly defined masculinity, they seek to celebrate, via sports, a plurality of identities.

***

What the chapters collected in this book cumulatively demonstrate is the profusion of ways in which sports influence, define, and assist in the creation and contest of identities, and do so at a series of levels and along a range of cultural domains. Far from being merely play or marginal unserious activities, they are key, multifaceted components in the complex constitution of most societies (certainly all modern ones) and a central aspect of the globalization of culture, and of the local resistances to it. Examining exactly, and in a systematic manner, the various roles played by these activities, both in the past and the present, is a legitimate, valuable task for social anthropologists. Their analytical and ethnographically rich accounts will help to detail and lay bare the specificities and the contexts within which all of us live our lives, however vicariously, through sport.

The reality of the opposition to the establishment of sport as a suitable topic for academic study can be illustrated by two events in the production of this book. One contributor to the seminar series on which this book is based gave a chapter on a sport which originated in that area of the developing world where she does her fieldwork and which has since became both prestigious and popular in many countries of the developed world. Her presentation was, in truth, more a detailed research proposal than a polished paper and when she applied to her university for a small grant to do the extra fieldwork necessary to complete her study, its rector tersely commented on her application, 'This one has to be NO.'

On 23 December 1992 *The Times* ran a head-of-the-page article on the seminar series, entitled 'Much hot air expended in the Oxford cricket test'. Its writer, who focused on the chapter by Pnina Werbner about British Pakistanis and cricket, discussed its content in a consistently jokey manner and chose to emphasize something the speaker had not even mentioned in her presentation: the supposedly deeply phallic symbolism of the game.

As these anecdotes reveal, sport continues to be seen by many as but a playful activity not worthy of, or not appropriate for, systematic investigation. How could something that is so much fun, these people seem to think, be studied seriously, and to any useful end? The common responses, whether by laypersons or academics (*The Times* journalist was, in fact, a Cambridge research fellow), to the analysis of sport are either outright rejection ('This one has to be NO') or an excuse for a smirk in the run-up to Christmas. This book is a contribution towards the revision of those attitudes.

Bibliography

Arbena, Joseph L. (1988), 'Sport and the Study of Latin American Society: An Overview', in J. L. Arbena (ed.), *Sport and Society in Latin America. Diffusion, Dependency, and the rise of Mass Culture* New York: Greenwood, pp. 1–14

Azoy, Whitney (1982), *Buzkashi. Game and Power in Afghanistan.* Philadelphia: University of Pennsylvania Press

Barnett, Steven (1990), *Games and Sets. The changing face of sport in television.* London: British Film Insitute

Blain, Nigel, Raymond Boyle and Hugh O'Donnell (1993), *Sport and National Identity in the European Media.* Leicester: Leicester University Press

Blanchard, Kendall and Alyce Cheska (1985), *The Anthropology of Sport. An Introduction.* South Hadley, MA: Bergin and Garvey

Brownell, Susan (1995), *Training the body for China. Sports in the Moral Order of the People's Republic.* Chicago: University of Chicago Press

Caillois, Roger (1969), 'The Structure and Classification of Games', in John Loy and Gerald Kenyon (eds), *Sport, Culture and Society.* New York: Macmillan, pp. 44–55

Chapman, Malcolm (1993), 'Social and biological aspects of ethnicity', in Malcolm Chapman (ed.), *Social and Biological Aspects of Ethnicity.* Oxford: Oxford University Press, pp. 1–46

Cohen, Sara (1994), 'Identity, Place and the "Liverpool Sound"', in Martin Stokes (ed.), *Ethnicity, Identity and Music. The Musical Construction of Place.* Oxford: Berg, pp. 117–134

Dobson, Roger (1995), 'City gents? Brokers use sexist sliding scale in the office', *The Independent on Sunday,* 9 July

Fleming, Scott (1991), 'Sport, Schooling and Asian Male Youth Culture', in Jarvie 1991a, pp. 30–57

Fox, Robin (1961), 'Pueblo Baseball: A New Use for Old Witchcraft', *Journal of American Folklore*, vol. 74, pp. 9–16

Frankenberg, Ronald (1990 (1957)), *Village on the Border. A social study of religion, politics and football in a north Wales community*. Prospect Heights, Illinois: Waveland

Gibbon, Edward (1966 (1776–1788)), *Decline and Fall of the Roman Empire*. H. Trevor-Roper (ed.) New York: New English Library

Goldhurst, John (1987), *Playing for Keeps. Sport, the Media and Society*. Melbourne: Longman Cheshire

Guttmann, Allen (1978), *From Ritual to Record. The nature of modern sports*. New York: Columbia University Press

— (1991), *Women's Sports. A History*. New York: Columbia University Press

Hargreaves, Jennifer (1994), *Sporting Females: Critical Issues in the History and Sociology of Women's Sports*. London: Routledge

Hargreaves, John (1986), *Sport, Power and Culture*. Cambridge: Polity

Hobsbawm, Eric and Terence Ranger (eds) (1983), *The Invention of Tradition*. Cambridge: Cambridge University Press

Holt, Richard (1989), *Sport and the British: A Modern History*. Oxford Studies in Social History. Oxford: Oxford University Press

Jarvie, Grant (ed.) (1991a), *Sport, Racism and Ethnicity*. London: Falmer

— (1991b), *Highland Games: The Making of a Myth*. Edinburgh Education and Society Series. Edinburgh: Edinburgh University Press

Jarvie, Grant and Graham Walker (1994) 'Ninety-minute Patriots. Scottish Sport in the Making of the Nation', in Grant Jarvie and Graham Walker (eds), *Scottish Sport in the Making of the Nation. Ninety-minute patriots?* Leicester: Leicester University Press, pp. 1–8

Kirk-Greene, Anthony (1989), 'Badge of Office? Sport and His Excellency in the British Empire', *International Journal of the History of Sport*, vol. 6, pp. 218–241

Leach, Edmund R. (1975), 'Review of "Trobriand Cricket"', *RAIN*, no. 9, p. 6

Lévi-Strauss, Claude (1966), *The Savage Mind*. London: Weidenfeld and Nicolson.

Lewis, J. Lowell (1992), *Ring of Liberation. Deceptive Discourse in Brazilian Capoeira*. Chicago: University of Chicago Press

Lowerson, John (1993), *Sport and the English Middle-classes 1870-1914*. Manchester: Manchester University Press

MacAloon, John J. (1981), *This Great Symbol: Pierre de Coubertin and the Origins of the Modern Olympic Games*. Chicago: University of Chicago Press

McCrone, Kathleen (1988), *Sport and the Physical Emancipation of Englishwomen 1870-1914*. London: Routledge

Maybury-Lewis, David (1992), *Millennium. Tribal Wisdom and the Modern World*. London: Viking

Powell, H. A. (1952), 'Cricket in Kiriwana', *The Listener,* 4 September, pp. 384–385

Pronger, Brian (1990), *The Arena of Masculinity. Sport, Homosexuality and the Meaning of Sex*. London: GMP

Riordan, James (1977), *Sport in Soviet Society: Development of Sport and Physical Education in Russia and the USSR*. Cambridge: Cambridge University Press

— 1991 *Sport, politics and communism*. Manchester: Manchester University Press

Scarborough, Vernon L. and David R. Wilcox (eds), (1991), *The Mesoamerican Ballgame*. Tucson: University of Arizona Press

Stoddart, Brian (1988), 'Cricket and Colonialism in the English-Speaking Caribbean to 1914: Towards a Cultural Analysis', in J. A. Mangan (ed.), *Pleasure, Profit and Proselytism. British Culture and Sport at Home and Abroad 1700–1914*. London: Cass, pp. 231–257

Sugden, John and Alan Bairner (1993), *Sport, Sectarianism and Society in a Divided Ireland*. Leicester: Leicester University Press

Vennum, Thomas (1994), *American Indian Lacrosse: Little borther of war.* Washington, DC: Smithsonian Institution

Wagner, Eric A. (1988), 'Sport in Revolutionary Societies: Cuba and Nicaragua', in J. L. Arbena (1994), pp. 113–136

Weiner, Annette (1977), 'Review of "Trobriand Cricket"', *American Anthropologist*, vol. 79, pp. 506–507

Whiting, Robert (1977), *The Chrysanthemum and the Bat. The game the Japanese play.* Tokyo: Permanent

2

'Strong as a Turk': Power, Performance and Representation in Turkish Wrestling

Martin Stokes

Anthropologists often have to negotiate a complex terrain of representations of 'popular' practice, and sport is no exception. In an analysis which is uncharacteristically hostile to popular cultural practice, and full of the scarcely concealed elitisms of post-war marxian cultural theory, Umberto Eco sees in sport the epitome of passive consumption: the feats of athleticism on the screen positively demand an admiration from the television viewer which is powerless and inert, and its battery of facts, figures and statistics fill proletarian minds with a knowledge which is both diversionary and deceitful (Eco 1987). If anthropologists respond that this kind of approach ignores the voice of the insider participant, they have problems here too.

The voice of the articulate fan is as often as not full of contradictions: sport is simultaneously everything and nothing. This kind of discourse is nowhere better exemplified than in Nick Hornby's eloquent account of football fandom in *Fever Pitch* (1992), which swings from descriptions of empowering, epiphanic revelation to moments of despairing negativism. In a significant passage in the introduction, Hornby debates the nature of sport as social knowledge. Whilst he is happy to assert that 'the way the game is consumed seems to offer all sorts of information about our society and culture' (1992: 11), he rubbishes the idea that football has any connection with 'the Falklands conflict, the Rushdie affair, the Gulf War, childbirth, the ozone layer, the poll tax, etc. etc.' (ibid.) This observation connects with his certainty that his engagement with the game is devoid of, to quote his own words, '*thought*, in the proper sense of the word.' He goes on to explain, 'There is no analysis, or self-awarenesss, or mental rigour going on at all. . . Obsessives are denied any kind of perspective on their own passion' (ibid.: 10). One must take issue with Hornby's remorselessly Cartesian notion of 'thought' as a form of abstract and disembodied mind-work, a detached viewpoint from which one 'gets a perspective' on other things. Sport literally embodies vital forms of social knowledge, and it does so in ways which bring into focus well established issues for anthropologists and cultural theorists.

For an outsider, an understanding of Turkish sport undoubtedly throws a great deal of light on other aspects of Turkish social life, and there is no sport which carries as much symbolic 'weight' in Turkey as wrestling. The sentiments evoked by wrestling are far from static or consensual. Interpretations of the symbols and imagery of wrestling can, of course, be used in different ways and appropriated as tools in hegemonic processes or their opposing counterparts. Indeed, wrestling is systematically used in the construction of myths of national strength and in a moral education in almost chivalric notions of contest and display. Turkish wrestling prowess is held to provide indisputable evidence of a machismo that has been globally celebrated since, in popular memory, the French monarch, Francis II, accepted a gift from an Ottoman Sultan and expressed the desire that this would make him 'strong as a Turk' ('*Türk gibi güçlü*'). The founder of the modern Turkish republic, Mustafa Kemal Atatürk, is reputed to have given the sport his blessing with the remark, 'Wrestling is a game of strength (*kuvvet*) and intelligence (*zeka*). The moment these two superior qualities are combined in a person, they can do great works'[1] (quoted in Sari 1992: 29). But wrestling can also be seen as a repository of subversive knowledge, as a recognition that all is not what it seems, that strength is not moral purity, that deceit and guile are necessary parts of social life, that one frequently has to cope with losing face, that compromise is sometimes better than contest. Wrestling might also be, and undoubtedly is, seen in Turkey as a cultural exploration of male relationships and of the deceits and inconsistencies of a pervasive masculinist ideology. The remainder of this chapter examines some of these assertions.[2]

Wrestling and Contest in the Mediterranean and Muslim Worlds

The significance of wrestling in Turkey can be attributed to the convergence of a number of related historical and social facts. Wrestling has a history in the Mediterranean area that long predates the arrival of the Turks in Anatolia in the eleventh century. Kinds of wrestling are portrayed in Babylonian and Ancient Egyptian art from the beginning of the third millennium BC. Wrestling was much cultivated by the Ancient Greeks, making its first appearance in the Olympics of 776 BC. Sari claims that wrestling was first recorded in Anatolia in the 41-44 AD Olympics in Antioch during the reign of Claudius (Sari 1992: 17). Following the collapse of the Roman Empire, Turks and Mongolians brought their Asiatic wrestling traditions with them to the early mediaeval Mediterranean and Middle East. In Anatolia the nomadic Turks would have encountered not just local forms of wrestling but also an entrenched tradition of public sporting events promoted by the political powers of the region.

There was more to the significance of wrestling amongst the Turks during this period than its powerful appeal to the nomadic bearers of a heroic-military ethos, in which the significers of strength were the object of intense cultural elaboration.[3] The Hadithic literature attests to the high significance attached to sporting pursuits, including wrestling, in the early Muslim world. In one famous quotation,[4] the Prophet claimed that the only leisure activities permitted to Muslim men were archery, horse-riding and making love to their wives (Uludag 1976: 124-7), thus indicating the imperatives of sexual reproduction and military readiness adopted by the early Muslims. This Hadith is often quoted in order to condemn most other leisure pursuits as *haram* (canonically forbidden). In a more positive vein, in other Hadith injunctions, the Prophet comes over as something of a sports enthusiast. He is reputed to have been an excellent sprinter and rider. One Hadith (from Buhari) relates that the Prophet and his camel, Adba, were unbeaten, until a race in which they were defeated by a Bedouin rider. He is reputed to have said, somewhat phlegmatically, 'This is the way the world is. Everything that is blessed with good fortune and raised up is made low' (Uludag 1976: 130). A Hadith (from Ebu Davud) relates that the Prophet was also a fine wrestler. According to this Hadith, he is challenged to a wrestling bout by a man named Rükane, and they agree to the prize of a sheep for the winner. The Prophet beats Rükane in one bout after another. Rükane eventually says, 'Oh Mohammed! I have never been beaten until now. What has defeated me is not you, but the spiritual power that you possess.' He becomes a Muslim on the spot, and Mohammed gives him the sheep (ibid.) This is significant not only in that it constitutes a kind of historical evidence of the significant role of sport in the early Muslim world, but also because Turkish commentators use Hadithic evidence (see, for example, Tekin 1992: 5) to assert the cultural importance of wrestling.

Wrestling and sport in general are seen by Turkish Muslims as means of honing the techniques of vigilance and combat, but they admire physical prowess also as a sign of spiritual power and blessing.

Finally, wrestling attests to a deeply rooted concern with the importance of male strength, and an aesthetic code reported widely by anthropologists throughout the Mediterranean world, in which male beauty is equated with physical prowess. It also attests to the significance of contest in circumMediterranean constructions of masculinity. As many anthropologists have pointed out, a man's standing in his community is crucially dependent upon his ability to compete in a public arena.[6] Even though these competitions are carried out in ways which ironize or send up the moment of contest, and which frequently have recourse to cunning, trickery and deceit,[7] a result is everything, and this result requires nothing less than the destruction, shaming and humiliation of one's adversary, performed in front of, and acknowledged by, 'the community'. A man's ability to compete is constantly on trial, and is demonstrated in a range of activities from cards, backgammon, and sports to the overtly violent conflicts that inevitably occur in relation to the protection of women and property. There is hardly a moment of the day when this ability is not under close scrutiny.

What makes wrestling significant in Turkey is that it constitutes a kind of theatrical enactment of the struggles and contests of everyday life. It takes the social materials of everyday life, but reworks and regulates them with a set of rules demanding the transparency and fair play which so conspicuously fail to operate in 'real life'. In a characteristically luminous phrase, Michel De Certeau pointed out that games 'constitute. . . a memory (a storage and classification) of schemas of actions articulating replies *with respect to circumstances.* They exercise that function precisely because they are detached from those everyday combats which forbid one to "show his hand", whose stakes, rules and moves are too complex' (1987: 22). The point of rules, then, is to provide observers of wrestling with a set of clearly articulated 'schemas of actions', that is to say, representations of the concept of contest, untrammelled by the messy and opaque transactions of 'real life'.

Turkish observers would probably agree with De Certeau. It is often asserted that wrestling is the simplest and most elemental form of contest. This perception is highly significant, for reasons that will be discussed below. At this point, however, it may be useful to describe a Turkish wrestling bout from the point of view of rules and techniques. The various forms of wrestling in Turkey would be described in international wrestling jargon as 'loose style', in that the opponents start separated, and 'touch-fall', and in that the wrestler wins by forcing his opponent's shoulders to the ground. The two main forms of international wrestling practised throughout Turkey are *serbest* ('free-style') and *greko-romen* (Greco-Roman). Greco-Roman was reputedly invented in France in the late nineteenth century, as an attempt to reconstruct Ancient Greek practice. It involves holds above the waist only, and uses a points system (based on the amount of time one contestant holds another in a position which will lead to a fall). *Serbest*, on the other hand, is a more recent version of 'touch-fall' wrestling, allowing leg-grips, and concluding only with a fall. Local forms of wrestling exist throughout rural Turkey, but the basic principles of touch-fall wrestling apply here as well. The best known is 'oily wrestling' (*yagli güres*), in the Edirne-Kirkpinar region of Turkish Thrace, in which the techniques and tactics of conventional touch-fall wrestling are transformed by the grips necessitated by slippery skin. *Aba* wrestling in the Hatay province of Southern Turkey transforms the same basic rules with a special costume, typical of many Asian 'belt-and-jacket' traditions and Russian 'Sambo' wrestling: here the costume creates a range of different possible holds.

Wrestling could more accurately be described as a game of balance and timing rather than force, in that the principal techniques are designed to disrupt one's opponent's balance. As in many other forms of wrestling (for example, Japanese *sumo*), an attacking move involves a moment of exposure which an opponent can quickly turn to his advantage. For the novice observer, then, wrestling consists of a long period of waiting in which both wrestlers hold each other by the shoulders, arms outstretched and slightly bent from the waist, followed by a sudden explosion of kicking intended to sweep the opponent's legs from under him (for example, in *Aba* wrestling, the techniques known as *cangal, yanbas, yandonme, sarma, koltuklamak*), pushing and shoving (*havalandirmak*) or holds designed to force one's opponent to the floor (*tekkol, koltuklamak,* or the headlock, *boyunduruk*). The bout ends either with a hurried scuffle on the ground and a quick decision by the referee, or with the dramatic *tus*[8], in which a particularly weak contestant is picked up with his legs in the air and thrown to the ground. Whilst the techniques may be elaborate, the principles and rules are particularly straightforward. This observation is readily endorsed by Turkish observers. Frequently, when I enquired about points of detail in the rules, people would say with a laugh, 'Rules? There's no rules. This is about strength (*kuvvet*)!'. Failure cannot be disguised in any way, and (compared to football, for example) adverse refereeing decisions, the poor performance of teammates, or the decisions of incompetent trainers or manager are no excuse. The winner is literally 'the destroyer' (*yikan*) and the loser 'the destroyed' (*yikilan*). Wrestling is considered to be simple, direct, conclusive and deeply 'traditional'. It is not surprising that wrestling should be a matter of considerable importance in Turkey today.

Wrestling, Football and Politics

Whilst wrestling and the figure of the wrestler are vital features of Turkish social life, wrestling is by no means the most popular sport in Turkey today. Football, and more particularly the big Istanbul clubs (Galatasaray, Besiktas and Fenerbahce), dominate sporting life and talk about sport throughout Turkey and beyond.[9] Football is widely considered to be progressive, European and sophisticated. Its vast popularity, indicated by the fact that most of the new satellite television channels broadcast live matches almost daily, owes something to the way it organizes the patterns of identity and belonging in cities which are held to disrupt and fragment this experience. It also owes something to the worlds of fantasy, glamour and political intrigue which Turkish football conjures up for those who follow it. The sums of money that change hands almost defy comprehension; footballers and their managers mix with politicians, film and music stars; the scandals of rigged games and transfer swindles fill the back pages of the daily papers. Above all, football involves a point of contact with a global audience for people whose capacity to travel is extremely limited.

Consequently, football is sometimes explicitly contrasted with wrestling, which is financially low-key, has less mass appeal, involves worthy but unglamorous personalities, and (since the global stage is largely occupied by Turkey and Eastern Europe) is not considered a properly 'international' sport. Sabahattin Özturk beat Klasiovatov in the 82-kilo final bout, and won the gold medal at the World Wrestling Championships in Toronto in August 1993, providing Turkey with a world championship wrestling medal for the first time in 23 years (since Ali Riza Alan won at Edmonton). This was not the only cause for celebration: in the same championships, Ilyas Sükrüoglu won a bronze at 48 kilos, and a number of other wrestlers finished high in their classes.[10] However, on his return to Turkey, Özturk was met by an extremely modest celebration, and one late-night television interview. News of his victory was relegated to page five of the major sporting weekly paper, *Fotomac*.

Committed sports fans watch wrestling as well as football, follow the Olympic wrestling keenly and are familiar with the names and personalities of those involved. When pressed, however, many more see football and wrestling as alternatives. Choosing to identify with football means presenting oneself as a modern European sophisticate. Wrestling, by contrast, evokes a traditional and oafish world, and constitutes evidence, in the opinion of many, of a pernicious Asiatic backwardness that the Turks are incapable of shaking off. When I attended a large wrestling festival in the Hatay province on 30 August 1992 (described in detail below), Ali, the man who ran the local *belediye*[11] hotel, was one of a number of people who stayed away from the event. He, like many in this town, had worked as a painter in France and in several Arab countries. He was fascinated by all things French, and constantly praised the abilities of the French colonial authorities to construct buildings, roads and bridges that were still in use today. This was seen as affected by other young men in the town, who embraced the ethos of *kabadayi* machismo more wholeheartedly (see below): his kindly but rather ponderous manner was considered to undermine his Francophile claims to sophistication. The wrestling festival was obviously a crucial test of identity for him. When it became clear that he wasn't going to make his way to the wrestling *meydan* with nearly everyone else in the town, I asked him why. His answer had a carefully rehearsed and often repeated ring to it. He would get up, he told me, at four o'clock in the morning to watch a live football match on one of the satellite channels on the television, and he would travel *anywhere* to see a decent game, but he was not going to get out of his chair and walk for five minutes to see the wrestling, even if they were the best wrestlers in the south of Turkey, and even if people were coming from far and wide to see the event. They were a bunch of rascals (*yaramaz*), and he would have nothing to do with it.

'Tough Guys': Maganda and Kabadayi

Ali's notion that wrestling is the mark of a backward rural world has many resonances. Wrestling is often associated in many of the popular cartoon satirical magazines with the figure of the *maganda* or *kabadayi*, the 'tough guy', defiantly celebrated in the south but widely ridiculed in the metropolitan north. Formerly the term *kabadayi* was used to denote urban 'men of honour', who had gained a reputation for protecting the honour of the neighbourhood (*mahalle*) and looking after its interests.

The political role of these urban notables in mediating new national politics in the post-Ottoman Middle East has been discussed at some length.[12]

In Turkey the contemporary political significance of the term *kabadayi* is quite different. For the metropolitan northerner, and those like Ali who have adopted metropolitan discourses about Turkish 'others', the *kabadayi's* adherence to an outdated ethic is both perverse and comic. The term *kabadayi* is frequently used in the papers to describe the participants in brawls involving small arms and knives in 'traditional' squatter-town districts: the term *maganda* is a contemporary slang version of the word *kabadayi*. The stereotypical hero of *Leman*, (a comic with an explicit political commentary highly critical of the war in the southeast, the human-rights record of Turkish security forces, police powers, legal corruption and, currently, privatization of state economic enterprises) is an 'intellectual' type, with a sparse beard, pipe and visible rib-cage who is constantly set upon by groups of oafish *maganda,* instantly recognizable by their hairy chests and medallions, elaborate moustaches, worry beads, trodden-down backs of shoes (indicating the traditional virtues of 'sitting' and ordering people to bring things to them), and cigarettes. In one cartoon the pipe-smoking hero finds himself in '*Maganda* Cafe', confronted by a carnivalesque scene in which half the *maganda* are wrestling with each other, and the other half sodomizing each other. In another, the same (or a remarkably similar) hero has a dream in which the *maganda* who have been making his life a misery on the beach are mysteriously sucked under the sea. He dons a mask and snorkel and finds himself observing a grotesque underwater '*Maganda* Olympics'. The ancestry of the *maganda* (although the term is not used) can be traced as stereotypes of an inflexible, traditional authority which is simultaneously comic and vicious in the literature of Kemal Tahir, Yasar Kemal and Orhan Kemal.[13]

The construction of the *maganda* figure in this urban popular culture has a clear political aim: the *maganda* emerged in this comic literature, probably with the gorilla character (complete with moustache and cigarettes) in *Fırt*'s 'Tarzan', almost immediately after the 1983 election of the first civil government, that of Turgut Özal's 'Motherland Party', after the military coup of 12 September 1980. For many commentators, his election marked the beginnings of a break with the state bureaucratic tradition established by Mustafa Kemal Ataturk. Özal embarked on a series of 'liberalization' reforms that for many meant the advancement of foreign capital and the dismantling of the state's patrimonial role in Turkish economics. The extent to which this process justified a return to 'traditional' Islamic values as a means of control following the civil unrest of the late 1970s surfaced during the 'Rabita' scandal of 1986, in which high-level military support for the Saudi finance of Turkish Muslims in Germany was revealed by *Cumhuriyet*'s investigative journalist Ugur Mumcu.[14] This congruence of the interests of military cadres (pledged to defend the secular state established by Ataturk) and business elites (who promote freedom to practise Islam as a means of opposing Ataturkian *étatisme*), outraged the Ataturkian secularist left. That the *maganda* surfaced as a figure of both fear and ridicule at this time owes much to the anxiety of these groups about the long term effects of the return to 'traditional authority' that was being promoted in many ways in the 1980s. The association of wrestling with traditional masculinist virtues and the *maganda* during this period is hardly coincidental.

Whilst the *maganda* (implicitly or explicitly associated with wrestling) has largely been constructed by the left as a means of criticizing newly emerging forms of 'traditional' authority, the journalistic celebration of Turkish champion wrestlers and the lament of their failures is clearly underpinned by a rightist political programme and scarcely concealed chauvinism. Following the poor performance of Turkish wrestlers at a meeting in Greece in April 1986 Mehmet Tekin, in an article entitled 'Are there NO wrestlers in the Hatay?' (*'Hatay'da Pehlivan YOK MU?'*, in *Hatay Gazetesi*, 14 July 1986) lamented the days in which a 'Turkish storm' blew through the Olympics and World Championships, and points to the decline in the sense of national responsibility (*millete karsi sorumluluk duygusu*) on the part of wrestlers, the commercialism of sport, the failure by the state to promote the sport in schools, and the fact that so many young people are now turning to Karate and Taekwando. There is indeed much to support the view that wrestling and its fetishization of the powerful male body underlies an unambiguously chauvinist political programme in Turkey (as elsewhere: one needs only to think of the role of Stallone and Schwarzenegger in Reaganite and post-Reaganite America). This programme has been encouraged by the fact that, on a longterm view the one international sport in which Turkey undoubtedly excels is wrestling. Since Yasar Erkan won a gold medal at Berlin in 1936, the list of Turkish Olympic medallists is a long one.[15]

It is, however, not just international success that appeals to a certain chauvinism, but the identity of the states with whom Turkey competes. Since most of the wrestling nations are Balkan states which acquired their independence from the Ottoman empire in the nineteenth century, wrestling evokes a world in which Turkey was the dominant power rather than a peripheral broker of European and American power in the Middle East.[16] Indeed, one might argue, that for many Turks, wrestling somehow reverses symbolically the military defeats which stripped Ottoman Turkey of its European territories. Murat Sertoglu's popular history of wrestling, published in 1987 in the Ministry of Culture and Tourism's 'Famous Turks' series, suggests just this. Sertoglu, puts wrestling and the life-stories of two of Turkey's most famous wrestlers, Adali Halil and Kurtdereli Mehmet, in a very specific historical and political context: the Ottoman-Russian war of 1878, Russia's and Europe's support for the Christians of the Ottoman Empire, and the increasing success of nationalist movements in the Balkans. Sertoglu suggests that whenever Turkish villagers found themselves and their customs threatened by Christians, wrestling emerged as a means of preserving the *kuvvet, kudret ve ahlak* (strength, power and morality) of the Balkan Muslim communities (Sertoglu 1987: 3). One of the first things the Bulgarian authorities did on achieving independence in 1878, Sertoglu claims, was to ban wrestling among the Muslim populations. Wrestling became a vital form of resistance to assimilation (Sertoglu 1987: 4). For precisely this reason, Sertoglu argues, the parts of Turkey which have the strongest wrestling traditions today are those villages in Turkish Thrace and the Marmara region which were settled with 'Turkish'[17] Balkan Muslims after the population exchanges of 1923. It is true that Kirkpinar (in Thrace) continues to host the biggest wrestling festival in Turkey, and other areas define themselves in relation to this place as, for example 'The Kirkpinar of the East',[18] 'The Black Sea Kirkpinar' and so on. The contemporary political resonances of the Balkan wrestling scene for those Turks who see themselves as Muslims besieged by hostile Christian neighbours, particularly a resurgent Christian Russia, cannot be overestimated, particularly in the climate of the current Balkan conflict. This kind of political posture was much in evidence in the Hatay in 1993, particularly among supporters of the Islamist *Refah Partisi* and the right-wing nationalist *Milli Hareket Partisi*.

Wrestling as Performance: Aba Wrestling and the Hatay

It would be easy to conclude from this excursion into written sources that wrestling is a symbolic expression of a kind of 'traditional' male authority, reshaped and reformulated in the now dominant political framework. But wrestling is a performance, and like all performances is capable of transforming rather than simply reproducing the power relationships in which it is embedded. My concluding case-study is based on observations of a wrestling festival in the Hatay province of southern Turkey.

The Hatay province today is part of the post-First World War French mandate eventually ceded to the Turkish Republic in 1937 in return for Ataturk's agreement not to involve Turkey in the Second World War. Since late Roman times this area has been a frontier contested by regional tribal confederacies, empires and states. After the collapse of the Roman empire Aleppo and Antioch came under Arab suzerainty in 638 AD. Omayyad and Abbasid control of the area was successfully contested by Byzantine power, the nascent Secukid states of Anatolia, and the migration of independent Turkmen tribes between the nineth and tenth centuries, a situation which allowed the crusading armies to walk through the entire Levant largely unopposed. In the early sixteenth century, when Antioch and Aleppo were major commercial centres and Payas a large Mediterranean port, the area was fought over by the Anatolian Ottomans and the Egyptian Memluks. Eventually, under Ottoman control, it was heavily fortified, and Turkmen nomads from Anatolia were settled throughout the triangle constituted by the cities of Latlakia, Aleppo and Antioch early in the eighteenth century: those Turkmen who inhabit the Senköy and Yayladag areas are still referred to by others as the *Bayir-Bucak Turkleri*, after the region in which they were settled. As Aswad (1971) has pointed out, the demographic mix of the Hatay in the eighteenth and nineteenth centuries was complicated by the migration of Turkish, Arab and Kurdish nomads away from the Jezira, an area of rich, and therefore heavily contested, grassland straddling today's borders between Syria, Iraq and Turkey.

Incoming nomadic pastoralists overcame settled villagers, and their power was subsequently entrenched and transformed by the land reforms associated with the administrative, military and economic 'reorganization' of the Ottoman Empire during the *Tatizimat* period (see Aswad 1971 and Van Bruinessen 1992). This period also saw the systematic absorption of the area into Northwest European-dominated patterns of trade. For reasons discussed by Keyer and others (Keyer and Tabak 1991), great landed estates organized around commercial agricultural production did not emerge in the Ottoman Middle East (as they did, for example, in Poland or South America), and the relations between capitalist and non-capitalist modes of production varied greatly throughout southern and eastern Anatolia. Agrarian relations in the area were, however characterized by an apparatus of coercive domination, which, as Gilsenan has suggested in north Lebanon, relied on a complex phenomenology of power, an obsession with the constant and frequently violent *appearance* of power (1986). It is this deeply rooted culture of coercion which has decisively shaped local constructions of manhood, and has undoubtedly contributed to the intense celebration of the *kabadayi* in the region. It has also undoubtedly reinforced the northern metropolitan notion that this culture of coercion is a peculiarly 'southern' and extremely backward state of affairs.

It is not surprising that this culture of coercion also informs local attitudes to the political process. After the massacres of Armenians during the First World War and the flight of those who survived them, the province is now divided between Sunni Turks and Alevi (heterodox) Arabs. This demographic split has given President Hafiz Asad of Syria (himself an Alevi) an opportunity to campaign against imposed colonial borders and argue repeatedly for the incorporation of the Hatay within the 'natural boundaries' of Syria. Whilst many Sunni Turks believe that Alevi Arabs wholeheartedly favour this, in fact most do not. During a conversation about identity that I initiated late one night in a hotel in Antakya, but was unable to keep up with, I heard one Arab telling another that, during the years after the 1980 coup, General Kenan Evren took Asad to task over his claims to the Hatay. According to this man, Evren had challenged Asad, telling him that if he was capable of wresting it away, he should take it; if not, he should forget it. Whether this unlikely exchange took place or not is irrelevant. The fact that international politics is seen as a kind of wrestling challenge between two *kabadayi* is deeply significant.

In a society such as this, in which the signs and symbols of conflict are very much on display and an integral part of its workings, wrestling has a special significance. The Hatay has its own form of wrestling called *Aba Güresi,* or in the local dialect simply *'Güles'.* Aba wrestling is more or less the sole preserve of the Sunni Turks of the Hatay, in particular those in the *Bayir-Bucak* villages and small towns of Senkoy, Altinözü and Yayladag, a distinct area of pine forests and craggy limestone hills below Kel Dagi mountain and the Turkish-Syrian border, largely given over to tobacco cultivation. It differs little from other forms of wrestling, and champion Aba wrestlers are often very successful elsewhere.[19] Though the point of it is still to force one's opponent's shoulders to the ground, it differs primarily in the fact that the contestants wear a sleeveless jacket of leather and cloth called 'Aba' (creating a set of different possible holds), and in having rules which create an altogether more direct and abrupt game. The technique known as *köprü* ('bridge, in which a wrestler can maintain himself in a 'safe' position when he has been forced to the ground) is forbidden in other forms of wrestling, since, in the opinion of proponents of Aba, it delays the likely outcome (article 15 of 1991 rules). When both contestants have forced one another to their knees, wrestling is stopped after one minute (article 10). Most significantly, at any rate for the non-local policemen who were on duty at the festival I attended, was the lack of weight brackets. In fact this situation is changing in order to give smaller wrestlers a chance, and perhaps, less overtly, to accept the dominant logic of *serbest* and *greko-roman* wrestling. Aba wrestling competitions take place at weddings throughout the summer, in local, semi-formal challenges, and public holidays.

The wrestling festival is a highly choreographed event. A small van carrying a *zurna-davul* duo (a shawm and drum combination indicating and quickening the emotional pace of any ritual event in rural Turkey) drove slowly through the town advertizing the event. At around half past five, people shut their shops and walked or rode their motorcycles out of town to the *meydan*, in fact the town's football pitch. The first few hours were given over to all comers, mostly men a little older than the main body of contestants. 'Warm-up' rounds took place between nine and midnight, and a series of knock-out bouts followed. By three o'clock in the morning most of the winners of each weight bracket had been decided. The final hour or so was taken up by the heavyweight finalists. The wrestling took place on a patch of ground (*mersah*) surrounded by a ring of possibly a thousand men about forty metres in diameter. Up to eight couples were wrestling at any one time, each with a referee. After each bout, each contestant would take it in turns to put his arms round his opponent and lift him in the air, and then walk off the *meydan* towards the trailer on which the judges were sitting. The drummer and shawm player, who were on this occasion conspicuously drunk, played infrequently, the drummer hopping and leaping in a huge circle round the *mersah* whenever he played. As in many rural gatherings of young Turkish men who do not often see one another, fights very often broke out as old scores were settled, or reopened. These scuffles constituted a kind of counterpoint to the wrestling in the *mersah*, which could easily be ignored if one was to see this purely as a 'sporting event'.

The Yayladag festival took place on August 30, the *Zafer Bayrami* ('Victory Festival') celebrating the defeat of the Greek forces by the Turks at Sakarya in Western Anatolia in 1921. Wrestling was the main focus of a number of events (including, for example, a torchlit parade organized by the local garrison), and people only turned their attention to the *mersah* when friends, relatives or fellow villagers were wrestling. Otherwise people walked back and forth between the *meydan* and the town, or sat around in the various stalls (selling ice-cream, tea and soup) set up for the event. The sense of being on view, and the festival atmosphere, both increased sensitivity to insult and intensified the banter amongst the young men. Fights very often broke out. Although they involved the use of knives, the fights were more social than physical, since they only ever took place in front of a large audience, which could be relied on to register the event and pull the protagonists apart before either got hurt. On occasions one would get the worst of a tussle and leave swearing violently and perhaps crying; but on the whole it was impossible to say that either had won or lost.

Similarly, the banter required both an audience and a sense of contest. Banter differs in the sense that it does not strictly require winners and losers. Verbal contests are constructed in ways which always provide the 'opponent' with an opportunity to provide a response. In successful banter, all parties 'win'. Banter among young men in Turkey is highly formalised, and revolves around what Dundes, Özkök and Leach (1972) have identified as a critical cultural and psychological configuration amongst Turkish males – the active male penis assaulting the passive male anus. Dundes et al focus on rhyming games in which 'the skill in the duelling process consists of parrying phallic thrusts and the would-be attacker is accused of *receiving* a penis instead' (ibid.: 135). The point of each 'return' is that it involves larger and larger objects, and the duel is conducted in rhyme. The conclusion is reached, in Dundes et al's conclusion, when one of the contestants has succeeded in verbally sodomizing his opponent with the entire citadel of the city of Aleppo, including its walls, turrets and minarets.

All inter-male contest in Turkey implies active masculinity and passive femininity. The merest suggestion that one cannot manage one's family, farm or business requires an active, violent response to negate the implied passivity. In the classic *namus davasi* (crime of honour), a man replies to a slight, whether predatory ploughing or grazing by a neighbour or a suspected insult to one's sister or daughter, by instant recourse to physical violence with gun or knife. The implied femininity is thus wiped out by an unambiguously phallic act. What is striking about verbal duelling is the lack of serious insult involved in what appears to be deeply insulting, confrontational language. Verbal duelling is, if anything, a celebration of collaborative wit and egalitarian friendship. Most forms of banter are not as formalized as those described by Dundes et al. What they have in common with Dundes et al's account, however, is rhyming and obsessive emphasis on the male anus (*göt*). The word *göt* is undoubtedly the most often used obscenity (i.e. in the same category as *küfür*, which men never use in front of women). 'Arsegiver' (*göt veren*) is not a foul insult but a comradely verbal invitation to a friend to respond in the same way. To take an example, which stuck in my mind at the time because it exhibited these two principles with maximum economy, one of the lads had invited another to sit down on a carpet that he had brought along, on which most of his group (like him, apprentice mechanics in a local garage) had huddled towards dawn. 'Any cunt around?' (*am var mi?*) he asked. '*Am yok, göt çok*', 'No cunt, plenty of arse', was the rhymed response.

This was scarcely the sophisticated celebration of wit and verbal skill described by Dundes et al, although it illustrates its essential elements. Whilst Dundes et al suggest that it constitutes a reproduction of the competitive honour ethos, what is striking is that it seems to obviate contest by using the most explicitly confrontational language (i.e. explicitly telling another man that he is a passive homosexual), and using the images of coercive domination, the 'fucker's' penis and the anus of the 'fucked'. Not only does it negate the ethos of contest, but it positively celebrates male communalism and the equality of male friendship, defiantly recognizing a far from perfect world and the flawed nature of a male sociality which exists in spite of, and not because of, the dominant male ethos of constant contest. If there is a 'counterpoint' (a choreographic metaphor would be more apt) between wrestling, fighting, and homoerotic banter, one could perhaps suggest that the latter construct a critique of the former with its remorseless duality of 'destroyer' and 'destroyed'. One might also suggest that the image of sodomy in banter, which excludes women, constitutes a recognition of the incompleteness of the claims made by a masculinist discourse and a wrestling ethos in which the wrestler ideally 'marries late' (Sertoglu 1987: 11). Most young men in provincial Turkey also marry late, but this is far from a matter of choice. The costs and time involved in getting through an apprenticeship, studying and doing one's military service, coupled with the costs of setting up a home, providing gold and frequently bride-price (depending on the area) increasingly prohibit marriage until a man is in his late twenties. Homoerotic banter constitutes a simple, direct comment on this state of affairs.

This ethos is questioned inside the ring as well as outside it. The connection between the wrestling ethos and the dominant constructions of masculinity lies in the idea that power should always be 'revealed'; power which requires secrecy is not power at all. The rules of Aba consequently preclude any form of *'anlasma'* (understanding), i.e. any prior agreement which conceals anything from the observers. And yet tactics in wrestling, as in anything else, require an understanding that one cannot always play 'by the rules'. A recurrent feature of local folklore is the wrestling bout between a young man (embarking on various trials of strength to demonstrate his worth) and a wrestler famous for his power: the young man enlists supernatural help, and gains the victory.[20] In 'real life', rules demand a transparency in which 'real' power can instantly be seen as such. When these rules are explicitly claimed to be inadequate, the ethos of a power whose legitimation and effect relies on its visibility is necessarily called into question.

The climax of the Yayladag festival took place in a final bout between two local heavyweights, Osman Çakir and Osman Kocaoglu (a regional champion). Both well knew that they were the centre of attention. They preceded the bout with a showy *pesrev*, the 'traditional' entry into the ring, which most wrestlers at this festival omitted. This indicated that what we were watching could easily turn into a display rather than a fight between two bitter rivals. They started the bout seriously, however. There was an expectant hush as they gripped one another's shoulders and leant forward. But they remained locked in a tense impasse for the entire seven-minute duration of the bout. In accordance with the rules there was a break, and another bout. This followed exactly the same pattern. At this point, one of the judges took the megaphone and addressed them from his trailer. His words, as I remember them, were as follows: 'You two have been wrestling for nearly half an hour. You realise these people have been waiting all night to see you. It's shameful (*ayip*)! For God's sake one of you, get a result!' The use of the term *ayip* did not have the desired effect. When the third bout started, the two wrestlers had evidently decided that the stakes were too high for both of them. After a few moments of exuberant slapping of thighs and the earth, which elicited a roar of anticipation from the crowd, the wrestlers entered what everybody knew was going to be the final clinch. Osman Çakir made a move that constituted an exaggerated, staged mistake. Kocaoglu immediately rolled him over on to his back, but before the referee had a chance to indicate him as the winner, Çakir had leapt to his feet, picked Kocaoglu up bodily and held him above his head with startling ease as he walked off the ring to clapping and cheering. When he got to the judges' table, however, Kocaoglu disentangled himself, picked Çakir up and paraded him around the ring in exactly the same way. The wrestling itself had become a total non-contest, whilst the gestures intended to indicate a respect for authority and a comradely acknowledgement of each wrestler's strength became the 'real' demonstration of physical prowess, in which no winner could be determined.

If anything, it was Çakir's decision to be the formal loser that attracted the onlookers' approval. It was, however, a moment enacted with some subtlety, and required careful 'reading'. Çakir could not simply fake the loss and then carry Kocaoglu off the *mersah* as victor. The claim to moral victory through defeat would have been too obvious and would have resulted in a serious humiliation of Kocaoglu, who would have been shown up as somebody who was taking himself too seriously. A symbolic levelling of the scores could only take place when Çakir had allowed himself to be paraded around the ring in turn. This dramatic, humorous performance left the conventions of wrestling firmly in place, but opened up quite different possibilities for interpreting them.

***

This analysis of wrestling in Turkey suggests a number of general assumptions about sport. Firstly, sport brings people together and coordinates them in special ways. In wrestling bouts in Turkish villages, men in the community and neighbouring villages are brought together in close physical proximity, their attention focussed on figures competing in a small brightly-lit ring. A heightened sense of occasion is created by the darkness, the excitement of outsiders in the village, and the sense of being outside normal social time. The specialness of the event, bringing together men who seldom gather in this way, is perhaps matched only by the gathering of men at the twice-yearly Bayram rituals (marking the end of Ramadan and the Feast of Sacrifices) in the central mosque in the town. Clearly sporting events are not simply opportunities for 'letting off steam', giving vent to 'natural' competitive instincts or expressing them through symbols, but elaborately structured public occasions, organized around social values of wide moral and political resonance.

Secondly, the ritual aspect of the sporting occasion focuses the townspeople's attention on the collectivity and people's activities in it in special ways. 'Normal' patterns of interpreting strategies and motives can be temporarily suspended. But this momentary suspension of disbelief is double-edged. One cannot forget, as an observer, that the strategies and motives, successes and failures, humorous inversions and ironies being represented and discerned in sport are precisely those of everyday life. Everyday life in Yayladag, for men at least, is governed by an ideology of honour and competition between honour equals. Everyday life also means realizing that this code of morality is impracticable; that some benefit from it while others cannot maintain themselves in its terms; and that constant manipulation and negotiation is needed if one is to make sense of oneself, in one's own eyes and those of others, according to this code of honourable contest. Wrestling in Turkey enables one to 'see' contest literally as well as metaphorically, in a different light. I would argue, therefore, that through sport we organize the means whereby we can deal creatively and critically with the contradictions of everyday life.

In this way, wrestling constitutes a dialogue on the operation and inherent contradictions of power in a society in which power is conceived in specific terms: masculine as opposed to feminine, active as opposed to passive, visible as opposed to concealed. It is a dialogue in the sense that it provides an opportunity to agree or disagree, or attempt to see the validity of a variety of proposals concerning how one should, or could, be a man. The extent to which these embodied concepts of masculinity assume specific and operational significance for the powerful, the powerless, or those struggling in between, lies beyond the scope of this chapter. I hope that I have succeeded though in demonstrating how wrestling makes them both visible and knowable.

Notes

1. 'Güres sudur: Kuvvet ve Zeka oyunu. Bu iki vasif insanda birlestigi vakit, büyük isler görebilir'.
2. This research was carried out in the Summer of 1993.
3. See, for example, the 14th Century *Book of Dede Korkuti*.
4. Related in the Hadithic traditions of Ibn Mace, Tirmizi, Ebu Davud and Nesai.
5. The introduction to Campbell's classic study points to the significance of concepts of male strength: 'Values based on concepts of honour, strength and pride . . .together . . .guide the conduct of the Sarakatsani in the apparent anarchy of their communal life' (1964: v).
6. Bourdieu's analysis of the 'dialectic of challenge and riposte' in Kabyle society (1965) is an early statement of this thesis.
7. Note, for example, Herzfeld's discussion of the nature of contest in rural Crete (1985).
8. From the Persian meaning strength, power or vigour (Redhouse Turkish-English Dictionary).
9. Istanbul clubs are, for example, keenly followed by Turkish speakers in Syria.

10. Sezgin Ayik came sixth in the 130-kilo bracket, and Ismail Faikoglu came fourth in the 62-kilo bracket.
11. Town council.
12. See, for example, Khoury's discussion of the Damascus *Kabadayat* (1992).
13. The 'three Kemals', celebrated particularly by the Turkish left as the founders of modern Turkish literature. In an English translation, Abdi Aga, the villain of Yasar Kemal's *Mehmet My Hawk*, is a classic example.
14. Ugur Mumcu was killed, apparently by Islamic activists, late in 1992. The event, along with the attack on Aziz Nesin by Muslim extremists in Sivas in May 1993 (when 37 writers, poets and musicians were killed) polarized the Islamic right and the Ataturkist and secularist left.
15. The 1948 London Olympics saw medals awarded to Mehmet Oktay, Mersinli Ahmet, Nasuh Akar, Gazanfer Bilge, Celal Arik and Yasar Dogu (who remains a household name in Turkey today). In 1952 (Helsinki), Hasam Gemici and Bayram Sit Altin won medals. Turkey also scored notable successes in 1956 (London) (Mithat Bayrak, Mustafa Dagistanli and Hamit Kaplan), in 1960 (Rome) (Ahmet Bilek, Mustafa Dagistanli, Hasan Gungor, Ismet Atli, Muzahir Sile, Mithat Bayrak, Tevfik Kis), in 1964 (Tokyo) (Ismail Ogan, Kazim Ayvaz), and in 1968 (Mexico) (Mahmut Atalay, Ahmet Ayik) (Sari 1992: 12–14). Sabahattin Ozturk's gold medal in the World Championships in Canada 1993 marks the end of a period in Turkish international wrestling that has been only relatively unsuccessful.
16. One could perhaps draw an analogy with cricket for English cricket fans as a symbolic means of mediating a post-colonial trauma.
17. The populations forcibly exchanged in this period were defined according to the Ottoman Turkish millet system, i.e. by religion, not language. There are still many villages in the Bursa and Balikesir region today in which some Bulgarian Slavic is spoken, and whose inhabitants are still described by other locals as *muhacir*, 'refugees'.
18. Wrestling enthusiasts in Yusufeli, a town in the North-Eastern province of Artvin with its own wrestling festival and tradition of champion wrestlers, describe local wrestling in these terms.
19. Fettah Yanaray, born in Antioch, occupies a significant place in Sari's local hall of fame (1992: 44). He not only won the 1984 Turkish wrestling championships and competed in the national team, but also came second in the national judo championships, is a professional karate trainer and has worked as a professional boxer.
20. Supernatural help arrives in the form of Hidir, the Muslim version

of the Prophet Elias, who traditionally turns up in the guise of an old man to help people in their moment of distress. See the story of the wrestling bout between the son of the King of Isfahan and the wrestler Karaduman in Silay 1988: 74.

Bibliography

Aswad, B. (1971), *Property Control and Social Strategies: Settlers on a Middle Eastern Plain*. Anthropological Papers. Ann Arbor: University of Michigan Press

Bourdieu, Pierre (1965), 'The sentiment of honour in Kabyle society' in J. G. Peristiany (ed.),*Honour and Shame: The values of Mediterranean society*. London: Weidenfeld and Nicolson. pp. 191–240

Campbell, John K. (1964), *Honour, Family and Patronage*. Oxford: Oxford University Press

De Certeau, Michel (1987), *The Practice of Everyday Life*. Berkeley: University of California Press

Dundes, A., B. Özkök and J. Leach (1972), 'The strategy of Turkish duelling rhymes' in J. Gumperez and D. Hymes (eds), *Directions in sociolinguistics*. New York: Rinehart and Winston. pp. 130–160

Eco, Umberto (1987), 'Sports chatter' in *Travels in Hyperreality*. London: Pan. pp. 159–165

Gilsenan, Michael (1986), 'Domination as social practice: patrimonialism in north Lebanon: arbitrary power, desecration, and the aesthetics of violence', *Critique of Anthropology*, vol. 6, no. 1, pp. 17–37

Herzfeld, Michael (1985), *The Poetics of Manhood: contest and identity in a Cretan mountain village*. Princeton: Princeton University Press

Hornby, Nick (1992), *Fever Pitch*. London: Gollancz

Keyder, Ç. and F. Tabak (eds.) (1991), *Landholding and commercial agriculture in the Middle East*. Albany: State University of New York

Khoury, P. (1992), 'Abu Ali al-Kilai: A Damascus Qabaday' in E.Burke III (ed.), *Struggle and Survival in the Modern Middle East*. London: I. B Tauris

Sari, Z. (1992), *Hatay'da Aba Güresi*. Antakya: Hatay Folklor Arastirmalari Dernegi

Sertoglu, M. (1987), *Rumeli Türk Pehlivanlari: Kurtdereli Mehmet ve Adali Halil*. Ankara: Kültür ve Turzim Bakanligi Yayinlari

Silay, M. (ed.) (1988), *Dr. Edip Kizildagli'dan Hatay Masallari*. Antakya: Hatay Yayinlari

Tekin, M. (1992), 'Hatay'da Aba Güresi Üzerine' in Z. Sari (ed.) *Hatay'da Aba Güresi*. Antakya: Hatay Folklor Arastirmalari Dernegi

Uludag, S. (1976), *Islam Açisindan Musikî ve Semâ*. Istanbul: Irfan

Van Bruinessen, M. (1992), *Agha, Sheikh and State: The Social and Political Structures of Kurdistan*. London: Zed Books

Acknowledgements

I am grateful to Richard English, Mark Burnett, and Lucy Baxandall for their comments on drafts of this chapter. I read a version of this chapter at a seminar in the Department of Sociology and Social Anthropology at the University of Hull, and I am grateful to Andy Dawson, Allison James and Sandra Wallman for their useful comments. I am also grateful to teachers at the Payas Meslek Endustri Lisesi for putting me up over the summer of 1993, when most of the research for this chapter was carried out, and those in Yayladag who made me so welcome.

3

Indigenous Polo and the Politics of Regional Identity in Northern Pakistan

Peter Parkes

Within the ethnography of sports, G. Whitney Azoy's *Buzkashi: Game and Power in Afghanistan* (1982) remains exemplary. By focusing on leaders's practical mobilization, for their own self-interested needs, of this highly dramatized equestrian game, Azoy moves well beyond a conventional interpretation of sport as ritualized play and display. Instead he highlights the overt referential functions of *buzkashi* tournamants. In northern Afghanistan, the minority Uzbeks exploit these tournaments as one means to wrest a distinctive identity, to convey their own regional aspirations of rugged autonomy from the alien hegemony of Pashtun officials in the capital, Kabul. What is so striking about Azoy's approach is his final analysis, which concerns contemporary transformations of this traditionally anarchic tribal game into an elaborately regulated national sport under central government sponsorship. In the process, the mobilizing powers of Uzbek *khans* (the managerial 'big-men' of tribal Uzbek society) are diminished and the *khans* themselves reduced to intermediary clients for the regional governor and his bureaucratic entourage of Pashtun athletic officials. These bureaucrats now impose an alternative, disciplinary apparatus of civilizing rules and penalties on the game, together with an appropriate civilizing discourse of government propaganda. Detailed historical ethnography of successive Afghan appropriations of the tribal Uzbek game from the 1950s thus serves to substantiate transformations of Weberian magnitude, which would otherwise only be conceivable in a much more abstract manner, i.e. it provides a concrete example of the shifts from traditional-patrimonial authority structures to national-bureaucratic ones within a single generation in Afghanistan. As the gory evidence of recent years demonstrates, the regional and sectarian strife stimulated by these transformations is still tragically unresolved.

This essay outlines a comparable ethnography of the similar equestrian sport of indigenous polo in neighbouring regions of northern Pakistan. I shall examine congruent political processes concerning nationalist appropriations of a regionally localized game, within much the same period as that treated by Azoy in northern Afghanistan, but under different circumstances in adjacent Pakistan. We shall observe the parallel transformation of native polo from a ceremonial game emblematic of regal authority and nobility, within formerly independent principalities, into a more organized athletic sport of national government and military patronage. A crucial independent variable, however, which makes ethnographic comparison between neighbouring regions of Afghanistan and Pakistan always a privileged conceptual experiment, is the peculiar political legacy of British colonialism in Pakistan.

Introduction: The Game of Kings, and Officers

Like Afghan *buzkashi*, the game of polo is plausibly derived from prehistoric equestrian sports of mounted Turkic and Iranian nomads of Central Asia, from which it was adopted as a symbol of state ceremony in Persia by at least the eleventh century (Diem 1942). By the sixteenth century, one might even conjecture a polo-centric 'arena state' within imperial Iran (*pace* Geertz 1980), when the Safavid ruler Shah Abbas specifically designed his new capital at Isphahan so that it focused on its central 'royal arena' (*maidan-i-shah*) for polo, with his own palace and mosque displaced to the periphery of the imperial sportsfield. The Persian game was then incorporated within the court rituals of Moghul rulers throughout South Asia, as evinced in an account of this 'football on horseback' by the Elizabethan Sherley brothers visiting the court of Akbar (Watson 1989: 51). It seems probable that the indigenous game played in the Hindu Kush was ceremonially shaped by this Moghul Indian form of Persian *chaughán-bazi* (the 'game of squared mallets'); for we encounter its similar ritual functions in state ceremonies persisting until the late 1960s. A Tibetan etymology of the widespread term *bulá*, 'ball' (hence Anglo-Indian *polo*), however, suggests a specifically Himalayan origin (Mahdisan 1981).

It was from just two peripheral Himalayan enclaves – on India's northwestern and northeastern frontiers – that all existent forms of polo derive, since the Moghul sport was elsewhere abandoned in the subcontinent by the eighteenth century. Although this essay concerns the indigenous game of the northwestern enclave, its other northeastern Himalayan survivor is also pertinent to our theme. For it was from Manipur, in Assam, that the game was ingeniously reconstructed as a British regimental sport, thence reintroduced to colonial India in the mid-nineteenth century. And it was through the reinvented British sport that modern polo has devolved as a Pakistani regimental preoccupation, whose civilizing rules have since encroached upon the Hindu Kush and Karakorum.

The curious story of polo's imperial reinvention and metropolitan reprocessing – its raw retrieval from Manipur to Hurlingham, and its re-export in finished form back to the subcontinent – is well enough known to aficionados of the game (Watson 1986; 1989: 50–59). It offers an unusually instructive paradigm for a historical anthropology of sport, precisely documenting the cross-cultural regenesis of a regionally localized game through an imperial world system, which thereby accumulates a sophisticated canon of civilizing rules which are ultimately re-imposed upon a primitivized and peripheralized parent-game. In the case of native polo, both its northeastern and northwestern Himalayan relics seem to have been discovered almost simultaneously by British officers, separately penetrating the northern frontiers of the subcontinent in the 1850s. But it was the Manipuri game that was famously adopted by Joseph Scherer, commandant of the Kuki Levy at Cachar in Assam. He arranged for the first British team of tea-planters to play against the Raja of Manipur, and established the Calcutta Polo Club in 1863, thereby instigating polo's contagious adoption by cavalry regiments throughout Bengal. Intriguingly, accounts of this Manipuri game are identical in all major respects with that witnessed within the same decade by Frederick Drew (1875: 380–92) in Baltistan and Gilgit. This Balti and Gilgit version is essentially the indigenous game still played throughout northern Pakistan. There were seven or more players per side, with games lasting up to an hour, without break, until a winning team had scored nine goals; and there were minimal rules, beyond such polite injunctions as against 'using teeth' in riding-off.

The modern sport of polo, however, stemmed from a written report of the Manipuri game in *The Field*, which inspired officers of the 10th Hussars on home leave at Aldershot to reconstruct their own 'hockey on horseback' with the aid of walking-sticks and a billiard ball. Devising basic rules adapted from British hockey, and from some other regimental equestrian sports, which defined criteria of duration and foul-play to safeguard their Irish ponies, it was this judicious Aldershot reconstruction of the Manipuri game which laid the regular foundations of regimental polo, enshrined in the Hurlingham Association Rules of 1876, and which was then carried back to the subcontinent.[1] Widely embraced by the British Indian army, and readopted by Indian princes, this modern sport survived the Raj as a disciplinary pastime of both Indian and Pakistani cavalry regiments, and was being incorporated into the recreational drill and display of civil service departments. There are now over a score of clubs in the Pakistan Polo Association (PPA), including many regimental stations in the northern Punjab and North-West Frontier Province, together with such government service teams as the Pakistan Railway Club and the Punjab Police Club. Yet the more numerous indigenous polo associations of the northern districts of Chitral and Gilgit have only 'affliliation' status within the PPA.

The Traditional Game

Frederick Drew's extensive early account of polo in Baltistan and Gilgit is an essential source on the traditional form and tactics of the indigenous game (Drew 1875: 380–92; cf. Leitner 1889; Frembgen 1988), for he was an enthusiastic 'participant-observer' of polo when serving as a mining engineer seconded to the Maharaja of Kashmir in the 1860s. As Drew then noted, polo grounds are found in virtually every village or large hamlet throughout Baltistan, Gilgit and Chitral (Fig. 1). Unlike the almost square regulation grounds of Hurlingham Association standards (200 x 300 yds), the equally long *shawaran* or *maidan* field is barely 40 yards wide, usually contained by a rough stone wall and with cairn pillars set four to eight yards apart as goals. In some settlements, such as Aiun in Chitral, the game was simply played between shopfronts along the bazaar. But in most villages the polo-ground is carefully irrigated to maintain a fine turf, serving as a central place of assembly for communal festivities, usually situated beside the local ruler's fort. A raised stone dais or 'throne' (*takht*) on the perimeter wall would accomodate such lords and attendant nobility, nowadays replaced or accompanied by local government officials (cf. Balneaves 1972: 48). Opposite this regal dais is the special place for low-caste musicians (*dom, bericho*), employed to orchestrate games with stirring melodies played on a barrel drum and two kettle drums accompanied by *surnai* reed flutes. Each player has an inherited or assigned personal tune, often a uniquely

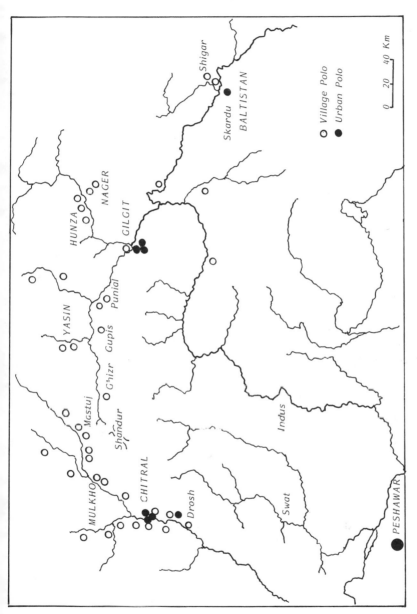

Fig. 1 Distribution of Polo in Northern Pakistan

composed melody that had been awarded as a royal boon to outstanding players and their descendants, which is especially played on the occasion of their triumphal 'taking off' (*tampuk*) after scoring a goal (Drew 1875: 383, 385; cf. Frembgen 1988: 208–9). The musicians also perform these ranked tunes for dances of victory or forfeiture at the conclusion of each game (Drew 1875: 385-86; Biddulph 1880: 85-86; cf. Tahir Ali 1981).

Drew further noted that there was no fixed number of players per side, observing teams with as many as 15 players in Baltistan. (Indigenous tournaments are nowadays limited to teams of five or six players.) He also saw little evidence of any tactical 'positions' in the traditional game comparable to the numbered team positions of what would become Hurlingham Association polo (i.e. numbers 1, 2, 3 and back; cf. Watson 1989: 15, 41–43). Rather, he described an anarchic and tactically individualized game, startlingly reminiscent of Azoy's (1982: 3) account of tribal *buzkashi*:

> The players do not take up their station at their respective goals, but *all* congregate at one end. Then from here one player begins the game by taking the ball in his hand, starting off at full gallop, and, when he comes to the middle of the ground, throwing it up and striking it as best he can towards the enemy's goal (i.e. *tampok*). . . But the leader is followed not only by his own side, but by all his opponents, galloping close behind, and the struggle comes for the second blow, if the ball has not reached the goal. Now when one of the other party gets the chance, he does not strike it back in the direction he wishes it ultimately to go, but carries it on *towards his own base*, for the sake of making the ball miss the goal and pass behind. If this happens, the practice is for a bystander to take up the ball and throw it as hard as he can in the other direction, so that now the second side have the advantage due to the impetus. And it is the rule that the game is not considered as again started until one of that side has touched the ball, this being done without interruption from the other side. Now probably will come the time when the ball gets checked and entangled among the horses' legs; then comes a *melée*, often amusing enough, when crowding of horses, pushing, hooking of sticks – intentionally as well as by accident, for it is an allowed thing – the ball remains for long confined and often invisible; till by some chance it gets clear and is carried away by some nimble-handed one; when a race again begins, to make or save the goal (Drew 1875: 383–4).

Drew further mentions that goals (*hal*) were confirmed only when one of the winning players dismounted and picked the ball up, prior to which any opponent could still strike the ball out. Goals would then be reversed, with the scorer galloping out in *tampuk* triumph to throw and strike the ball in the opposite direction. Unlike Hurlingham polo, there are thus no short 'chukkas' of seven-minute play, nor any changing of ponies. Traditional games could wearily persist for an hour, until one side had scored nine goals, as in Manipur. Nowadays, tournament games are divided into halves of 30 minutes' duration, with a rest break of ten minutes.

Drew and other mid-nineteenth century British observers also detailed the ceremonial and ritual functions of polo within mountain principalities of this region, which persisted until their dissolution barely twenty-five years ago. In Chitral, the spring polo season was inaugurated with state rituals conducted by the ruling prince (Mehtar) during the pre-Islamic New Year festival of Nauroz, held at the vernal equinox (Lentz 1939: 148f.) In Hunza, more elaborate rites of inauguration were held during the spring barley-sowing festival (*bóphao*), after the king had been invited by his hereditary chancellor (*wazir*) to inaugurate ploughing, the latter initiating the first *tampuk* strike on the royal polo-ground, and then galloping through the goal with a cry that 'Many sons will be born!' (Lorimer 1979: 75).[2]

Polo games were also more profanely expressive of regal authority and patronage in the mountain principalities of this region, where it was expected that fit rulers should be seen to participate in demonstration games, if not in competitive tournaments. Sponsorship of new polo-grounds, together with the hosting of communal feasts at sporting festivals, were essential policies of populist legitimation for tyrannous princes, otherwise notoriously prone to sell off their subjects into slavery, sometimes to subsidize further their polo expenses (Müller-Stellrecht 1981). There were also substantial royal grants (*meherbani* benefices) of horses or whole estates awarded to favoured players.

Yet polo had seemingly ambivalent connotations of both courtly hierarchy and populist democracy, where princes, courtiers and commoners might all be witnessed playing and competing together on an athletically equal footing:

All people are passionately fond of the game; those of rank look upon the playing of it as one of the chief objects for which they were sent into the world; but not to them is the pursuit confined; all who can get a pony to mount join in it, and the poorest enter thoroughly into the spirit of it (Drew 1875: 380–81).

In the 1930s another British traveller, witnessing the game in the small principality of Yasin, comments similarly on indigenous polo's

> real democracy. . . where the Raja, the headman and all the ragbag and bobtail of the countryside – in fact everyone who possessed a horse – played together in perfect good-fellowship and complete indifference to person (Schomberg 1935: 51).

Again in Gilgit:

> It is a wonderful democratic game; it is a curious paradox in a land of autocracy to see the Raja, his sons, and wazir all jostling and crashing together with any peasant who has a pony and cares to play. There is no respect for persons whatever (Schomberg 1935: 192).

In contrast to the elaborate court etiquette which surrounded the hierarchical ranking of caste-like tributary estates in these mountain principalities (Biddulph 1880: 61-68; Schomberg 1938: 213–18; cf. Barth 1956: 81–83), the public competition of teams of mixed rank might well be represented as a 'democratic' spectacle, subordinating courtly distinctions to merits of athletic skill. Yet participation was necessarily restricted to those who could afford the upkeep of horses, i.e. a knightly nobility of 'true human beings' (*adamzada*), who always formed a small fraction of the predominantly pedestrian population of 'miserable poor' (*fakir mishkin*) in such arid and fodderless states as Chitral.

Polo was thus essentially a fraternizing ceremony of this equestrian elite, which was itself both internally stratified by rank and hypergamy, and interrelated by ties of foster allegiance, or 'milk kinship' (Biddulph 1880: 82; Schomberg 1938: 225–26). These 'kin' ties further allied petty nobility with commoners throughout the district (cf. Schomberg 1935: 90-92; Hussam-ul-Mulk n.d.) Thus the competitive performance of polo by the powerful, irrespective of court rank, played out wider coalitions, transcending caste and locality, whereby the lowliest spectator could identify with the sporting fortunes or mishaps of 'his' prince and quasi-kinsman. In view of the perpetual internecine struggles of princes over rulership of these petty states, such coalitional identification of spectators with players on the polo-ground signified far more than mystified fanship; for these allegiances were ever ready to erupt in violent support of princely pretenders to the throne, as recurred notoriously in Chitral at the end of the nineteenth century (Robertson 1898: ch. 4; Alder 1963:

287–99; Parkes n.d.)

Peripatetic polo tournaments were also traditionally employed to consolidate the fragile regional alliances of the rulers themselves, who travelled from district to district in order to reactivate local allegiances of their own dependent foster-kin and supporters. But sponsorship of such games, together with other expenses of these royal tours, was largely borne by a hereditary yeoman estate of 'food-providers' (*ashimadek*; Biddulph 1880: 64–65), a substantial 'middle class' of smallholders which had long resented their enforced subsidy of such royal largesse (Schomberg 1938: 217–18). These unacknowledged and resentful sponsors of the traditional game would ultimately rally against the obligatory provision of their services, which they did through political mobilization within the anti-royalist Muslim League, in the troubled years following Partition and the gradual incorporation of the northern principalities within the new nation of Pakistan (Ghufran 1962: ch. 15).

The Colonial and Post-Colonial Game

As the formerly autonomous mountain principalities of the Hindu Kush and Karakorum became subject to imperial annexation from the 1890s, we can observe a gradual appropriation of royal polo patronage by British Political Agents. These foreign patrons also enthusiatically suggested various improvements upon the local game, in which their officers were now regularly participating. One should note, however, that an earlier generation of civilian explorers in the 1870s, such as Gottlieb Leitner and Frederic Drew, considered that there might be more to learn here than to teach in adopting indigenous polo as a British regimental sport:

One cannot help allowing considerable weight to the fact of three, if nor four, Englishmen having lost their lives at this game within the first ten years of its introduction into Upper India. . .(But) in Baltistan, fatal accidents at polo are hardly known, and it behoves us to examine whether this may not be due to their different way of conducting the game. I have little doubt that this freedom from accident arises from the galloping being done in the same direction at one time; there is no meeting; both sides start together and ride together after the ball. This is a very different thing from two sides being drawn up opposing each other, as in a tournament, and galloping towards each other. As to the commencing, the Balti plan of striking the ball in the air at a gallop is much more workmanlike – requiring as it does some considerable skill – than any other (Drew 1875: 390).

But such suggestions for apprenticeship of the indigenous game were scarcely heeded by Hurlingham, nor by Drew's successors in Gilgit and Chitral. Within two decades, such professional soldiers as E.F. Knight had 'no doubt that, though this game is native to the country, we have much improved upon it, and polo as played by British officers in India is a far superior sport' (1897: 185). Officers' concern about damage to their lowland regimental ponies, which were brought up to their outposts in the Karakorum, encouraged slight modifications of indigenous rules and penalties along Hurlingham guidelines, at least in regulating matches with native teams. Padded flags replaced the stone goal-posts; the rule of dismounting to seize the ball after making a goal (somewhat like grappling the goat carcass of *buzkashi*) was waived as a criterion of scoring; a rest period was introduced; intentional hooking of sticks above shoulders, or across a pony, was discouraged as foul-play.[3]

These imposed regulations, applicable only in matches with the foreign soldiers, were no doubt considered a small accomodation to the otherwise generous sponsorship of the indigenous game by such popular Political Agents as Major Cobb, who outrivalled local rulers in founding polo-grounds in virtually every village within Gilgit Agency by the late 1930s (Frembgen 1988: 198). In Gilgit, Cobb's vigour for the game is even enshrined in the saying 'I would rather be a donkey and carry wood from (distant) Harelli than play number one on Cobb Sahib's polo team' (Staley 1982: 256). Such Political Agents also helped to support the game and its princely patrons during the occasional rebellions by members of hereditary service estates against the feudal regimes of this region. By the mid-1940s these rebellions had escalated thanks to Muslim League agitation. Major Cobb then famously broke a strike of hereditary *dom* musicians, who had refused to perform for polo matches in Gilgit (Staley 1982: 264).

After Partition in 1947, British Political Agents were replaced by their Pakistani counterparts.[4] The majority of these civil administrators were also mainly regimental officers, often from the Punjab, who continued the tradition of military sponsorship of the still popular local game, despite occasional Islamicist protests against polo's frivolity and profanity, with its 'un-Islamic' music and dance. By the 1960s, polo-playing Punjabi and Pakhtun officers were beginning to introduce their own thoroughbred lowland ponies to the game, and were therefore encouraging further regulations and improvements of tactics according to the Hurlingham conventions of their lowland regimental practice.

The Modern Game

We arrive at the era of my own fieldwork experience of polo-playing in Chitral in the early 1970s. The feudal principality of Chitral State had already been dissolved by presidential decree in 1969, the local rajaships of Gilgit and Baltistan Agencies in 1972, and finally the Mirdom of Hunza was abolished in September 1974. Polo-playing Deputy Commissioners were now enthusiastically encouraging a safer and tactically more civilized training for the game. Although resisted by an older generation of courtly players, and having little impact on the village game in remote regions of Upper Chitral, these innovations were more eagerly adopted by a younger generation of players stemming from the old noble families of the court, as well as by officers of the old state militia, the Chitral Scouts (see Trench 1985). For these elite players had already embraced several changes to the game introduced at Chitrali tournaments a generation earlier, as explained to me recently by a champion player, an English-speaking advocate of courtier descent:

> The only small difference between the way we play here, and how they still play in Gilgit, is over what we call 'catch tampok' (*tamphok dosik*): when the ball is hooked up in the air and you catch it, and take it to the goal, and throw it through; or you take your horse with the ball in your hand through the goal; or else you give it to a companion who can do this. This 'catch tampok' is still played in Gilgit. But not in Shandur, or anywhere much in Chitral now. We stopped this in '56 or '57. There was too much quarrelling on those occasions, too much hitting of the horses and each other.

The same player, currently a leading member of Chitral's civil A-team, further explained how fouls and tactical 'positions' (very similar to those of Hurlingham polo) might have developed:

> The game has perhaps developed a bit, but without any real changes. That would affect the charm of the game. But even our rule-less game (*bekanun bazi*) has conventions or 'unwritten laws', you might say. You cannot hit someone intentionally, or hit his horse's legs if there is no ball there; and you should be calm and quiet in defence. So we

have a judge (umpire) there, but he has no work at all to do in most games. If rules were introduced, well there would be no end of introducing new rules then, to make it a 'gentleman's game'. But the people would lose interest in it, because the people are interested in too much courage, too much danger. These are the circumstances. Some techniques and positions have developed, because our horses are more trained than in the past, and we now practise too much. More sweetness is also coming into the game, because our horses are Punjabi 'first breed'. But there were positions in the past too: that number *one* guards number *six*; and number *six* keeps the goal, although sometimes carrying the ball even to the other goal if there is an open space; while numbers *three* and *four* stay in the middle. In the past there were those numbers too.

Confronted with Drew's account of a positionless and seemingly individualistic game, this champion player further speculated that strategic 'positions' might have naturally emerged with improved breeds of ponies:

The old Badakshi horses were not trained, not expert, nor as sensual, as Punjabi horses. Those horses are sweet by nature, they are quick to your heart, even if they lack stamina. But in twenty-minute games it's more the quickness of the horse – his response to orders, his handiness in turning – that really counts. Maybe with Badakshi horses the game then depended on just one or two good horses, so there could be no fixed positions. But some tactics have always been there. It's the same as what they call 'collective defense', that German way of thinking, even in war. I have gone through an article of Kissinger (a former President of World Polo), and I definitely agree with him: not only in football, not only in war games, but in polo also, everywhere there are the *same* tactics. So changes may take place, but not very much. The game itself has not changed.

Chitrali polo-playing has, however, changed noticeably since the introduction of Punjabi horses around 1974, when an enthusiast Deputy Commissioner had a string of regimental ponies flown in to Chitral. I well remember this friendly DC's confided ambitions of 'uplifting' the primitive local game, then a subject of some bemused mockery by elite polo-players, including my informant's now deceased father, a former counsellor of the last Mehtar. With the teaching of new tactics appropriate for foreign horses came such new code-calls as 'Leave it!' or 'Turn!' in place of the old argot of Khowar phrases (cf. Frembgen 1988: 206; Azoy 1982: 95). Already by the end of my main fieldwork in spring 1977, all Scouts and civil teams in Lower Chitral had converted to Punjabi ponies, so only remote village teams in the Upper District retained the old Badakshi horses. Apart from discrepancies of cost, there were insurmountable differences of size (12–13 hand Badakshis; 15-hand or higher Punjabis), with a consequent slight lengthening of polo-sticks, which now rendered tournament play between village and elite teams a pointlessly handicapped exercise. The once homogeneous and 'democratic' indigenous game had finally ruptured into separate class and regional fractions, mainly as a result of tournament sponsorship.

Direct government subsidies of polo-playing in Chitral had long been limited to performing officers of the Chitral Scouts, who received free horses and rations as well as extensive training as professional players. Those of the Chitral Police Team still receive an ordinary Constable's wages of 3,000 Rupees per month, and otherwise have to purchase and maintain their own ponies. All other teams are self-financed, with estimated annual costs of Rs. 25-30,000 for maintaining Punjabi ponies nowadays, which only hereditary rentier landlords can afford.[5] The Pakistan Tourism Development Corporation awards selected tournament players a small bursary of Rs. 1,000 for the season; but that is all. As another civilian A-team player of elite descent, but lesser means, explained:

> It is very difficult for people who are not big landowners, but who just have an enthusiasm (*shauki*) for polo. Their life becomes miserable, spending everything they have at home on horses. When Chitral was a State, perhaps not *every*one played polo; but those who did considered it a service (*khesmat*) to the Mehtar; and they were rewarded with horses, or given good dinners; they were 'patronized' by the Mehtar. Now we really need such sponsorship, either from the government or from semi-agencies. But it should be given to those players at least according to their standard: A-category, B-type or C-type. These players *must* be helped; for it is important for tourism; it supports Kho (Chitrali) culture, which the government is bound to preserve; it contributes to health; it increases the competitiveness of the region.

Despite escalating costs of maintaining horses, Chitral still has an estimated 50 village teams, although barely half are selected to participate in regional tournaments. As my A-team friends concurred: 'It is not that *those* teams are discriminated against in any way by the Chitral Polo Association; those teams are simply not of *that* calibre'. 'Those teams', of course, were the rural village teams of Mulkho and Mastuj, who still play the anarchic traditional game on Badakshi ponies.

Village teams in Gilgit Agency and Baltistan have suffered more devastating setbacks of modernization. Polo-playing in these regions, as in Upper Chitral, had always been associated with the necessity of horse transport for conveying trade and tribute. With the building of jeep and truck roads in recent decades, the always costly maintenance of horses has become a redundant extravagance. After the completion in 1978 of the Karakorum Highway, a metalled road linking Islamabad with Kashgar through the gorges of the upper Indus and along Hunza valley (Kreutzman 1991), polo-playing has virtually disappeared along its length. Of formerly six teams in the Ghujal District of upper Hunza, who arranged spring and autumn tournaments in the 1970s, just two horses survived by 1990 (Kassam pers. comm.). But two teams from the former polo mecca of Nager persist, their selected players still dominating tournaments in Gilgit (cf. Frembgen 1988: 198, 204); while rural teams from the still poorly accessible villages of Ishkoman, Punial, and Ghizr continue to flourish, although they are rarely invited nowadays to tournaments at the prestigious Agha Shahi Stadium in Gilgit town. Here, as in Chitral, the dominant A-teams are comprised of professionally salaried and equipped players of the old Gilgit Scouts milita, renamed the Northern Light Infantry (NLI), together with the Northern Areas Working Organization (NAWO), and the Public Works Team (PWT). Notoriously, all poach their star Nager players from each other, with ever inflated transfer bids for these prima donna 'Imran Khans of the Northern Areas' at major tournaments (Kassam pers. comm.) The NLI team is thus rudely referred to as the 'Nakedly Lucrative Infantry' (Urdu *nanga luch infantri*) by civil players.

District and regional polo tournaments in Chitral and Gilgit stem from the enthusiastic administrative arrangements of British Political Agents, like Major Cobb, who regularized the more informally orchestrated peripatetic tournaments of roving princes as these waned in the 1930s and '40s. In Chitral, the polo spring season is now officially inaugurated by the Deputy Commissioner during government celebrations of Pakistan Day on the 23rd March, almost coinciding with the Mehtar's ancient equinoxial rites of Nauroz (ca. 21 March). Heading a selection committee of polo veterans, predominantly of princely descent, the DC supervises the 'Commisioner's Cup' tournament in May, comprising separate games for the elite military or civil A-teams and some 20 rural village teams invited from Upper Chitral, with small cash prizes financed from District Council development funds. A second 'Chief Minister's Cup' is presided over by North-West Frontier Province officials coming up from Peshawar to celebrate Pakistan Independence Day on August 14, a convenient occasion for government propaganda and election promises to be delivered to attendant spectators. Another traditional tournament, 'the Inspector General Frontier Corps Cup', used to be held in June; but it was withdrawn in the early 1990s, as was a spring tournament once sponsored by Pakistan International Airlines (PIA). The PIA indeed once flew in their own prestigious Hurlingham Association team for a demonstration match at their tournament in 1990. But this was not a felicitous experiment. As Chitrali players politely remember: 'Our game did not really suit their big Arab horses; they could not turn in our little *junali* ground, and they seemed worried about hurting them. This "free-style" was just not *their* game: it was too costly, their chances of winning were dim, and there was no thrill even for the people'. The same year also witnessed a brief adoption of the bad poaching habits of Gilgit, when the Chitral Scouts at Drosh began offering lucrative transfer bids to civil players; but this malpractice was debarred on the advice of the DC's Committee in autumn 1994.

Similar regional tournaments in Gilgit were formerly sponsored by Pakistan International Airlines, but have since been replaced by stipends and horse allowances awarded by the Pakistan Tourism Development Corporation (PTDC), which also hosts its own tournament cup in April. A second autumn tournament is sponsored by the Commissioner for Northern Areas to commemorate the patriotic 'Gilgit Freedom Struggle' (*Jashni Azadi Gilgit*) against Indian Kashmir in November 1947.[6] Local District Council Tournaments are also held in some remoter areas, like Ghizr, just before the Commissioner's Cup, when civil and military B-teams occasionally compete with rural players; but as in Chitral, such local teams with their 'rough and ready' (*andarun*) manners, and little Wakhi ponies, are no real match for even second-grade professional teams, with their sophisticated regimental 'techniques' (*nafarsat*) of blocking and backhand passing. The spectacular culmination of all these district matches is, however, the inter-regional Shandur Tournament, sponsored annually by the central government Ministry of Tourism and Culture around the end of June.

Shandur: The Post-Modern Game?

Located on an otherwise deserted high mountain pass between Chitral
District and the Northern Areas of Gilgit Agency (see Fig. 1), over 12,000
feet above sea level, the Shandur Tournament is justly touted as the
supreme tourist attraction of Pakistan: 'Polo on the Roof of the World'
(with an appended 'World's Highest Golf Tournament' and 'All-Pakistan
Trout Fishing Competition'). This inter-regional tournament has,
however, its own contested local history. It was supposedly initiated in
1938, when local polo teams from Rajaships in Gilgit Agency first visited
Chitral, with sporadic return matches of these village teams played in
1958 in Gilgit and at Shandur in 1966 (Shahzad 1995: 40).[7] From 1989,
it was effectively reinvented as a traditionalized annual contest between
'Gilgit Agency' and 'Chitral District' teams through the promotional
efforts of the Pakistan Tourism Development Corporation: 'The ancient
game of polo was born in Central Asia, grew up in Persia. . .and reached
maturity at Shandur, in the majestic Northern Areas of Pakistan' (PTDC
brochure, Gilgit 1990).

The Shandur Tournament is a truly national event, well covered by
the Pakistan Television Corporation, whose highlights can be almost
simultaneously viewed through satellite dishes sprouting on the mud
roofs of the remotest villages of Upper Chitral and Gilgit. It is also a
vast government function, regularly attended by Presidents and Prime
Ministers (both Nawaz Sharif and Benazir Bhutto in recent years), by
the Chief of Army Staff, and by the Ministries of Culture and Sport from
both Central and Provincial Governments. Many such VIPs are flown
in by military helicopter, and accommodated in elaborate marquees
erected around the high-pasture *mahuran bagh* stadium, where they are
regally entertained by Colonel Khushwaqt, ex-prince of nearby Mastuj,
and an outstanding former polo-player of Chitral, who now manages an
international Karakorum trekking company from his crumbling royal
fort. The tournament already costs hundreds of thousands of Rupees,
specially allocated in 1995 to the NWFP Provincial Government (no
doubt to sooth regional fractions within the Pakistan People's Party). But
such funds are wholly accounted in 'VIP and VVIP budgeting', i.e. in
providing security and support staff for government officials and
diplomats, together with their transport and accommodation costs.
Lowlier prize money for A-team and B-team polo-players (Rs. 100,000)
is sponsored by Red and White Cigarettes, Coca-Cola (Pakistan) or PIA,
while the meagre subsistence of civil teams can only be partly covered
from District development funds. Local polo-playing is indeed becoming

a barely noticed backdrop for the Shandur Season, Islamabad's Royal Ascot.

The revamped Shandur Tournament has had further widespread effects on the nature and reception of polo-playing in Chitral and Gilgit. Prior to its annual institutionalization from 1989, all Chitrali teams had traditionally five players. But in order to compete with the six-player teams of the champion Northern Light Infantry of Gilgit Agency, Chitral A-Teams needed to practice with an additional player. Now six-player teams are conventional in regional Chitrali tournaments, requiring a reconfiguration of all positional tactics according to Gilgiti techniques which further alienates the elite and professionalized game from that persisting in rural villages.

The co-option of Deputy Commissioners into the extravagant ambitions of the Pakistan Tourism Development Corporation has also caused unintended political reactions which recall the social protests mobilized by Muslim League agitators against the princely games of the 1940s. Recently, one of the great polo-sponsoring DCs of contemporay Chitral was obliged to seek transferral as a consequence of his all too visible support for the game, which he had partly provided from his own pocket (according to his own account). After the rebuilding and widening of the main *junali* polo ground of Chitral in 1989, and the construction of a splendid tin-roofed pavilion for tourist spectators, Islamicist agitators of the opposition *Jamaati Islami* party began disseminating scandalous rumours of his misappropriation of Chitral Area Development Project funds. The people's allocated money, intended for productive projects, was being lavished upon the un-Islamic pastimes of the old courtly elite, the mullahs sermonized over their mosque loudspeakers (and there were further intimations of impropriety with those pretty young English school-teachers attending the game). Piously outraged demonstrators against this DC's supposed profligacy were soon interrupting tourist polo-games throughout the summer and autumn of 1990. Chitrali polo's briefly powerful patron was transferred before the end of the year.

Conclusions

Following a simple chronology of observed transformations in the indigenous polo of northern Pakistan, we have witnessed subtle shifts in the game's practices and discourses as it has accommodated to successive alien administrations. We have particularly examined the ambivalent legacy of British colonial patronage, whereby a similar elite anglophone administration (Punjabi officers) has perpetuated an alternative lowland tradition of regimental (Hurlingham) polo, so lending some recognizable affinity between the sporting habits of rulers and ruled which could be fruitfully grafted onto the traditional stem of princely patronage. Improving the indigenous game according to their own regimentally instilled dispositions of sporting excellence and fair-play, neither British nor Punjabi administrators probably ever intended to 'change' the game through arrogation. Rather they wished to nurture what they perceived as its intrinsic qualities, sensed through their own more civilized sporting habits. Polo-playing administrators indeed boast of their demotic participation in a 'wild game' (*jangali tamasha*) which would shock fellow civil servants and regimental colleagues posted to tamer districts. They would therefore regard themselves as caretakers of an indigenous and endangered local tradition, whose authentic preservation (for foreign appreciation) is also an objective of the Pakistan Tourism Development Corporation.

Justification for each slight modification introduced by these foreign benefactors has peculiarly concerned the welfare of horses – a justification again stemming from the sporting sensibilites of an originally British regimental equestrian tradition. For the fine feelings of a foreign spectator, the anarchic traditional game certainly does appear unnecessarily cruel at times, when the little Badakshi ponies get bloodily gouged with spurs and whips as well as with sticks in the chaotic frenzy of a massed challenge (e.g. Balneaves 1972: 46–53). Yet one might dispassionately reconsider Drew's vigorous defence of the traditional game against its original animal welfare detractors:

> I must try to efface an impression that has lately got abroad, that polo is a cause of cruelty to the ponies. It can only be so if racing be cruel to race-horses, and hunting to hunters. The truth is that the game brings out a horse's capabilities, exercises his faculties, and so makes him fulfil the object of his life, in the highest degree. In the heat of the game a blow from the ball on his shin or his knee (a joint by no means so tender as our own knee, with which it does not correspond in structure) is hardly felt. . .If one exposes the ponies to no greater risk of injury than we do ourselves at polo – and I cannot think their risk is greater – then the best friends of animals should be satisfied (Drew 1875: 391-92).

As we know from the historiography of animal welfare (e.g. Turner

1980), the contemporary liberal (proto-feminist) concerns which Drew addressed here implicated broader moralizing sensibilities of a modernizing civility, as elsewhere treated by Norbert Elias (1978). Similar civilizing senses and rhetorics evidently still inform the sporting motives of our polo-playing Deputy Commissioners, in their attempts to correct what they cannot help but experience as a sometimes brutal local game.

A second major theme of our account has been the gradual, almost imperceptible division of a once socially coherent indigenous game into separate elite and rural village fractions, belying a still widely upheld belief in local polo's epitomization of participatory democracy. DCs and ex-princes may still be seen playing with local players, irrespective of administrative rank. But tournament play has inevitably introduced a distinctive competitive grading of military and elite civil teams. Their incremental evolution, under the influence of regimental Hurlingham conventions, has further resulted in the distinct speciation of a technically hybrid polo that can no longer fruitfully interact with the original game. There are now physical incompatabilities (e.g. of height or team numbers), redefining the mutual tactics of play, that mark a saltatory divide from former differences of relative skill. This leap into a separate, quasi-professional pool of competing civil A-team and Scouts players in Chitral may be dated to the onset of major tournament promotion in the early 1970s; in Gilgit it seemingly occurred earlier, under the special predatorial pressure of the Northern Light Infantry, which still dominates all indigenous polo teams in northern Pakistan.

The courtly fathers and grandfathers of my champion polo-playing friends in Chitral were still regularly playing the indigenous game with commoners from local village teams 25 years ago. But their A-team descendants are understandably more anxious that their well-practised skills be recognizably differentiated from those of their backwood country cousins (and local village teams typically include ex-nobility who are related and intermarried with Chitral's young urban professionals) in their desperate lobbies for government or corporate subsidies. We witness, in their plaintive English, a further rupturing of moral sensibilities concerning the former solidarity of Chitrali players, irrespective of merit, in their resistance to the civilizing pretensions of DCs and Scouts officers, which I well remember being discussed with disrespectful mirth at their family homes in the 1970s. This necessary compliance with the authoritative tournament game (always with a hopeful if sceptical ear to long-heard promises of further PTDC or Provincial Government subsidy) seems indicative of a broader class division isloating this educated and increasingly professionalized urban elite of ex-nobility.

Differences in sporting practice may thus be emblematic of a wider recreational culture, including language (Urdu and English) and musical tastes (a conservative connoisseurship of Chitrali court melodies and eschewal of popular Hindi film music) which now irrevocably divides this elite from their barely literate relatives as well as their social inferiors. For these amateur players, whether professionally employed or idle gentry in what little spare time is left from daily polo practice, are also typically private contractors (*tikadar*) for the many lucrative development projects which are now flooding into northern Pakistan. Their fortunes and lifestyle are thus becoming more intimately associated with outside (Punjabi, Pakhtun or European) administrators than with their rural compatriots. Their detachment from the indigenous village game accompanies a more general disinterest in hereditary (and now distastefully paternalist) obligations to dependents and foster-kin, obligations which once welded these mountain principalities into socially interlinked, although ranked, sodalities. Rifts in the tactical playing of polo seem again tokens of a more general type of distinct class formation which is occurring throughout northern Pakistan.[8]

Yet we should note that polo is still an immensely popular spectator sport in Chitral and Gilgit, just as Drew noted long ago: '(all) the children of an early age get their eye and hand in accord by practising it on foot – playing indeed the ordinary hockey of our country' (1875: 381). Such juvenile polo, played on foot or bicycle, still beats football, while the bazaars of Chitral and Gilgit still close shop whenever a tournament match begins. Rural village players continue to flock to the regional tournaments of Chitral, Gilgit and Shandur, commonly deprecating their own 'wild' (*jangali*) game at home in contrast to the 'regulated' (*kanuni*) sport of their civil and army superiors. Indeed, they employ the very same meiotic terms of ironic and resistant self-mockery as those used by elite champions reflecting on the relative 'barbarism' of *their* indigenous game in relation to the lowland regimental sport. A shared discourse of collective self-deprecation, from an imagined national perspective, together with fiercely patriotic and enthusiastic spectatorship, thus papers over the class fissures of polo that we have diagnosed here, which were indeed mirthfully denied by my Chitrali friends. I should state, however, that I share their hopes for sponsorship of the elite game, which may well be necessary if indigenous polo is to survive at all in Pakistan.

My slight parody of the novelistic pretensions of anthropological colleagues, especially in describing the extraordinary Shandur Tournament, is similarly intended in good faith: I suggest being careful, especially in the bourgeoning ethnography of contemporary sport and leisure, not to adopt feuilleton preoccupations with the international debris surrounding such sporting spectacles, which are precisely the surface preoccupations of their supercilious audience. Rather I have tried to document the more mundane local effects of a long history of sporting tournaments on the practical techniques and regulations of the indigenous game – hence its significance in the overtly debated or evidently implicated concerns of various players about regional ethnicity, family rank or class identity. Taking inspiration from Azoy's fine monograph on Afghan *buzkashi*, and more especially from Bourdieu's (1990) progamme for a comparative sociology of sport, we might relegate to anthropologizing journalists our old interpretivist tricks (of reading imaginative 'texts' over the shoulders of performers and informants) and instead attend to what players and spectators and officials are actually saying and doing (cf. Asad 1981), as well as heeding the historical testaments of such neglected proto-ethnographers of sport as Frederick Drew.

Notes

1. This received history of the game (Watson 1989: 52–53) is characteristically disputed by G.W. Leitner, a cranky explorer of the northwestern enclave, which he called 'Dardistan' (see Keay 1979: 14-22). I reproduce here his apparently unnoticed claim to precedence in introducing polo from Ladakh, which might be further investigated:

   'Although our first practical knowldgc of "Polo" was derived from the Manipuri game as played at Calcutta, it is not Manipur, but Hunza and Nagyr, that maintain the original rules of the ancient "Chaughán-bazi" so famous in Persian history. The account given by J. Moray Brown for the "Badminton Library" of the introduction of Polo into England (Longmans, Green & Co. 1891), seems to be at variance with the facts within my knowledge, for it was introduced into England in 1867, not 1869, by one who had played the Tibetan game as brought to Lahore by me in 1866, after a tour in Middle and Little Tibet. Since then it has become acclimatised not only in England, but also in Europe. The Tibetan game, however, does not reach the perfection of the Nagyr game, although it seems to be superior to that of Manipur' (Leitner 1889: Appendix IV.1 'Polo in Hunza-Nagyr'; cf. Frembgen 1988: 198 n.5).

2. It is subsequently explained that 'If the horse and ball go through the goal, there will be a favourable year and sons will be born. On the other hand, if the ball goes out, they say that there will be a difficult year and daughters will be born' (Lorimer 1979: 255). The significance of the *wazir* thus serving as an auspice of human fertility is elsewhere illuminated by a conjugal analogy: 'The *tham* (king) is husband, the *wazir* is his wife. The prosperity of the house depends upon the wife, the prosperity of the country depends on the *wazir*' (Lorimer 1979: 126). On other court rituals surrounding polo, see Müller-Stellrecht (1973: 78–79; 260-64) on Hunza and Frembgen (1988: 205) on Nager; cf. Jettmar (1975: 267–69).

3. Cf. Drew (1857: 386–87), who foresaw many of these modifications as desirable for English players. Schomberg similarly noted: 'To anyone used to Indian polo, the roughness of the game is remarkable. There is "crossing" of an outrageous nature, hitting your opponent's pony very hard with a polo stick, catching the ball with the hand, puting the arm round a man's waist, and a number of customs that would not be tolerated down country' (1935: 193).

4. The federally administered Northern Areas formerly comprised Political Agencies in Gilgit and Baltistan. After the dissolution of states and rajaships in this region (1972–74), Political Agents were redesignated Deputy Commissioners. Chitral State also had a Political Agent advising its Mehtar, prior to its dissolution in 1969, when the former principality was incorporated as a subdistrict of Malakand Agency (NWFP) under a Deputy Commissioner.

5. A Punjabi polo pony now costs Rs. 25–30,000. A trained groom (*sais*) expects a monthly payment of Rs. 1000, with similar additional monthly costs for his subsistence together with fodder.

6 On the peculiar 'independence struggles' of Gilgit in 1947–48, then claimed by India as a dependency of Kashmir, see Dani (1989: 326–401), Staley (1982: 265–69), and especially Lamb (1994: 118–22).

7. There is a less exalted reference in the official history of Chitral to the unexpected arrival, on 24 May 1938, of a composite polo team from three minor Rajaships of Gilgit Agency at the Mehtar's Darbar and District Tournament in Chitral: 'It was led by the three brothers of the Governors (or Rajas) of these areas. . . Some interesting matches were held. . . The Chitral team distinguished themselves in the game. . . They were, however, beaten by the Punial team' (Ghufran 1962: Ch. 14). A more alluring account was entrusted to me by Advocate Wali Rakhman of Chitral: 'The tournament really started when Major Kirkbride (P.A. Gilgit 1934–37) came to Shandur Pass in the case of some elopement or abduction of a noble girl from *this* area (Chitral) by men of Ghizr at Yasin. The party from Chitral went on horseback to settle this dispute there, and then they played polo.

English gentlemen were playing on *both* sides with the local gentry (as respective adjudicators from Chitral and Gilgit): they did not know that there would be any competition; but all of a sudden they started playing at *mahuran*. This was all recorded by Babar Jan, Governor of Gupis, in his Diaries, which I have in my possession. There he mentions that Major Kirkbride was actually captain of *our* (Chitral) team, so *we* really won that first match'. (Chitral has since won just two Shandur tournaments, in 1986 and 1993).

8. See Staley (1982: 259–65, 270–71) for a sympathetic acount of such ruptures already evident in the 1960s; also Haserodt (1989) on more recent social and economic developments in Chitral.

Bibliography

Alder, G. J. (1963), *British India's Northern Frontier 1865-95: a Study in Imperial Policy*. London: Longmans (for the Royal Commonwealth Society)

Asad, T. (1981), 'Anthropology and the Analysis of Ideology', *Man* (N.S.), vol. 14, pp. 607–27

Azoy, G. Whitney (1982), *Buzkashi: Game and Power in Afghanistan*. Pennsylvania: University of Pennsylvania Press.

Balneaves, E. (1972), *Mountains of the Murgha Zerin: between the Hindu Kush and the Karakorum*. London: John Gifford.

Barth, Fredrik (1956), *Indus and Swat Kohistan: an Ethnographic Survey*. Oslo: Forenede Trykkerier.

Biddulph, J. (1880), *Tribes of the Hindoo Koosh*. Calcutta: Office of the Superintendant of Government Printing

Bourdicu, Pierre (1990), 'Programme for a Sociology of Sport', in his *In Other Words*. Cambridge: Polity, pp. 156–67

Dani, A. H. (1989), *History of Northern Areas of Pakistan*. Islamabad: National Institute of Historical and Cultural Research

Diem, C. (1942), *Asiatische Reiterspiele: Ein Beitrag zur Kulturgeschichte der Völker*. Berlin

Drew, Frederik (1875), *The Jummo and Kashmir Territories: a Geographical Account*. London

Elias, Norbet (1978), *The Civilizing Process*. Oxford: Basil Blackwell

Frembgen, Jurgen (1988), 'Polo in Nager: zur Ethnographie eines orientalischen Reiterspiel', *Zentralasiatische Studien*, vol.21, pp. 197–217

Geertz, Clifford (1980), *Negara: the Theatre State in Nineteenth-Century Bali*. Princeton University Press

Ghufran, M. M. (1962), *Nai Tarikh-e Chitral*. (New History of Chitral, in Urdu, Mirza Ghulam Murtaza (ed.)) Peshawar

Haserodt, K. (1989), 'Chitral (pakistanischer Hindukusch): Strukturen, Wandel und Probleme eines Lebensraumes im Hochgebirge zwischen Gletschern und Wüste', in K. Haserodt (ed.), *Hochgebirgsräume Nordpakistans im Hindukusch, Karakorum und Westhimalaya: Beiträge und Materialen zur Regionalen Geographie*. Berlin: Institut für Geographie der Technischen Universität Berlin, pp. 44–180

Hussam-ul Mulk, Shahzada. (n.d.), The Traditional Administration of Chitral State. Karl Jettmar (ed.) Unpublished Ms.

Jettmar, Karl (1975), *Die Religionen des Hindukusch*. Stuttgart: W. Kohlhammer

Keay, J. (1979), *The Gilgit Game: the Explorers of the Western Himalyas*. London: John Murray

Knight, E. F. (1897), *Where Three Empires Meet*. London: Longmans, Green

Kreutzmann, K. (1991), 'The Karakorum Highway: the Impact of Road Construction on Mountain Societies', *Modern Asian Studies*, vol. 25, no. 4, pp. 711–36

Lamb, A. (1994), *Birth of a Tragedy: Kashmir 1947*. Hertingfordbury: Roxford

Leitner, G. W. (1894), *Dardistan in 1866, 1886 and 1893*. Woking: Oriental University Institute

Lentz, W. (1939), *Zeitrechnung in Nuristan und am Pamir*. Berlin: aus den Abhandlungen der Preuâischen Akademie der Wissenschaften, Phil.-Hist. Klasse Jg. 1938

Lorimer, D. (1979), Ms. 'Notes on Hunza', authored by I. Müller-Stellrecht (ed.) as *Hunza: Materialen zur Ethnographie von Dardistan (Pakistan) aus den nachgelassenem Aufzeichnungen von D. L. R. Lorimer*, I. Graz: Akademische Druck-u. Verlagsanstalt

Mahdisan, S. (1981), 'Chaughan or Polo in Pakistan: its Etymology and History', *Journal of Central Asia*, vol. 4, no. 2, pp. 29–31

Müller-Stellrecht, I. (1973), *Feste in Dardistan, Darstellung und Kulturgeschichtliche Analyse*. Arbeiten aus dem Seminar für Völkerkunde der Johann Wolfgang Goeth-Universität Frankfurt-am-Main, vol. 5. Wiebaden: Franz Steiner

— (1981), 'Menschenhandel und Machtpolitik im westlichen Himalaja: ein Kapitel aus der Geschichte Dardistans (Nordpakistan)', *Zentralasiatische Studien*, vol. 15, pp. 392–472

Parkes, Peter (n.d.), 'Chitral 1895: Minority Historical Perspectives'. Paper delivered to *3rd International Hindu Kush Cultural Conference*, held at Chitral in Pakistan on 25-30 August 1995. In E. Bashir (n.d.), *Hindu Kush Studies, vol. 2*. Karachi: Oxford University Press for Anjuman-e-Taraqqi Khowar. Forthcoming

Robertson, G. S. (1898), *Chitrál: the Story of a Minor Siege*. London: Methuen

Schomberg, R. C. F. (1935), *Between the Oxus and the Indus*. London: Hopkinson

— (1938), *Kafirs and Glaciers: Travels in Chitral*. London: Hopkinson

Shahzad, M.Y. (1995), 'A Brief Note on the Shandur Polo Tournament' in *Chitral: the Heart of the Hindu Kush*, Souvenir of the 3rd International Hindukush Cultural Conference, 26-30 August 1995. Chitral: Anjuman-e-Taraqqi Chitral

Staley, J. (1982), *Words for my Brother: Travels between the Hindu Kush and the Himalayas*. Karachi: Oxford University Press.

Tahir Ali (1981), 'Ceremonial and Social Structure among the Burusho of Hunza', in C. von Fürer-Haimendorf (ed.), *Asian Highland Societies in Anthropological Perspective*. Delhi: Sterling Publishers

Trench, C.C. (1985), *The Frontier Scouts*. London: Jonathan Cape

Turner, J. (1980), *Reckoning with the Beast: Animals, Pain and Humanity in the Victorian Mind*. Baltimore: Johns Hopkins

Watson, J.N.P. (1986), *The World of Polo: Past and Present*, London: Sportsman's Press

— (1989), *A Concise Guide to Polo*, London: Sportsman's Press

Acknowledgements

I am grateful to the Leverhulme Trust for a research fellowship at the Queen's University of Belfast (1988-90), where this paper was conceived, and to the ESRC for the award of a travel grant (R000 22 1087) for research in Chitral and Gilgit in 1989. The Department of Sociology & Social Anthropology of the University of Kent generously supported my attendance, at short notice, of the 3rd International Hindu Kush Cultural Conference in Chitral, in August-September 1995, when I was able to update and improve a hitherto casual knowledge of polo-playing. I further benefited there from discussion of the game with its erudite ethnographer in Nager, Jurgen Frembgen, and especially from interviews with the Chitrali polo champions, Nasir and Wali Rakhman, who suffered unrelenting interrogation. My knowledge of contemporay polo in Gilgit is largely derived from answers to enquiries kindly collected in the field by Ms. Sabrina Kassam (pers. comm.) Lastly, I thank Jeremy MacClancy for allowing me a precious week, beyond all editorial deadlines, to recompose this essay on returning from Chitral in September 1995.

4

Female Bullfighting, Gender Stereotyping and the State

Jeremy MacClancy

To many Britons the traditional image of Spain is one of baroque religiosity, bloody bullfights and lovers impelled by their passion. This was an image built to a great extent on ignorance, for Spain was not included in the Grand Tour of Europe: young British gentlemen, concerned with their self-education, did not visit its cities; its spas were not fashionable; it was not part of any modern religious pilgrimage. Indeed, Spain

> remained unsanctioned by habit and convention, and most Victorians and Edwardians found (it) vaguely intimidating and even suspect from (its) association with the excesses of Romantic sensibility. . . Spain, until quite late in the nineteenth century, still seemed as remote as it had seemed in the eighteenth. 'No country is less known to the rest of Europe', said Dr Johnson in 1761. 'There is no country in Europe so little known and yet so well worth visiting', wrote Dr Madden in 1864 (Pemble 1987: 48).

Unlike Italy, Spain was not 'a wreck of paradise'. English visitors educated in the classics did not experience the same 'light of recognition' that they felt on viewing Italian sites. Through ignorance, Spain became a land of mystery, a peninsular home for the exotic, culturally separated by the Pyrenees from the continental landmass. Kirkpatrick, commenting on the work of Richard Ford and Borrow, says they make the reader feel that 'Spain is a detached fragment of the orient', a country of brutal contrast, whether geographical, economical, emotional, or cultural' (Kirkpatrick 1916: 251). In 1954 V. S. Pritchett was still able to say:

Spain is the old and necessary enemy of the West. There we learn our history upside down and see life exposed to the skin. Neither in France nor in Italy can one be so frankly frightened. All the hungers of life are blankly stated there. We see the primitive hungers we live by and yet, by a curious feat of stoicism, fatalism, and lethargy, the passions are sceptically contained (1954: 7)

Spain is a way for Britons to reveal, by contrast, the Anglo-Saxon norm. Like the image of the Eastern city discussed by Gilsenan, Spain can represent Britain 'both as its opposite. . . and as its concealed, secret dispositions, secret, longed-for, feared, enticing, and shameful all at once' (Gilsenan 1986: 13). In the Mediterranean, Puritan Victorians saw pleasures and freedoms not available to them in Britain, and yet they simultaneously condemned and repudiated 'the Latin way of life' with startling violence. Taking their high morality with them, they were both fascinated and appalled by the seeming excesses of Spanish Catholicism and bullfighting.

Spain was a land of strong contrasts where the dichotomies underlying any notion of civilization were more vividly expressed than elsewhere in the Mediterranean. In Spain life was seen to be more exposed, its roots more visible. British travellers to Spain could exploit these Hispanic contrasts to underline the difference between Spain and Britain. Thus reading a book on Spain indirectly reminded the reader what constituted Britain, what made it distinct. These attitudes have persisted into recent decades, stimulated greatly, in the case of bullfighting, by Hemingway's almost mystical interpretation of the practice (see e.g. Tynan 1955; Welles 1968).

British anthropologists have not been immune to the effects of this traditional image, which was propagated in travelogues, novels, plays, paintings and song. In this paper I wish to demonstrate how even the most influential British anthropologist of Spain, Julian Pitt-Rivers, has – perhaps inadvertently – helped to perpetuate this image in his representations of bullfighting and gender relations. In his published work, Pitt-Rivers puts forward singular timeless interpretations of these phenomena. In contrast, I wish to speak of plurality, of the obligation to site our studies historically, and of the need to investigate the links between the ideology of the state and that of local communities.

I do not want my effort to be misunderstood. I do not wish to write a triumphalist Whig history of the anthropology of Spain, with Pitt-Rivers as my bogey-ethnographer of hegemony. I only single out his work because it has been so influential, and because his *People of the Sierra* (1954) is one of the very few contemporary documentary and analytical accounts we have of rural life in the early decades of the Franquist regime.

***

Pitt-Rivers (1984) sees the *corrida* fundamentally as a religious rite, and more specifically as a sacrifice. Interpreting the ceremony in predominantly sexual terms, he regards the matador in the early stage of the *corrida* as a feminine figure and the bull as a masculine one. The roles reverse as the fight proceeds. The man, by progressively dominating the bull, regains his masculinity and makes the bull feminine. Pitt-Rivers interprets the fatal wounding of the animal by the matador as a form of rape. Moreover, since the sword is a penis and the bull's wound a menstruating vagina, the matador, by penetrating the bleeding part of the animal, symbolically violates the traditional, local taboo against having sexual intercourse with a woman who is having her period. Pitt-Rivers, wishing to expand the significance of his analysis, then claims that the conflict between man and animal in the *corrida* symbolizes the conflict between man and woman in Andalusia. At its death the bull, 'an emblem of bestial masculinity', transmits its procreative power to its killer, who by breaking the menstrual taboo returns Andalusian men and women to their culturally appropriate positions: 'Men go back to being true men, since they are no longer afraid of women, and women transform themselves into true female animals, finally capable of signing the peace pact in the war between the sexes.'

When Garry Marvin, who did his fieldwork specifically on bullfighting in Andalusia in the late 1970s, gave bullfighters and non-intellectual aficionados the gist of Pitt-Rivers' argument, he was met with looks of surprise and incredulity, as well as the odd guffaw. 'Is *that* what intellectuals get up to?' they seemed to imply (Marvin, pers. comm.) Matadors may admit, as some of them do, that the excitement they feel during a *corrida* is akin to sexual thrill, they may confess that they have an orgasm during their contest with the animal, but neither of those statements by any means implies that bullfighters swap and alternate sexual roles with the bull they are fighting.

It is true that Andalusians, and many other Spaniards, use bullfighting terms as metaphors for the relations between the sexes. But this should not make us think, as both Pitt-Rivers and Douglass (1984) claim, that the bullfight is an enactment of the contest between Andalusian men and women. As Mitchell points out, this is to confuse metaphor with essence.

People *do* talk about men as bullfighters and about women as bulls, but they also use many other metaphors to describe the bullfight: a *corrida* may be discussed as the domination of man over woman, as the triumph of light over darkness, of good over evil, of guile over force, of vertical over horizontal, of plebeian over aristocrat, of son over father, of Christian over Moor, of life over death, and of death over life (Mitchell 1986, 1988: 132– 5). People may also refer to men as bulls and to women as bullfighters (see for example the poems in Boada and Cebolla 1976: 80–6). In *Matador*, a film made by the Spanish director Pedro Almodovar, the female protagonist swords the male to death. In this complex context, where various metaphors can be applied to the bullfight, it would seem that almost the only uncontroversial definition is a minimalist one: a *corrida* concerns a bullfighter's skilful domination of an animal that can kill.[1]

Pitt-Rivers (1993) sees female bullfighters as something to discuss in an appendix, as though they were but a footnote to a male history. He tries to dismiss them: 'Around the turn of the century there was a vogue for lady matadors in the same epoch when circus-like shows were put on in the bull-rings such as a combat between a fighting-bull and a tiger. . . But Spanish machismo won the day and ladies were finally forbidden to fight in the ring.'

In fact, females have participated in bullfights almost since they began, some achieving great renown.[2] The earliest recorded case is of a *matadora* who in 1683 performed in the Plaza Mayor of Madrid, on the occasion of a visit to Spain by the Prince of Wales, later Charles I. The greatest of the eighteenth-century *toreras*, La Pajulera, sketched by Goya, was compared with some of the greatest matadors of her day. Banned by Ferdinand VII when he came to power in 1814, female bullfighting resurfaced in 1820 at the start of the 'liberal triennium'. By the late 1830s the managers of bullrings were being overwhelmed by the petitions of female *cuadrillas* (a bullfighting team consisting of a bullfighter and his/her *picadores* and *banderilleros*), while the most skilled women came to rival even the most famous male bullfighters in popularity. In 1868, shortly after the flight of Isabel II, female bullfighting again gained great popularity. From 1886 until 1908 female bullfighters, including the veteran Martina Garcia, then in her 60s, once again competed against their male counterparts for fame in the ring. Prohibited during the dictatorship of Primo de Rivera, female bullfighting became so common under the Republic that some critics spoke of 'a feminist plague'. There were more than 60 female bullfighters during this period, the most skilled of them all, Juanita Cruz, even managing to fight in Las Ventas in

Madrid, one of the most prestigious bullrings in the country. Though the practice was banned by Franco, during the course of his regime, some women spontaneously jumped into the ring to fight, and if they wanted to develop their skill went on to fight in Portugal, France or South America. The only famous female bullfighter of this time was Conchita Cintron, a Peruvian who in Spain could only *rejonear* (fight bulls with lances from horseback). The prohibition was only lifted in 1974 after a sustained campaign, supported by over a hundred of her male colleagues, by Angela Hernández, who had learnt to bullfight in Latin America. Within a year there were over thirty women fighting in rings. There has been a new wave of enthusiasm in recent years, the most prominent of this latest group being the much-publicized Cristina Sánchez (Hooper 1991; Rozsnyai 1992). To close the 1994 season she and two of her peers held a special women-only bullfight in Malaga, which was broadcast live on national television.

This brief list of female bullfighters over the last three centuries demonstrates the persistence of the tradition. If that tradition appears to be uneven, this is mainly because from the early nineteenth century until the present day female bullfighting was usually banned by conservative or absolutist governments and normally allowed by liberal ones. Ferdinand VII banned the practice, his liberal successors allowed it; Primo de Rivera prohibited it, his republican successors repealed the prohibition; and so on. In other words, it does not seem to be the case that women did not want to fight, but that for long periods they were not given the opportunity. The epitaph on Juanita Cruz's grave is clear on this point: 'Despite all the damage done to me in my *patria* by those responsible for the mediocrity of bullfighting in the years 1940–50. . .'

Pitt-Rivers sees female bullfighting as on a par with circus-like shows. While it is true that during the later nineteenth century female bullfighters often had to participate in taurine masquerades, it is also true that many female bullfighters during this period fought bulls in the same way as their male contemporaries: they took the same risks, and came to bear the same kinds of scars.

Active and recently retired female bullfighters discuss their experiences in almost exactly the same way as men, for they have to be just as ready to react. As one put it, 'A man is a man and a woman is a woman. But when you're facing a bull, it's all the same. The bull won't ask for your identity card.' They play down the killing as a necessity, choosing to emphasize instead the need to dominate the bull and perform their task well. They say that their bullfighting technique is no different from that of their male colleagues. What is important is to be able to fight the bull and to do so with style. They say that the anatomical and physiological differences between the sexes make no difference to the way they fight bulls; periods, they add, do not normally affect their performance as they are already so fit. Yolanda Carabajal, a recent leading bullfighter, says that if on the first day of menstruation it hurts to bullfight, she quickly forgets it through force of will. Many of these women say they had wanted occupations involving physical activity. Cristina Sánchez says that if she had not become a bullfighter she would have been a firewoman or a police officer. Like their male counterparts, today's female bullfighters stress the distinctive emotion they have when in the ring. 'I can't explain or describe the feelings I have when the bull comes out,' said one, 'but when I'm fighting well, I feel a sense of tranquillity, satisfaction, pleasure; I feel at home.' (Conchita Cintron makes a very similar comment in her autobiography (1968: 105)). Cristina Sánchez admitted, 'When things go well with the bull is something indescribable. You are at one with it. I do not know if it could be defined as something sexual, as many of my companions say. What is certain is that, for a woman, it is no less marvellous' (Gómez 1991).

Women in the contemporary group of female bullfighters seem quite content for taurine correspondents to tell their readers that they are part of a long, undeservedly neglected history within the chronicle of Spanish bullfighting. But at the same time they do not wish to be seen as merely the latest representatives of a long tradition. Underlining the difference between themselves and those who went before them, they say they wish to be known as *toreros*. Unlike some of their predecessors in the 1970s who were prepared to pose scantily clad in bullfighting postures and did not remain long in the profession, these women affirm their commitment to bullfighting as a career (if they can manage to make it pay). It must also be stated that opposition to female bullfighting is diminishing nowadays as the male-privileging ideology of the difference between the genders is today much more openly challenged than was the case formerly.

Who were, and are, these women? Lack of information precludes any definitive generalization but it seems from the evidence available that they came, or come, from the same backgrounds (i.e. impoverished or taurine-centred) as most male bullfighters. La Pajuelera was a street-seller of matches (*pajuelas*); las Noyas, one of the most famous of fin-de-siècle bullfighters, was born and brought up in the administrative quarters of a ring; many were the wives or daughters of bullfighters or *banderilleros*. In popular nineteenth-century stories female bullfighters were usually portrayed as the daughters of bullfighters killed in the ring.

Angela Hernández was an orphan, Cristina Sánchez is the daughter of a *banderillero*, and Yolanda Carabajal is the daughter of a lorry-driver. Like their male counterparts it seems that women bullfighters sought, and seek, fame, money and public recognition of their skills: Conchita Cintron (1968: 135), remembering her feelings just before her first bullfight (in Mexico), stated, 'I felt my heart pounding, but above all I felt a compelling drive to fight, to show these aficionados what I had learnt.' In these respects there seems to be no difference between them and their male counterparts.

What was, and is, the public's attitude to these women? Male bullfighters were usually opposed to them, as potential rivals in an already highly competitive profession. Bullfighting correspondents for periodicals were often vehemently opposed to women killing bulls. The ring was not an appropriate place for them who were, moreover, ignorant of the subtleties involved in bullfighting. Women were meant to be sewing socks, not sticking swords into bleeding animals. They were not supposed to be displaying bravery in a public space, but maintaining the moral order in their homes and raising their children in the fear of God. In 1849 *El Clamor Público* argued that female bullfighters 'offer an indecorous spectacle and one which does not dignify a cultivated people'. Conservative and absolutist authorities presented similar arguments. In 1811 Jose Bonaparte's Minister of the Interior did not allow a woman to bullfight, on the grounds that 'one must be mindful of decency and public decorum, which would be violated by such a spectacle, whose influence on public morals is clear'. Almost exactly a hundred years later the current Minister of the Interior, Juan de la Cierva, gave the same justification: 'The act in itself constitutes an unbecoming spectacle and one so opposed to culture and to all delicate emotions, that under no circumstances should the gubernatorial authorities allow its celebration, it being an act which offends morality and good customs'. According to the dominant ideology, the appropriate place for women in a bull-ring has been on the stands, from which they are meant to be able to admire the public demonstration of male prowess. Women were supposed to be merely spectators, not skilled killers.[3]

Marvin (1988: 142–165) found that the Andalusian bullfighters and aficionados with whom he spent time believed that men, and only men, should evince the personal qualities of courage, assertiveness, desire to influence and competitiveness, and that they should be seen to manifest these qualities in public domains such as bars. They thought that women, because they have no *cojones*, lack courage, that it would be *fea* ('ugly') for a female to dominate in public, and that it would be *fea* for her to be injured, since men would be forced to stand by and watch the wounding, and some men would take pleasure in the gory event. When in 1991 I attended the graduation fight of Cristina Sánchez at the Madrid School of Tauromachy (she had come top of her class of over 100 pupils), the man sitting next to me was very surprised to see a woman entering the ring. Between gasps he said this could not be, because bullfighters had to face grave danger, otherwise it would not be bullfighting; thus if a woman donned the traditional 'suit of lights' and went to fight, she stood the chance of being hurt, and that was totally inappropriate. After arguing with me briefly, he said that women could be as brave as men, but that they were not so good at killing. The group of women behind us, to whom I repeated all these words, agreed that women could be as brave as men, and that, yes, it was true that female bullfighters were not so good at the kill.[4]

Some male taurine aficionados told me that women's anatomy makes it inappropriate for them to fight bulls. One claimed that a *matadora*'s breasts were a great disadvantage for her: 'No matter how supple the costume, she will always have a vulnerable spot the bull can attack.' Some emphasized to me that a *corrida* was an aesthetic event. Since, they said, women have broader hips and larger behinds, they would not look good in a suit of lights. Watching them fight bulls, these men claimed, would not be an aesthetically appealing event.

Given that matadors performing in the same *corrida* will strive to outdo one another in courage, skill, and mastery, bullfighters told Marvin that they would not wish to appear on the same bill as a woman, since women were not meant to be competitive and they did not wish to be compared with women. Thus when discussing a *matadora* whose ability was generally recognized, they either deny her femininity or classify her as an exceptional case. Perhaps one of the confessional statements of such an aficionado as Orson Welles (ibid.: x) reveals the underlying anxiety of these men: 'There is a kind of cuckoldry in the spectacle of a pretty girl making public nonsense of our hairy-chested pretensions.'

Welles (ibid.: viii), who attended his first *corrida* at the age of 12, is fluent and explicit about the appropriate sex for a bullfighter:

> The bull-fighter is a knight without armour who slays his dragons for pay, a mercenary who does battle by a code as strict as the duello. . . Folk-hero, circus star, gladiator, he is nothing without courage, and his function is inexcusable without art. It is as an artist that he must be praised or condemned: as a sculptor working in the most difficult of raw materials, a ballet dancer with the most deadly

dangerous of partners, a tragic actor, bright in the spangles of carnival and the harlequinade, shedding – and bleeding – real blood. He is many things. But he is not a woman.

Today female bullfighters complain that large sectors of the taurine world do not take them seriously. They say it is difficult to find an *apoderado* (financial backer) prepared to take them on. (Many of their predecessors suffered the same difficulty). Without a backer it is very difficult, given the costs of maintaining a *cuadrilla* to give bullfights around the country and so gain fame. And it is only the more famous who get the opportunity to fight in the most prestigious rings. Some male bullfighters refuse to enter a ring with them, in case their performance outshines their own. While women bullfighters no longer have to put up with the comments (such as 'Get back to the kitchen!') shouted from the stands that Angela Hernández had to suffer, they suspect that many spectators still view them as but amusing novelties.

In contrast to all these attitudes, several nineteenth-century taurine correspondents (like most of their modern counterparts) looked favourably on female bullfighting; liberal Ministers of the Interior tended to tolerate the practice; and many female bullfighters, both in this century and the last one, have been assisted by some of their male colleagues. (It is worth pointing out in this context that some Latin American countries, whose non-indigenous male population is characterized as being far more machista than its Spanish counterpart, have never banned women from bullfighting.) Moreover the public always seems to have been willing to pay to watch female bullfights. But just what the public thought of these women we do not know; and there is no socially necessary reason why there should be one common sort of reaction to female bullfighters. The fact that there was a dominant ideology of gender difference which constructed men as domineering and women as passive implies not that many did not maintain different beliefs, only that the latter were often more difficult to express. It may be, as Pitt-Rivers says, that many members of the public saw them as entertaining exceptions. But it is also possible that many saw them as equal to their male colleagues. I met many people who spoke in these terms. One male aficionado interviewed by a British television journalist ('Euroexpress', Channel 4, 1992) praised Yolanda Carabajal's style:

I came here today to see her bullfighting. I love to see her fight. She's extraordinary. She is as good as any matador. She puts such feeling and spirit into it. I can only compare with singing. Some sing and it is just off-key. Others sing and it is soul-shattering. That is what the aficionados here want.

Revealing though that quotation is, the truth quite simply is that we do not yet have sufficient information to enable us to ascertain in detail, and with any certainty, the evolving complexity of spectators' reactions to females in the ring. What we do know is that at times the public has made its collective support absolutely evident. Perhaps the most dramatic example occurred during Conchita Cintron's last fight (in Jaen): when she dismounted from her horse to cape the bull, the crowd shouted so fervently in her defence that the President of the fight was forced to pardon her for her illegal activity, and then, because the crowd went on shouting, to honour her in the traditional manner for the skilfullness of her performance by having her presented with the bull's ears and tail (Verrill 1961: 275; Cintron 1968: 275–279).

Given this variety in people's attitudes to female bullfighters, perhaps the one generalization that can be made is that those opposed to the practice tend to see themselves as traditionalists concerned to uphold what they take to be the time-honoured moral system. To them the sight of women publicly demonstrating their ability to dominate disturbs the 'natural' order of things. Seeing gender difference not as historically and culturally contingent but as the expression of fixed, ultimately biologically-based essences, they regard female bullfighting as a threat to their rigid classification of the world. Therefore, they reason, it ought to be denigrated or prohibited.

***

There is a further point to be made, however, for this all too rapid survey suggests not only that Pitt-Rivers has misrepresented bullfighting as an essentially male activity, but that he has misrepresented gender relations in Spain as well.

There is already an anthropological literature critical of the relatively stark way that he portrayed sexual difference. In the Galician fishing community studied by Kelley (1991), women are seen as capable of doing anything men can do and are not perceived as needing a man to establish a successful household. Cole (1991), who studied Portuguese fisherwomen, ascertained that there are different levels of gender construction which enable, and even require, that men and women negotiate their gender identities and gender relations. As Corbin (1987), who worked in the town of Ronda (only a few dozen kilometres from

Pitt-Rivers's field-site), has suggested, 'women may not regard themselves as inferior or dominated, may not consider their own activities less valuable than men's, may be as ambivalent about men as men are about them.' Del Valle (1985: 292) discovered that while Basque anthropology had presented a unitary vision of women, in reality there are a multiplicity of modes of female expression. Lever (1986), who worked in Castile, found that Pitt-Rivers had concentrated on the views of middle-aged married men who were fathers and carried economic weight in pueblos. Regarded by the villagers with whom he lived as a *señorito* and addressed by them as '*Don* Julian', he seems to have transmitted the views of those males in a structurally similar position to himself. Other villagers, of a different age, family position or gender, might merely have paid lip service to the values of the dominant group, while holding very different values themselves.

An important point to emerge from this clarification of gender differences is that Pitt-Rivers, who (it is important to remember) did his fieldwork during the height of the Franquist dictatorship, appears to have paid too little attention to the interlocking relationship between the ideology of the family promulgated by the fascist state and that upheld by powerful male villagers at that time. In the first decades of the Franquist regime in particular, the dictator's minions were very concerned to re-establish and reinforce a traditionalist dichotomy of gender relations (Gaite 1987): men were entrusted with authority, the earning of money, and the acquisition of prestige; they were meant, to evince of courage, if necessary, and were allowed to be sexually aggressive. In contrast, women were meant to be subordinate and to care for the home and the upholding of religious values; they had to maintain a high degree of sexual reserve, and if they could, to evince beauty and delicacy.[5] Thus important male villagers, by reproducing the dominant ideology of their rural home, simultaneously legitimated their own leading position within the pueblo, their links with the state administration, and the ideology of the state itself. The dictatorship bolstered their status and vice versa. (This relationship was not just ideological: for instance, the mayor of the village was not elected by the populace but designated by the provincial governor.) In this context and at this time, there was little or no opportunity for the effective communication of other views about the nature of gender difference. The self-interests of the state and village leaders combined to suppress them.[6] And Pitt-Rivers either chose not to discuss these alternative voices in print or was not privileged to hear them (perhaps these were then considered very private opinions which one did not discuss with a resident foreigner). For even during the time of his fieldwork (1949–1952), the regime was still imprisoning people for '*sus ideas*' (their ideas).

That the images of the active male and the passive female were integral parts of the dominant, and not the sole, ideology of gender differences in this period was made very clear during the first decades of the century. The first feminist organizations, formed in the 1910s, met with much male hostility and resistance to reform, however mild the changes their leaders proposed (Scanlon 1976; Nash 1981; Ugalde 1993a; 1993b). Indeed, the response was so violent that the Hispanist Shirley Mangini (1995: 6), discussing the vitriolic male reaction to the founding in 1926 of the first women's club in Madrid, wrote, 'One wonders how any women of those times had the energy to combat such relentless misogyny and patriarchal hysteria.'

During the Republic feminist ideas were to a some extent adopted by anti-traditionalist forces: communists, socialists, and left-wingers generally (Nash 1989). Some women were elected to the Cortes, others were given positions of great public responsibility, yet others bore arms. During the Civil War, those Republican groups who saw the conflict as an all-encompassing social revolution were determined to construct a new status for Spanish women. For instance, anarchist-feminists formed Mujeres Libres ('Free Women') groups which fostered 'radical views on sexual and family relations, campaigned against the exploitation of women in prostitution, worked hard to further working-class women's interests through training courses in everything from typing to electrical skills, encouraged women to join trade unions and engage in political activity, and generally promoted the image and reality of a new, independent, trained, working woman' (Lannon 1991: 223; see also Fraser 1979: 286–290; Ackelsberg 1991). Representatives of Mujeres Libres who toured rural villages were well aware of local women's attitudes to the dominant ideology of gender differences. As one stated, remembering the exuberance of her audiences,

> The ideas which grabbed them the most? Talk about the power men exercised over women. . . There would be a kind of uproar when you would say to them, 'We cannot permit men to think themselves superior to women, that they have a right to rule over them.' I think that Spanish women were waiting anxiously for that call (in Ackelsberg 1993: 381).

It was against this sort of revolutionary effort that the forces of reaction fought. It was because of these attempted changes that the fledgling dictatorship was keen to reimpose traditionalist images of man and womanhood.

During the Franquist regime, that attitudes diverging from the officially propagated ideology of the family did exist is shown by the facts that some women *did* try to bullfight during this period, and that many people did start openly to express other views on gender differences as soon as they could, i.e. during the dying years of the dictatorship. 'One finds disillusionment, indignation and sometimes great bitterness,' writes the Hispanist Ian Gibson (1992: 89), 'among many middle-aged and older women today. They feel that they have been cheated. In the Andalusian hill town of Ronda, elderly female pensioners spoke sadly to me about their married lives, the drudgery in the home, the endless children, the impossibility of escape.' Rarely did women have the strength to rebel. Gaite (1987: 44) mentions the story she heard of the young woman who reacted against pressure to get married by deceiving her fiancé about her real intentions. When at the altar the priest asked her if she wished the man at her side to be her husband, she replied, 'No, sir!' Turning to the congregation, she proclaimed before walking out, 'And if I have come this far, it is so that all of you will know that if I remain a spinster, it is because I wish to!'

During my own fieldwork, carried out in the mid-1980s in a village in the northern Spanish province of Navarre, middle-aged democrats repeatedly emphasized to me the sense of repression they felt during the decades of dictatorship, and the obligation to toe the line publicly. Many villagers also stressed to me the great sense of relief they felt once the transition to democracy was well under way. One sign of this change was that at open meetings in the town-hall women were for the first time prepared to shout their opposition to measures they disagreed with. When I asked a particular friend of mine about a spinster neighbour of ours, she revealed to me that when in the 1950s the woman had become engaged, the local priest had put pressure on her parents to prevent the marriage, which they did. In reaction, the woman publicly struck the priest, an almost unimaginable act given the power of the Church in those times. As punishment, she was confined to a mental asylum for a period: in the eyes of the authorities, a woman who deviated from the norm in this way was not a rebel, but mad.[7]

***

Today anthropologists of Europe recognize that the concept of a village as a community unto itself was an ethnographic fiction that can no longer be sustained; that instead of celebrating unity we need to investigate plurality; that we need to integrate many levels of analysis (from the parochial to the international); and that we have to be aware of the possible interrelations between nationally-transmitted ideologies and those maintained at local levels. They also recognize that foreign anthropologists need to adopt a suitably critical attitude to those images of Spain transmitted by compatriot writers. Given these caveats, it is perhaps noteworthy that recent British writers on Spain (e.g. Hooper 1986; Elms 1992; Jacobs 1994) have deliberately tried to break with the traditional representations of the country. Not for them an exotic image of mystery based on ignorance.

Notes

1. This minimalist statement is a development of that presented by Mitchell (1986) and refined by Cambria (1991).
2. The data on which this brief historical analysis relies come from Boada and Cebolla 1976.
3. Given the association of bullfighting and domination in public, perhaps it is not surprising that the rock star Madonna, who is often lauded as subverting traditional gender differences, presents herself in a recent video as a bullfighter.
4. Some claim that women are not good at killing because their forearm muscles are not as developed as men's.In Spanish slaughterhouses, only men kill the animals; the only job women do is to cut up the carcasses.
5. Women were also kept busy rearing children. The regime encouraged large families and regularly awarded prizes to the most prolific. Unsurprisingly, given the attitudes of the regime, most of the credit went to the father, not to the mother (Gibson 1992: 88).
6. A similar conjuncture occurred in Portugal during the rule of Salazar (Cole ibid.: ch.5).
7. It is very likely that there were many domestic, minor and local acts of opposition to the Franquist regime (such as graffiti and the woman who assaulted her parish priest). But local historians of Spain have on the whole yet to study them. The few historical studies specifically about women in Spain strongly suggest that in the past many women did challenge the dominant ideology. Dillard (1984), in his analysis of mediaeval women, details the various ways in which some of them rebelled. Perry (1990), in her analysis of Sevillian women in the

sixteenth century, focuses on women's subversive strategies against the contemporary strengthening of the gender division.

Bibliography

Ackelsberg, M.A. (1991), *Free Women of Spain. Anarchism and the Struggle for the Emancipation of Women.* Bloomington: Indiana University Press
— (1993), 'Models of Revolution: Rural women and Anarchist Collectivism in Civil War Spain', *Journal of Peasant Studies*, vol. 20, pp. 367–388
Boado, Emilia and Fermin Cebolla (1976), *Las señoritas toreras: Historia, erotica y politica del toreo feminino.* Madrid: Felmar
Cambria, Rosario (1991), 'Bullfighting and the Intellectuals' in Mitchell (1991), pp. 199–230
Cintron, Conchita (1968) *¡Torera! Memoirs of a Bull-fighter.*London: Macmillan
Cole, Sally (1991), *Women of the Praia: Work and Lives in a Portuguese Coastal Community.* Princeton: Princeton University Press
Corbin, M.P. (1987), 'Review of D. Gilmore and G. Gwyne (eds.) "Sex and Gender in Southern Europe: Problems and Prospects"'. *Man*, vol. 22, p. 756
Del Valle, Teresa (ed.) (1985), *Mujer Vasca: Imagen y realidad.* Barcelona: Anthropos
Dillard, H. (1984), *Daughters of the Reconquest: Women in Castilian town society, 1100–1300.* Cambridge: Cambridge University Press
Douglass, C. (1984), 'Toro muerto, vaca es: An interpretation of the Spanish bullfight', *American Ethnologist*, vol. 11, pp. 242–258
Elms, Robert (1992), *Spain. A portrait after the general.* London: Heinemann
Fraser, Ronald (1979), *Blood of Spain: The experience of civil war 1936–1939.* Harmondsworth: Allen Lane
Gaite, Carmen Martín (1987), *Usos amorosos de la posguerra española.* Barcelona: Anagrama
Gibson, Ian (1992), *Fire in the blood. The New Spain.* London: Faber and Faber
Gilsenan, Michael (1986), *Imagined Cities of the East.* Oxford: Clarendon Press.
Gómez, P. (1991), 'Estocada a los prejuicios', *El País*, 22 October
Hooper, John (1986), *The Spaniards. A portrait of the new Spain.*London: Viking
— (1991) 'Keeping the red rag flying', *The Observer* Magazine, 11 August, pp. 12–16
Jacobs, Michael (1994), *Between Hopes and Memories. A Spanish Journey.* London: Picador
Kelley, Heidi (1991), 'Unwed mothers and household reputation in a Spanish Galician community', *American Ethnologist*, vol. 18, pp. 565–580
Kirkpatrick, F.A. (1916), 'The Literature of Travel' in A. W. Ward and A. R. Waller (eds), *The Cambridge History of English Literature*, vol. XIV, pp.

240–256.

Lannon, Francis (1991), 'Women and images of women in the Spanish civil war', *Transactions of the Royal Historical Society,* Sixth series, vol. 1, pp. 213–228

Lever, Alison (1986) 'Honour as a red herring', *Critique of Anthropology,* vol. 6, pp. 83–106

Mangini, Shirley (1995), *Memories of Resistance: Women's voices from the Spanish Civil War.* New Haven: Yale University Press

Marvin, Garry (1988), *Bullfight.* Oxford: Basil Blackwell

Mitchell, Timothy J. (1986), 'Bull-fighting: The Ritual Origin of Scholarly Myths', *Journal of American Folklore,* vol. 99, pp. 394–414

— (1988), *Violence and Piety in Spanish Folklore.* Philadelphia: University of Pennsylvania Press

— (1991), *Blood Sport: A Social History of Spanish Bullfighting.*Philadephia: University of Pennsylvania Press

Nash, Mary (1981), *Mujer y Movimiento Obrero en España.* Barcelona: Fontamara

— (1989), *Las Mujeres en la Guerra Civil.* Salamanca: Ministerio de Cultura

Pemble, John (1987), *The Mediterranean Passion: Victorians and Edwardians in the South.* Oxford: Clarendon Press.

Perry, M.E. (1990), *Gender and Disorder in Early Modern Seville.* Princeton: Princeton University Press

Pitt-Rivers, Julian A. (1954), *The People of the Sierra.* London: Weidenfeld and Nicolson

— (1984), 'El sacrificio del toro', *Revista de Occidente,* vol. 36, pp. 27–47

— (1993), 'The Spanish bull-fight and kindred activities',*Anthropology Today,* vol. 9, pp. 11–15

Pritchett, V.S. (1954), *The Spanish Temper.* London: Chatto and Windus.

Rozsnyai, S. (1992), 'Tackling machismo by the horns', *The Times* Saturday Review, 4 January, pp. 24–5

Scanlon, G. (1976), *La Polemica Feminista en la España contemporanea (1868–1974).* Madrid: Siglo Veintiuno

Tynan, Kenneth (1955), *Bull Fever.* London

Ugalde Solana, Mercedes (1993a), 'La evolución de la diferenciación de género e identidad feminina (I): Las nacionalistas vascas en las primeras tres décadas del siglo XX', in A. Campos and L. Mendez (eds),*Teoria feminista: identidad, género y política.* San Sebastian: Universidad del Pais Vasco. pp. 117–131

— (1993b), 'La evolución de la diferenciación de género e identidad feminina (II): Las nacionalistas vascas durante los años treinta', in A. Campos and L. Mendez (eds), *Teoria feminista: identidad, género y política.* San Sebastian: Universidad del Pais Vasco. pp. 133–145

Verrill Cintron, L. (1961), *Goddess of the Bull-ring*. London: Muller

Welles, Orson (1968), 'Introduction' in Cintron 1968, pp. v–xi

Acknowledgements

My thanks to Vicky Hayward for generously lending the cassette-tapes she made of her interviews with female bullfighters, and to Rodney Needham, Peter Parkes, and Sarah Pink for comments.

5

'Our Blood is Green': Cricket, Identity and Social Empowerment among British Pakistanis

Pnina Werbner

Introduction: The Cricket Team's Visit and Other Celebrations

'Pakistan zindabad!'
'Islam zindabad!'
'Pakistan forever!'
'Islam forever!'

This is the cry from the terraces by young British Pakistani supporters of their national cricket team. The same cry is to be heard when youngsters drive their cars with horns blaring and green flags waving, in the Manchester Asian shopping district on the *eid* (a major celebration held at the end of Ramadan), or when British Muslims march in processions to celebrate the Prophet's Birthday, *eid-milad-un-Nabi*.

In June 1987 the Pakistan National Cricket team, captained by the revered and legendary Imran Khan, came to Manchester to play at Old Trafford in the World Series. The team's visit generated wild excitement among Manchester's Pakistanis. In particular, the competition to host the team was intense. Anyone who knew anyone related to a member of the team activated his links in an attempt to gain the privileged chance to throw a party for Imran Khan and his illustrious team mates.

The result of this competition was that three parties were held for the visiting cricketers within the space of five days. Two were hosted by wealthy businessmen at exclusive events. The third, by far the largest, was a Benefit Dinner for Imran Khan, 'Prince of Pakistan, Crowned King of All-Rounders' as the poster declared, organised by three young businessmen friends. The Benefit Dinner, held in Stockport Town Hall, was an open event. Tickets were £25 a person, and about 700 predominantly young men gathered to honour their hero. Although the organization was good, and a good deal of money and care had been invested in the function, it was sabotaged from the start. Before it took place, a number of businessmen tried to prevent its staging, spreading rumours about its cancellation and threatening the organizers. During the dinner a young man went up to Imran Khan and wiped a £5 note in his face, saying 'Here's some money if you want it!'. Although he was immediately removed from the hall, and the benefit dinner raised £6,000, the event was later construed by establishment members of the community as a total failure. My companions at the dinner, respectable businessmen, said, 'What do you expect at such an open event?' The young organizers were bitter. One them told me: 'I don't want to have anything more to do with Pakistanis. I just don't care about them any more. If I saw a Pakistani hurt in the street, I wouldn't help him.'

A week earlier, three other parties had been held in Manchester on a single day to celebrate the *eid*. The parties revealed some of the underlying cultural dilemmas faced by Pakistani immigrants, as Muslims, in Britain. The first party was simply a cultural failure. It was a children's party hosted by the male management committee of the Pakistani community centre, and it consisted of two incongruous halves: a first half devoted to children's reading of passages from the Koran, which was lugubriously solemn; and a second half devoted to an act by two English entertainers who told funny English jokes and sang funny English songs in heavy Lancashire accents. I doubt whether this schizophrenic cultural experiment was ever repeated. The second *eid* party was quite different. It was an urban elite affair held in a restaurant with a buffet dinner and bhangra band. The highlight of this party, which included whole families, came when the organizer, a millionaire in the clothing trade, and his best friend, a successful accountant with a large firm, performed a drunken dance in the centre of the floor. This was followed by the very public opening of a magnum of champagne. The evening was enlivened by amateur South Asian singing and dancing by the guests. Most remarkably, there was open and ostentatious drinking of alcohol, flouting the rules of Islam in public on a Muslim holiday.

The third *eid* party that day was an all-male affair without drink but with speeches, which erupted into a major quarrel between several community leaders and the *maulvi* (Islamic scholars) of the Central Mosque, almost ending in a physical fight.

Other events also indicated that the space of fun, of popular culture, was contested and problematic. An entertainment evening held some months later in an Indian restaurant exemplifies the cultural tensions in the South Asian Muslim community. In a nightclub atmosphere, a rather sleazy Bombay group of instrumentalists and female dancers entertained the gathering, which consisted of Hindu Gujaratis and Punjabis, sitting in family groups, and Pakistani men standing along the walls and drinking somewhat surreptitiously, unknown to their wives, while they enjoyed the live women's sensual dancing.

Contested Spaces

It is evident that the space of fun is, for Pakistanis, a highly contested space. On the one hand, fun can be delegitimized and marginalized. To have fun is to sin, and being sinful is fun. But this implies a cultural 'gap': an absence of a domain of popular culture which could bridge the austere religiosity of the mosque and official occasions, and the transgressive breaking of religious taboos; a popular cultural space for entertainment, fun and laughter which could be said to be at once Pakistani and yet acceptable from an Islamic religious point of view. Religiosity in the city is not only austere but also contentious and politicized. Even devotional sufi music, *qawwali*, is rarely performed. Local sufi orders are reformist, sober and sometimes highly political (on Bradford see Baily 1990). The Central Mosque during the 1980s was the focus of religious conflicts and struggles for power and dominance, often involving public arguments and fights, sometimes quite violent. On the face of it, my observations led me to believe, there were no Islamic cultural traditions which were neither mosque-based nor religiously focused; no cultural space which Pakistani parents in Britain shared with their children and which constituted a publicly legitimate substitute for British popular culture. I was, as it turned out, wrong.

In 1992 Al Masoom ('For the Innocent'), a Pakistani women's voluntary organization, held a series of functions dedicated to fund-raising for a young Pakistani boy's bone-marrow transplant. The female voluntary workers set about raising money through amateur shows and fairs, held in school halls in the various neighbourhoods where Pakistanis live. Altogether the functions raised £27,000 in two months, virtually all of it from working and lower middle class members of the community. The chief organizer is a very pious Muslim, and the shows are held for an all-women and children audience. The women are careful not to be accused of un-Islamic conduct. Nevertheless, the shows focus around

South Asian music, dance and performance. Mrs. Khan, the organizer, explains, 'I believe that music is not religiously acceptable in front of men, but it is fine when only women are present. It is for happiness and our religion does not prohibit us from being happy. Otherwise the events would be far too boring. Some (religious) people are', she adds, 'too extreme.' Apart from food, arts and crafts, a fashion show and an auction of jewellery donated by some of the middle class ladies, the highlight of the events is the dramas put on by the women voluntary workers. All the parts, both male and female, are acted by young women and teenage girls from the local high schools, who dress up as men for the male roles. This in itself creates a sense of fun, evoking the transvestite masquerading and joking at the *mhendi* pre-wedding rites which I have described at length elsewhere (Werbner 1990: ch. 9). The drama on one occasion enacted a morality tale of a young Raja seeking an intelligent bride. The moral of the story was, I was told: who is more intelligent? The king or the poor man's daughter? Each of the dramas culminates in a *mhendi* ritual on stage, which provides an excuse for singing and dancing. The dramas lampoon men and stock South Asian comic characters, and often deal with contemporary dilemmas facing women as immigrants in the context of marriage.

On the face of it, one would expect the women's efforts for such an obviously humanitarian cause to be praised by community leaders and supported by the Pakistan High Commission. Instead, the women have encountered general opposition from established businessmen and even anonymous threats of violence (on male opposition to APWA in Pakistan, see Metcalf 1987: 149; Mumtaz and Shaheed 1988). One businessman greeted their fund-raising efforts with the words, 'Have all the men died in the community?' (i.e. why are women fund-raising). A similar response was encountered by the young men in their efforts to sell tickets for their cricket benefit dinner. They were asked, 'Why are you the organizer? And who is he (Imran Khan)? What good has he done for Pakistan? He just chases women!' 'They,' the young organizer told me bitterly, 'who have all their women on the side and go out to bet on the cricket game at the bookies. I think Imran Khan has done more for Pakistan than anyone else. He has given Pakistan a good name. A man at the top of his profession, whatever he is, a chemist or anything, has the responsibility to represent his country. Yes, he has done more for Pakistan than anyone else.'

To understand why attempts were made to undermine both the young cricket fans' benefit dinner and the women's philanthropic efforts, these need to be seen in a broader context. Both religious institutions and

Pakistani national communal associations are controlled by older men, mainly first-generation immigrants from Pakistan. Though engaged in bitter factional disputes with one another, they recognize the legitimate right of their rivals as male elders to compete to represent the 'community' in the public realm. This is the realm of public moral responsibility and hence of prestige, where cultural capital is created through fund-raising and visible public organization (see Werbner 1990: ch. 10). This is the social space in which male elders acquire honour and status. There is no room in this space for young upstarts, political unknowns, or women.

Islam, Nationalism and Popular Culture

To consider further the implications of this series of events, seen together, I want to turn now to a more general discussion of the relationship between Islam, nationalism, popular culture and identity. In Britain it has been widely noted that Muslims originating from Pakistan in South Asia have in recent years stressed their Islamic identity, distancing themselves from a more neutral 'South Asian' racial and cultural ascription, from a politically activist 'black' self-labelling, and, most recently, from a nationalist identification as 'Pakistanis'. I wish to argue here that this apparent identity shift disguises a continuing tension between different dimensions of a complex cluster of personal identities. Islam, as 'high culture' to be defended at all costs, cannot suppress popular cultural traditions rooted in the South Asian and Pakistani nationalist origins of immigrants and their descendents.

Unlike high cultural Islamic traditions, South Asian popular culture is 'fun': it celebrates the body and bodily expressiveness or sensuality through sport, music, dance and laughter. If Islamic high culture is controlled, rule-bound and cerebral, South Asian popular culture is transgressive, openly alluding to uncontrollable feelings, sex and other bodily functions. It glorifies physical strength, beauty and prowess. It mobilizes satire, parody, masquerade or pastiche to comment on current affairs, to lampoon the powerful and venerable, to incorporate the foreign and the Other beyond the boundaries.[1]

The celebration of South Asian popular culture as 'fun' is not merely a pastime or a moment of licence, peripheral to an understanding of British Pakistani society's 'culture'. If this was the case it would be difficult to explain why excessive shows of force by powerful authorities are needed to attempt to suppress such celebrations of fun. Nor is popular culture, whether in the form of cricket, music or drama, reducible to singular identities – nationalist, ethnic or religious, to be entirely 'captured' and manipulated by political leaders (see Cohen 1991; 1992).

Part of the reason for this insuppressible, irreducible quality of fun lies in its symbolic elaboration of emotion and passion, and its 'democratic' accessibility to all social strata. Fun creates powerful counterdiscourses and it is these which cannot be rooted out. Where one cultural identity encloses the group in a purified fortress of difference and otherness, other Pakistani and South Asian popular cultural identities constantly breach the barricades, appealing to groups beyond the boundary and human sentiments which incorporate otherness in parodic self-mockery or humanitarian love and caring.

In contemporary hierarchical societies, whether South Asian or European, popular culture, as Bourdieu (1986) has argued perceptively, empowers not only subordinate but also superordinate groups, often those concerned with the innovative production of high culture or elites wishing to set themselves apart from the conservative middle strata. The need is, however, to go beyond this generalization and locate the social contexts in which specific modes of popular culture valorize different class fractions, social categories and ethnic identifications in South Asian Muslim Punjabi Pakistani society.

All symbolic practices, whether of 'high' or popular culture, are embedded in social situations. If fun is the special prerogative of subordinate and elite groups, these groups – as social agents – must create the 'spaces' or social situations in which fun is culturally produced. Distinctively, immigrants from Pakistan have had to create not only fun spaces but the sacralized spaces of high Islamic and nationalist culture as well. A focus on these immigrants as social agents creating their own spaces thus entails a shift in theoretical perspective from an analysis of 'culture' or 'religion' as a disembodied system of meanings, religious approaches and social organizations to a focus on the symbolic practitioners themselves – men and women engaged in specific discourses in particular settings. These symbolic practitioners are not *only* Muslims, and the social spaces they create and participate in are not only, or even primarily, religious ones. Social identity is indexical. It is constituted situationally, within a particular social and historical context, both as practical knowledge and purposeful action. It is publicly negotiated and objectified by social actors in relation to their imagined audiences.[2]

The question then needs to be raised: given the indexicality of social identities, do the multiple identities any particular individual possesses form a coherent and consistent set of identifications?[3] And secondly, to the extent that an individual's social identities are in practice *incoherent* and *inconsistent,* how is this inconsistency managed? Is such an individual moved by schizophrenic forces beyond his control?[4] Or are individual social identities hierarchically ordered by value and saliency in relation to a series of encompassing symbolic domains and social spaces?[5] More specifically, what happens to social identities in the course of migration, or in the encounter with modernity and post-modernity?

Since individual identities can be schizophrenic and inconsistent, British Pakistanis (who are also Muslims, South Asians, mostly Punjabis, more or less Westernized)[6] tend to sustain different symbolic domains of activity and to keep these domains separate. In particular, the purely sacred, formal and serious activities of 'high' Islam and the profane, (a syncretic, hybrid amalgam of Islamic and Asian/Western cultural and symbolic practices) are compartmentalized, or, to use Clifford Geertz's term, kept in 'disjunction' (Geertz 1969: 17–8, 105–7). The formation of distinct symbolic spaces in which distinct practices and discourses are created and publicly negotiated are thus determined both by *symbolic content* and *audience.*

What produces and sustains the social spaces in which particular symbolic discourses and practices are created, negotiated and elaborated?[7] In order to answer this question, we need to consider first, what resources of time, wealth, effort and symbolic imagination social actors in a given historical context are willing to *invest* in a particular symbolic domain, and second, the extent to which they are willing to *mobilize to defend* and protect that domain when and if it is threatened 'externally'. *Investment* is an act of creation; *defence* is an act of preserving that which has been created.

Migration thus entails more than cultural production or reproduction. It entails acts of cultural and material *creativity.* Social spaces and symbolic discourses, as well as their material and organizational embodiments, all need to be created from scratch. These creations may meet resistance from the receiving society since migrants are not creating their social spaces entirely in a void. Yet not all new ethnic and religious creations meet such resistance or are perceived to threaten existing social arrangements. Within the general conditions of post-modernity the potential exists for an almost infinite creation of new social spaces, given appropriate investment and the existence of receptive audiences made up of cultural or religious consumers. As long as social spaces do not threaten to *displace* or encroach upon other people's symbolic spaces, they remain – at least in Britain – almost invisible, and certainly tolerated. Civil society is by its very nature pluralistic and continuously inventive.

Popular culture in South Asia has its traditional spaces sited in two major domains: a feminized youthful domain I shall call popular wedding culture, and a youthful male domain of sport. The first domain, that of popular wedding culture, draws its symbolic inspiration from female pre-wedding ritual celebrations, and especially the *mhendi* rite (see Werbner 1990), a ritual initiation of the bride and groom which licenses fun, music, dancing and transvestite masquerade. *Mhendis* are traditionally held in purdah, in the secret enclosure of the women's quarters, by an intimate circle of female friends and kinswomen.

While Muslim South Asian male wedding culture is also marked by licensed behaviour, lewd joking and transvestite dancing, it is less elaborate, arguably because the tension between what is legitimate and permissible is not so great. Islamic high culture expects young women to hide their sensuality and exhibit extreme modesty and bodily control. Music and dance are usually prohibited, and the only permissible expression of sexuality is in marriage. Men, especially young men, are by contrast expected to be more 'natural' and wild since they must engage with the outside world of danger and honour (see Boddy 1989 for a similar argument in relation to the Sudan). Men and women are segregated in public, and women must cover their bodies and heads in front of male elders and strangers.

From this space of absolute segregation and female enclosure popular wedding culture has been projected in contemporary South Asia on to the widest space of mass media commercialized popular culture – films, television, live entertainment, music, dance, singing – in which love, sensuality, comedy, parody, romance and passion are literalized and objectified in commodified aesthetic forms for the widest possible consumer market. What was feminized, restricted, hidden and marginal has become inclusive and dominant. What was sexually segregated is now publicly mixed. What was unofficially licensed as satire in hidden female celebrations is now licensed in public. Popular cultural stars – male and female – are adored and hero-worshipped. Women stars appear in public as sensual beings who sing, dance and openly fall in love.

Against the feminized space of popular wedding culture, sport, and especially cricket, is an expression of controlled masculine aggression and competitiveness. The intense enthusiasm for cricket as spectacle in South Asia amounts to a cult glorifying the human body, not as a denied vessel to be transcended by ascetic Sufi practices, but as an active, valorized vehicle to be nurtured and cultivated in order to enhance human physical capacity *in* the world. Hence sport is the masculinized domain of popular culture. Cricket, the game of the 'Other', the former oppressor, which has become a national and international sport, has also become a popular cultural expression of modern Pakistani nationalism and friendly competition in the international arena. It is a sport of the Commonwealth, a medium of communication, along with the English language, between erstwhile colonies. It is a sub-culture with its own values of *noblesse oblige*, fair play, upright conduct, sportsmanship, correct public behaviour, team spirit, and so forth. It is also symbolic of the nation-state as a 'Western' invention. Since cricket has become a part of professionalized mass media entertainment, its stars have become national heroes. The huge financial stakes involved in the international game make it more exciting, competitive and contentious than its imperial predecessor, and subject to highly controversial public disputes, screened live on television, between national teams or team captains and umpires, and to allegations of corruption and bribery involving hundreds of thousands of pounds. All this adds to the masculine glamour and politicization of the game.

Here, then, are two popular cultural domains which Pakistanis share and which are not specifically Islamic, although they mesh with Islamic traditions as domestic manifestations: a feminized domain of popular 'marriage' culture and a masculinized domain of male 'honour', power and aggression. Both run counter to Islamic high culture with its stress on purity, bodily containment, spirituality and intellect. Both also transcend and hence transgress (from the Islamist point of view) the boundaries of *umma*, the Muslim community. Popular wedding culture encompasses a Pan-Asian Urdu- and Hindi-speaking population, including Muslims, Hindus and Sikhs, who share common aesthetic traditions, similar wedding songs and dances and musical instrumental genres, as well as comic and satirical tropes which cut across religious and even regional linguistic boundaries. Cricket too transgresses the boundaries of the *umma*, creating links between nations of different religious persuasions, while at the same time it poses an alternative to the religious community in the nation-state, promoting a very different definition of order, law and morality from that of Islam. Pakistani identities thus draw on three intersecting transnational cultural spaces, *none of which coincides with the nation-state*.

Performative Space and Identity

As a performative space, each cultural domain also represents a source of personal gendered and generational identity empowerment, and dramatizes a powerful aesthetic tradition through voluntary activities enacted by opposed social categories: Islam – by male elders; popular wedding culture – by women; and cricket – by men, especially young men. The divisions can be summed up as follows:

Table 1

Cultural Domain	Gender/ Age	Aesthetic/ Morality	Boundaries	Empowerment
Islam	Male elders/ (Female elders)	Purity, spirituality, self-denial, solemnity	Religious community *umma*	Dominant male elders
Wedding Culture	Young women (Women)	Sensuality, love, comerdy, satire, sexual expressiveness	Pan-Asian	Women and non-orthodox elite families
Cricket (Men)	Young men	Physical power/ aggression, individual responsibility, team spirit	Commonwealth nation-state	Young men and non-observant elite men

A paradoxical situation has thus emerged in which South Asian wedding culture is both the highest and the lowest, the most exclusive, restricted and segregated and the most inclusive, universal and tolerant, having the broadest appeal in terms of generation, gender and religious divisions. While Reformist Islam is inclusive in its transcendence of linguistic and hence regional ethnic boundaries, and tolerant in its transcendence of class and race, it remains intolerant in its rejection of alternative aesthetic and ethical expressions. Religiosity attacks popular culture and hence the relationship between them is one of powerful contestation. The status of the 'owners' of the religious domain – clerics, saints and male elder community leaders or spokesmen – has been rendered ambiguous by the mass commercialization of popular culture. Film and cricket stars compete for popular supremacy with saints, *ulema* (the clergy) and politicians. Although religious and political leaders use the press and media to gain publicity, they cannot, on the whole, compete against the sheer seductiveness and glamour of film or TV stars and cricket heroes.

In Britain Pakistani immigrants have had to create the domain of high culture and its spaces; and these, as mentioned, have until recently been entirely controlled by male elders. Domestic wedding *mhendi* rituals, held by women in the confines of their homes, were early revitalized by immigrants as young girls and boys reached marriageable age (see Werbner 1990). Sports and mass popular wedding culture remained, however, 'imported' commodities, packaged in South Asia. This left a public sphere in which men, whatever their political and religious persuasion, predominated. The contours of this space of 'high' culture and politics that they created was sober, earnest and intellectual, while being also a domain of passionate political argument and artistic rhetorical creativity, a testing-ground of individual leadership qualities in an endless game of factional power alignments (see Werbner 1991b).

This implied a certain communal *closure*. Though the religious-cum-political domain had come to be increasingly fractionalized since the mid-1970s, it nevertheless remained encapsulated, with religiosity, wealth, elderhood and leadership conjoined. Non-observant Pakistanis remained marginal in the community.

Sporadic attempts to form women's organizations had all failed. Young men's organisations (with the exception of radical Islamic associations) were conspicuous by their absence. The empowerment of these two subordinate groups – women and young men – relates to the maturation of second-generation immigrants and the cultural dilemmas generated by permanent settlement. Dispersed urban living, and the need to provide alternative forms of entertainment for youth and children in order to compete with the power of Western popular culture have underlined a growing predicament: how to preserve and reproduce community not merely as a domain of religious observance but as a site of fun, leisure and celebration in which young Asian Muslim men and women can be socialized.

This has entailed the movement of popular wedding culture from the interiority of the domestic out to the public sphere. The transformation has been associated with an assumption by women and sports fans of voluntary leadership roles, threatening the hegemony of male elders.

What is this public sphere?[8] The problem is one of theorizing the nexus between popular and political cultures, between mass media images and simulations and local-level voluntary communal public culture. The latter is the space in which ethnic ideologies are negotiated publicly by local-level leaders and activists in front of a local audience. This communal public culture is by its very nature pluralistic since it harnesses segmental aesthetic, moral or religious sentiments in order to mobilize audiences or congregations for specific communal ends, either for the solidaristic celebration of religious and national festivals or for philanthropic and charitable causes.

This public sphere can be located in a hierarchy of progressively inclusive social spaces, from the domestic and inter-domestic to the mass cultural. At each scale of social inclusiveness different cultural narratives are negotiated. The most inclusive – that of commercial mass media – penetrates the other cultural spaces and is thus all-pervasive. It also cuts across national boundaries and ethnic or religious communities, and enhances both the awareness of otherness and physical access to an alternative cultural Other.

I have argued elsewhere that the domestic *mhendi* ritual has an incorporative capacity to comment on and absorb alterity which stems from its liminal deployment of parody, pastiche, satire and cross-over (P. Werbner ibid.) This is true also of South Asian mass popular culture, which can borrow Western popular genres, themes and consumer goods selectively, without losing its distinctive South Asian flavour. This incorporative capacity is enhanced by the common stress in Western and South Asian – and indeed, Islamic – popular cultures on bodily expressiveness and enjoyment. Reflecting this incorporative capacity of popular culture, new Pakistani professional pop groups are beginning to emerge in Britain which celebrate hybridity through an amalgam of South Asian, Western and black hip-hop genres. These groups often satirize familial themes such as arranged marriages, and attack racism, while glorifying Asian and Muslim masculinities

Since South Asian mass culture is openly for sale, it is fundamentally indiscriminate, especially in its packaged forms as TV programmes, films, and audio-video cassettes, books, newspapers and periodicals. In seeking mass consumer markets, its genres not only celebrate collective values but revise, channel and reshape these values.

At the other end of the scale, domestic and inter-domestic celebrations objectify the specific culturally shared images and symbols negotiated in intimate family circles. *Communal* voluntary public culture lies at the point of greatest ambiguity between the utterly private and exclusive and the fully public and inclusive. This is why diasporic ethnicities and religiosities are formed, celebrated and transgressed within this sphere.

The social events described here transgressed in one way or another currently accepted ethno-religious ideologies. On the one hand were events which were *morally* transgressive, drawing on Western or South Asian forms of entertainment to infringe Islamic ritual prohibitions, without challenging hegemonic Western or Asian values. As morally transgressive, these events were marginalized as deviant in communal constructions, and remained semi-private. They thus defined a diasporic ethnicity which was unofficial and delegitimized, a space of 'sinful fun', and set apart a class fraction (Westernized Pakistanis/Asians) who had shed one facet (Islam) of a multi-faceted ethnicity, while continuing to celebrate their national and regional cultural attachments. This fraction, being wealthy and politically powerful, could not be ignored or entirely marginalized. Nevertheless, it remained peripheral to the central arena of diasporic politics since it was perceived to promote an ideological capitulation to Western dominance. Moral transgression was merely a means of defining an exclusive, elitist social status in a social context in which the ethnic majority remained deeply religious. It consisted simply of a conjuncture between normatively separate cultures (Western and South Asian Muslim) which empowered a fraction of an already powerful group – male elders, internally divided – without fully challenging structures of dominance within the community.

That such celebrations should move into a semi-public arena nevertheless points to the fact that these Westernized elites are making a hidden political bid for dominance against the more religiously conservative elite fractions. At present, however, the appeal of Westernized genres of cultural transgression is limited, and these Westernized Asian Muslims are unable to mobilize broad constituencies. Their empowerment is one of wealth and connections with the wider society. Few of the organizers at present even pretend to assume ethnic leadership roles. Hence this form of cultural transgression may be said to be syncretic without being creative.

By contrast to events that are merely culturally transgressive – drinking in public or the public celebration of sexuality – there are other events which empower previously subordinate, culturally constituted social categories, in the communal arena. Their transgression is more radical since it challenges established hierarchies by harnessing the sentimental power of mass popular culture (sports and entertainment) for the self-empowerment of groups previously denied access to the public arena altogether.

The clash has been generated, as argued, by the opening up of a space for the expression of pluralistic interests in the public sphere, characteristic of Western modernity. This allows for the challenging of a monolithic conception of a bounded community which ethnic leaders aspire to preserve. For these men, mainly first-generation immigrants from Pakistan or India, it is only within such a bounded community that high status and leadership are meaningful constructions, given the subordinate position of their group in the wider society and their own peripheral status within this broader arena.

Thus both women and young men are discouraged from holding independent prestige events in the communal public arena. As we saw, Pakistani women have in the 1990s founded a number of active philanthropic organizations concerned with fund-raising for welfare causes and the rights of women and children. The early efforts of Al Masoom were followed by more spectacular philanthropic drives. The women have taken goods, clothes and medical supplies for Bosnian refugees, including an ambulance, and, following that, to Albania too. Among the more spectacular public events staged by a consortium of Pakistani women's organizations in Manchester was a 'women in black' march through the city streets to protest against the continuing violence in Kashmir and Bosnia. Participating in the march was a British MP, Gerald Kaufman, and it was hosted by the Lord Mayor of Manchester. Al Masoom ('For the Innocent'), the women's organization spearheading this move into the public domain, was initially subjected to a campaign of harassment and physical threats and to allegations of corruption and mishandling of public money, all in a clear effort to prevent the women from assuming a legitimate leadership role in the community. The solidarity of local Pakistani women in the face of this sustained attack has been quite remarkable, many of them ignoring their husbands' criticisms in their determination to join and participate in the organization's activities.

Young men's empowerment as an autonomous social category has been hampered by their 'failure' to stage an 'open' event successfully. However, this leaves unclear the limits of legitimate public popular culture they can enjoy beyond the religious sphere. Playing cricket, rather than entertaining cricket stars, is clearly regarded as legitimate, and the control of male elders in this domain is minimal. Unlike women, young men are gradually incorporated into elders' associations as they mature. The line between 'youth' and 'elderhood' is highly ambiguous and depends on the achievement of further status attributes (wealth, professional or political standing, etc.) Young men are often recruited to meetings requiring factional shows of physical strength or voting power (see Werbner 1991b). Their exclusion from leadership in the prestige public domain is thus temporary, yet it remains particularly significant in Britain. For it is in the field of sport, through support of the national team, that young British Pakistanis express their love of both cricket and the home country, along with their sense of alienation and disaffection from British society.

It is at the level of mass cultural stardom that the publicly official and the unofficial merge, so that the feminized domestic sphere of popular entertainment and the young male cult of masculinity as sports receive the seal of male elder legitimacy as expressions of Pakistani nationalism. At this point, however, the organization is taken over by male elders who dominate throughout. Nevertheless, the other social categories (women and youth) are not excluded, hence the space is defined as simultaneously *public and familial*, Islamic and universal. This is a truly creative innovation, a revolution rather than a rebellion.

On Cricket, Fund-Raising and Tolerance

All of which brings us back to cricket. A few months before the fund-raising drive by Al Masoom, Imran Khan returned to Manchester once again, this time to appeal for a charity he himself had founded to build a cancer hospital in Lahore. Like the Al Masoom philanthropic events, this one combined Muslim and Asian popular culture in a blend which was uniquely Pakistani and Muslim South Asian. Although the appeal took place on the eve of the Gulf War, at the height of the Rushdie affair, no mention was made of either of these political time-bombs. Instead, the Imran Khan Hospital Benefit Dinner was an evening of fun, laughter, singing and music. It embodied, in a taken-for-granted natural way, what the world could be like if there were no wars, no racial or religious bigotry, and no ethnic intolerance and violence.

The appeal took place in the most exclusive hotel in Manchester, in front of all the Who's Who of the region. Tickets were £50 a head and most groups consisted of ten family members and friends, seated at round tables, each representing a donation of £500 for the cause. Seats at the high table, sitting along with the celebrities, were £3,000 each. The performers were international stars including Dilip Kumar, the beloved Muslim Indian film star, 'King of the Bombay Screen' and his wife, herself a celebrity. All had come to assist the hero of the evening, Imran

Khan, the sun in the celestial firmament, adored and adulated by young and old alike. The evening raised £115,000 for the appeal, the largest sum raised in one evening in the whole of Britain, topping Birmingham's £100,000.

In the audience were men and women, all dressed in their best. At some tables people were drinking wine discreetly but this passed without comment. It was a sophisticated gathering, such as could be found in elite circles in Delhi, Lahore, Karachi or Bombay. It was not a place for religious bigots or narrow minded *ulama*. The evening was set apart as a moment of universal harmony and humanitarian brotherhood.

The speeches were particularly revealing. Dilip Kumar spoke of the the world as a global village in which human beings should learn to live at peace with one another, to fight against pain and illness:

> It is an irony, when the world is growing towards not just internationalism but towards universalness, that we are talking about nationalities, we are talking about ethnic identities; we, the people and some of the leaders of human society talking about religion, practising irreligiousness. . . Yes, we've had too much of this religion. There is but one religion that is preached by all the gospels, by all the sacred books, and that is the decency of man towards fellow human beings. And I stand here with that stamp of Indian nationality to support the cause of my brother (Imran Khan) in this exercise in humanism, universal humanism. . . '

In all the speeches, Islamic themes were interwoven into the public domain of charitable giving. The celebrities, and above all Imran Khan himself, were likened to Muslim Sufi saints, *awliya*, friends of God, close to God. And giving to the hospital was giving to God, a sacrifice which would increase a person's merit in the next world. Whether or not these sportsmen and entertainers flout Islamic rules in their private lives (whether they drink or chase women), was suppressed during the evening, because in the official public domain they behave as exemplary Muslims, and are seen to be working for the public good of the whole community, performing *khidmat* public service. This is political pop Islamic style, and it appeals to the same powerful ethical and aesthetic emotions as the alliances between political activists and pop stars, from Pete Seeger to Bob Geldof.

Initially, the sums raised by the cricketer were still comparatively modest. To put these sums in perspective, at a mosque cornerstone laying ceremony in Birmingham which I attended a year later, £160,000 was raised for a new mosque building in less than an hour! Pakistani disaster and war appeals in Britain raise millions. Importantly, however, the Imran Khan Hospital Benefit Appeal was the first of its kind in Manchester. It was the first legitimate event to be devoted to fund raising for a welfare cause in Pakistan, using the appeal of media stars, music and song to mobilize an elite mixed audience of men, women and youth in an atmosphere of mutual tolerance, and the first serious event for a serious cause celebrated by serious people in a non-serious manner. The revolutionary nature of the appeal and its populist style was to become more apparent as the Imran Khan roadshow gathered momentum and donations for the hospital began to pour in from Pakistanis at home as well. In December 1994 the hospital opened in Lahore amid widespread expressions of adulation for the cricketer- turned-philanthropist and mass shows of popular support from ordinary citizens. At the same time the press alleged that Imran Khan had assumed the mantle of sainthood and was plotting to overthrow the Pakistani government, while a court case against him was pending for failing to register his charity with the proper authorities (see, for example, Chaudhury 1995 and Malik 1995). In a televised interview in February 1995 Imran Khan defended his actions; he made it clear that in his view the Pakistani elite had betrayed its leadership role in abandoning Islam and the masses in Pakistan: 'Islam plays a very important part in my life because Islam means humanity for me', he told a BBC2 Newsnight reporter. 'There is nothing anyone can give me. I give people', he added, underlining the Islamic stress on *khidmat*, selfless giving and devotion to the community which had earned him his current saintly title. The saint in Islam is always a giver, never a receiver.

From a sociological point of view, the achievement of Pakistani nationalists such as Imran Khan or Kaifat Khan, the leader of Al Masoom, has been their capacity to legitimize an alternative 'humanitarian hybridity': by celebrating Islam through humour and music, they invoke a vision of a less defensive, more open society, one which contrasts sharply with the current Islamist stress on closure and external threat.

Ironically many (but significantly not all) of the donors in the audience attending Imran Khan's Manchester appeal had also during the *same* period attended public communal events at which speakers declared their support for Saddam Hussein's invasion of Kuwait (see Werbner 1994). Yet the framed spaces of ultra-nationalist religious rhetoric and patriotic charitable pop were kept totally separate, and remained in disjunction.

In April 1992 the Pakistan international cricket team, captained by

Imran Khan, won the World Cup Limited Overs Cricket Competition in Sydney. The cliffhanger between Pakistan and England revealed a hidden but obvious truth: that when it comes to sport, there is no such thing as being British. While the English mourned their defeat, British Pakistanis all over the United Kingdom were celebrating their team's victory. When it comes to cricket, it seems, blood is thicker than the English rain.⌈A young Pakistani, born and bred in Britain, told his English friends, 'I'm proud to be British but when it comes down to the hard core, I'm really Pakistani.'⌉Young Pakistanis in Manchester field a large number of amateur cricket teams, playing in local amateur leagues. The average age of team players is about 30, and the vast majority were either born or grew up in Britain.

British Pakistanis' taken-for-granted support of their national team apparently needs no additional explanation. Loyalty to the Pakistani national team appears to be natural and instinctive, something, they seem to feel, they imbibe with their mother's milk, or inherit along with their father's blood. As one celebrating young man told a *Guardian* reporter, 'If you cut my wrists, green blood will come out.' The Pakistani flag is green. Green is the colour of Islam.

Two years previously, in a controversial speech in the House of Commons on the eve of the Indian test series, Norman Tebbitt, the hard-line Tory MP, castigated British Asians and declared that they should demonstrate their loyalty by supporting England. 'If you come to live in a country and take up the passport of that country, and you see your future and your family's future in that country, it seems to me that is your country. You can't just keep harking back.'

Tebbitt's remarks, greeted by a storm of protest at the time, were clearly absurd in a country which regularly fields four national teams for any sporting contest (Irish, English, Scottish, and Welsh). The equation between national loyalty and team loyalty made here is quite evidently spurious, despite attempts by the Right to impute apparent support for the home country's team to unwillingness on the part of Asians, and especially Pakistanis, to 'integrate.'

Sporting contests both objectify social divisions and nationalist sentiments and point to an alliance between contesters, a shared fanaticism. There is a sense of friendship and fun in the competing loyalties. Sporting contests are, it would seem, like *moka* in Melanesia, a *substitute* for war, a domain of symbolic agonism, a token not of hatred and disloyalty but of friendly rivalry in the midst of peace.

The context in which my chapter is set is one in which there has been an apparent shift in communal discourse: from a stress on national to a stress on religious identity, linked to a growing realization by immigrants from Pakistan that their stay in Britain is permanent, and that the most pressing need is to fight local battles for religious rights (see Nielsen 1988; 1992). The publication of *The Satanic Verses*, however, revealed a deep clash between Islam and British nationalism. 'Islam' was now a term to be defended at all costs, a matter of personal and communal honour. British Pakistanis 'became', officially, in the media and in their own eyes, 'Muslims'.

Yet publicly paraded identities, however sacred and universal, conceal deeply-felt communal sentiments. If cricket reveals the sentimental depths of nationalism, having 'fun' reveals Pakistanis' deep South Asian cultural roots and identity. Outside prayer times or politics, British Pakistanis love having fun. They watch Indian movies, hero-worship Indian film stars, listen avidly to modern bhangra music, dance and sing, celebrate and enjoy life like all other South Asians. Thus Al Masoom raised money by providing amusement and fun for other Pakistani women and children, drawing on familiar South Asian genres of entertainment. The women lampooned men, sang and danced. Their fund-raising was aggressively attacked by businessmen and community leaders, despite the women's piety and the clear sanctity of their cause.

If official religion, nationalism and economic production are the domain of male elders, then sports, entertainment and consumption are the domain of youth, women, and families. The sacred which is elevated above the profane is thus elevated as a *compartmentalized* preserve of elder male honour. To challenge this ranking of values by controlling fund-raising or by hosting dignitaries is to provoke the hostility of male elders. It is only an international mass media celebrity such as Imran Khan, adored, classy and elitist, who can successfully challenge this hierarchy and reach out to a broader humanism *with* elder male approval. Yet daily life, the quotidian, which is profane, is dominated by women and youth. As diaspora Pakistanis sink roots in Britain and come increasingly to resemble their hosts in matters of fund raising and celebration, so too women and young men are likely increasingly to claim their share of the prestige public domain.

Just as male elders create the cultural genres and social spaces where Pakistani nationalism is celebrated officially or religious worship is conducted in the utmost seriousness, so too young men and women create the cultural agendas and social spaces for fun and amusement, for consumption and imaginative artistic expression, which also celebrate nationalism and religiosity, but through unofficial genres of parody or sport. Women create public spaces for the family, and especially for children and teenage girls, to enjoy themselves in a distinctive cultural milieu they can share with their parents. The children come to all the wedding *mhendi* celebrations, and so too are brought into the dancing, singing, music and masquerade of the women's public performances. Popular culture, the aestheticization of everyday life (Featherstone 1992), draws families together and creates a counter-culture to the pervasive English popular culture and music, something distinctively Asian and Muslim which yet can be enjoyed as sheer fun.

Through situational disjunctions, blendings and juxtapositions, British-Pakistanis (who are Muslims-Asians-Punjabis-more-or-less-Westernized) create internally coherent sets of symbolic practices which are set apart and 'disjuncted'. The separation between spaces is never, however, as we have seen, complete. There is constant inter-situational 'commentary' and 'leakage' between spaces and domains. Different symbolic discourses, produced in particular situations, cross-refer to one another while the symbolic spaces in which they are produced are also subject to internal local-level ethnic political contestations. These sometimes involve a symbolic (and even physical) attack on the cultural premises and autonomy of both the organizers and the specific symbolic domains they control. In other words, 'situational inter-reference' may become *interference*, a clash, implicit or explicit, between discrete symbolic spaces.[9]

Because, however, each symbolic domain consists of a 'lived-in' world of meanings and connotations, of primordial sentiments, of material objects, of interests and power struggles, of 'natural', quotidian, taken-for-granted personal identities, these attacks are basically doomed. Sometimes, however, one symbolic domain, such as the 'purified' religious space of knowledge practices, may gain ground temporarily at the expense of another, within a particular community, at a particular historical moment.[10]

The extent to which 'fun' and the spaces of fun are constitutive of identity and subjectivity – whether ethnic, gendered or generational – remains to be fully theorized, although discussions of youth subcultures and popular culture have highlighted certain dimensions of this conjuncture. By juxtaposing a variety of 'social situations', all of them equally typical and pervasive among British Muslims (who are also Pakistanis, mostly Punjabis and more-or-less Westernized) the present chapter has considered not only how identities shift in their situational salience, but how they are differentially imaged and constituted in internal ethnic contestations for power and influence. Rather than a pure, unchanging vision of Islam, I have attempted to illuminate the ways in which Islam is differentially objectified or denied, in a context which incorporates both South Asian and English themes, comments on them, and plays upon them.

One thing is evident. Young diaspora Pakistanis do not deny their national roots. Their loyalty and sentimental attachment to the home country is as deep as ever. Indeed, the charity shows which they stage for welfare in the home country are part of a new trend towards the establishment of lasting attachments between diaspora British Pakistanis and Pakistan. In these events an old-new hybridism between Islam and popular culture is created, in which the two are inextricably intermeshed culturally and emotionally.

In mid-March 1992 an acquaintance was returning home late at night from a party, and happened to drive through Manchester's main Asian retail centre. Unexpectedly, without warning, she found herself in a gigantic traffic jam, with cars hooting all around her, drivers driving down the wrong lanes, green flags flying from windows and sun roofs, and shouts of 'Long Live Pakistan' amidst the general pandemonium. The pavements were packed with policemen. The drivers were all young Asians. Terrified her car would be damaged, she sent her husband to enquire what was happening. The young people told him: 'We are celebrating *eid*. It is our Christmas.'

Two years previously, young men like these had gathered in Manchester from many towns in the North West and had run amuck, breaking shop windows in their enthusiastic 'celebrations'. Now, apparently, there is talk among elders of providing an appropriate social space where these young Pakistani teenagers can celebrate *eid* and enjoy themselves without causing damage or public disturbances.

The amalgam of Islam and Pakistani culture, religion and nationalism, are both objectified in the green flag and continued loyalty to the home country. But they are also objectified in cricket and bhangra music, and these are *forcing* their way into the official public arena, despite the resistance of elder males and religious officials. Serious politics, like puritanical Islam, must necessarily give way to the need to create public spaces for the young to celebrate, as well as to the universal humanism of public Pakistani celebrities such as Imran Khan.

Conclusion

My interest in the present paper has been not with global and national public spaces of identity but with the autonomous spaces urban diasporic ethnic groups create for themselves. It is in these spaces that 'culture' becomes a contested terrain, as social classes and categories, positioned differentially *vis-a-vis* each other, struggle to define the cultural shape of their shared collective identities.

This was evident also in the Rushdie affair: in *The Satanic Verses* Salman Rushdie utilised the Islamic South Asian space of fun and satire to create a radical commentary on puritanical Islam.[11] But in attacking the persona of the Prophet he transgressed the boundaries between symbolic spaces, to incur the wrath not only of puritans but of the vast majority of ordinary Muslims. He went beyond the acceptable amalgams or hybrids of Islam and South Asian satirical creativity. In radically subverting the hierarchy of values between the sacred and the profane publicly, in front of a Western audience, he violated the prescribed disjunctions between symbolic spaces and domains.

The creation by British Pakistanis of distinct symbolic spaces in which distinct practices and discourses are created and publicly negotiated, draws on prior experiences to create new mythologies played out in front of contemporary British Pakistani audiences. A 'space' includes both actors and audience. In challenging the hegemony of Pakistani male elders, Pakistani women and young men, positioned differently yet sharing dual or even multiple worlds of lived-in realities, are, it seems, now transforming the imagining of their ethnic group's shared collective identities in Britain.

Notes

1. On bodily transgression as counterhegemonic see Bakhtin 1968; Bourdieu 1986; on incorporation of otherness beyond the boundary through satire and ritual masquerade see Handelman 1981; Boddy 1989; R. Werbner 1989: ch. 3; Werbner 1990: ch. 8; on postcolonial cricket see Appadurai 1995.
2. For a discussion of my use of the 'indexical' see Werbner 1990: 260–1. For a general review of early literature on social situations see Garbett 1970.
3. On inconsistent identifications see Clifford 1988: 338; Werbner 1991a.
4. This question is also raised by Fischer 1986: 195.
5. I use 'encompassment' in the sense used by Dumont 1983.
6. On the multiple identities of British Pakistanis see Werbner 1991b.
7. I use 'social space' here in the triadic sense defined by Lefebvre 1991: 33.

8. For the debates surrounding the notion of the 'public sphere' see Habermas 1989.
9. For a general discussion of inter-referentiality, and in conjunction with 'interference' see Fischer 1986; Fischer and Abedi 1990: xxiv, xxxi–ii.
10. I use the notion of 'knowledge practices' to refer to an explicit discourse and its associated prescriptive practices, in the sense discussed by Foucault (e.g. Foucault 1977). This contrasts with the taken-for-granted, common-sense assumptions embedded in the quotidian, Bourdieu's 'practical knowledge' (Bourdieu 1977).
11. See Werbner 1992, and Fischer and Abedi 1990, chapter 7.

Bibliography

Appadurai, Arjun (1995), 'Playing with Modernity: the Decolonization of Indian Cricket', in Carol A. Breckenridge (ed.), *Consuming Modernity: Public culture in a South Asian World*. Minneapolis: University of Minnesota Press

Bakhtin, Mikhail (1968), *Rabelais and His World*. H Iswolsky, trans. Cambridge Mass: MIT Press

Boddy, Janice. (1989), *Wombs and Alien Spirits*. Wisconsin: Wisconsin University Press

Bourdieu, Pierre. (1977 (1972)), *Outline of a Theory of Practice*. Richard Nice, trans. Cambridge: Cambridge University Press

— (1986), *Distinction*. London: Routledge

Chaudhary, Vivek (1995), 'The Prince of Pakistan', *The Guardian*, 7 February

Clifford, James (1988), *The Predicament of Culture: Twentieth Century Ethnography, Literature and Art*. Cambridge, Mass: Harvard University Press

Cohen, Abner (1991), 'Drama and Politics in the Development of a London Carnival' in Pnina Werbner and Muhammad Anwar (eds.) *Black and Ethnic Leaderships in Britain*. London: Routledge (1992). *Masquerade Politics: Explorations in the Structure of Urban Cultural Movements*. Berkeley: University of California Press.

Dumont, Louis (1983), 'A Modified View of Our Origins: the Christian Beginnings of Modern Individualism', *Contributions to Indian Sociology*, (N.S.) vol. 17, no. 1, pp. 1–26

Featherstone, Mike (1991), *Consumer Culture and Postmodernism*. London: Sage

Fischer, M.J. (1986), 'Ethnicity and the Post-Modern Arts of Memory,' in James Clifford and George E. Marcus (eds), *Writing Culture: the Poetics and*

Politics of Ethnography. Berkeley: University of California Press, pp. 194–233

Fischer, M. J. and Mehdi Abedi (1990), *Debating Muslims: Cultural Dialogues in Postmodernity and Tradition*. Madison: University of Wisconsin Press

Foucault, Michel (1977 (1975)), *Discipline and Punish*. Alan Sheridan, trans. London: Penguin

Garbett, Kingsley G. (1970), 'The Analysis of Social Situations', *Man*, (N.S.) vol. 5, no. 2, pp. 214–27

Geertz, Clifford (1968), *Islam Observed*. New Haven: Yale University Press

Habermas, Jurgen (1989 (1962)), *The Structural Transformation of the Public Sphere*. Thomas Burger, trans. Cambridge: Polity Press

Handelman, Don (1981), 'The Ritual Clown: Attributes and Affinities', *Anthropos*, vol.76, pp. 321–70

Lefebvre, Henri (1991 (1974)), *The Production of Space*. Donald Nicholson-Smith, trans. Oxford: Blackwell

Malik, Sohail (1995), 'Acheson Man', *Q News*, 20–27 January. Melucci

Metcalf, Barbara (1987),'Islamic Arguments in Contemporary Pakistan', in William R. Roff (ed.), *Islam and the Political Economy of Meaning: Comparative Studies in Muslim Discourse*. Berkeley: University of California Press

Mumtaz, Khawar and Farida Shaheed (1987), *Women of Pakistan*. London: Zed

Nielsen, Jorgen S. (1988), 'Muslims in Britain and Local Authority Responses', in Tomas Gerholm and Yngve Georg Lithman (eds), *The New Islamic Presence in Western Europe*. London: Mansell, pp. 53–77

— (1992), 'Islam, Muslims, and British Local and Central Government: Structural Fluidity'. Paper presented at the Conference on 'European Islam: Societies and States', Torino

Werbner, Pnina (1990), *The Migration Process: Capital, Gifts and Offerings among British Pakistanis*. Oxford: Berg

— (1991a), 'Introduction II: Black and Ethnic Leaderships in Britain; a Theoretical Overview' in Pnina Werbner and Muhammad Anwar (eds), pp. 15–37

— (1991b), 'Factionalism and Violence in British Pakistani Politics' in Hastings Donnan and Pnina Werbner (eds), *Economy and Culture in Pakistan: Migrants and Cities in a Muslim Society*. London: Macmillan, pp. 188–215

— (1992), 'L'affaire Rushdie et l'integration musulmane en Grande-Bretagne', in Sophia Mappa (ed.), *L'Europe des Douze et les autres: intégration ou auto-exclusion?* Forum de Delphes. Paris: Karthala

Werbner, Richard (1989), *Ritual Passage, Sacred Journey: The Processes and*

Organisation of Religious Movement. Washington DC: Smithsonian Institution Press

Acknowledgements

This paper has benefited greatly from comments made by participants at the conference on 'European Islam: Societies and States' in Torino, May 1992; at the International Centre for Contemporary Cultural Research's seminar series on 'Creative Social Spaces', University of Manchester; and at the Oxford University 'Ethnicity and Identity' seminar series on 'Sport and Identity'. Research was conducted in Manchester with the support of grants from the UK Economic and Social Research Council. I am grateful to the Council for its generous support.

6

Angling: A Live Issue

Jeremy MacClancy

Angling, the most popular participant sport in Britain, is also among the least publicized. Though over 3,500,000 people practise the sport it very rarely gains headlines in national newspapers and almost never appears on national news programmes. Unlike football its leading practitioners are not household names and do not accrue small fortunes. The most patent reason for this apparent neglect by the media is that, at least until very recently, angling has been regarded as an essentially uncontroversial, traditional activity predominantly practised by solitary characters. In televisual terms, the sight of a man sitting quietly on a riverbank for hours on end is not a strong image. For television producers, the moments of intense excitement are too few, their timing too unpredictable. Angling, in other words, is popular for precisely the reason that makes it unsuitable television material: it is not a spectator sport for the masses but a participant activity for patient individuals.

Angling writers eulogize their pastime as an all-embracing gentle activity of manifest benefit to both its practitioners and society. They claim learning to pursue fish appeals to the intellect, develops analytical abilities and stimulates constructive thinking. An aid to the formation of character, fishing offers relief from life's pressures, educates anglers in the virtues of patience, teaches calmness in the face of adversity, 'procures contentedness' (Cox 1697), 'purifies thoughts' (Cholmondeley-Pennell 1870: 15), and engenders a 'philosophical' turn of mind (O'Gorman 1845: 9). Eminently therapeutic it provides good exercise, 'like yoga with exciting bursts' (Milner 1993: 5). It supplies an opportunity to observe nature at first hand and develops anglers' aesthetic sense, opening their eyes wide to the splendours of the living world: 'A newly landed fish can be a beautiful thing. I can't help but admire some the fresh, sparkling fish which I have caught' (ibid.) It exercises our competitiveness without kindling the extremes of violence found in other sports. It supports a million-pound industry and keeps people in work and kids off the streets (Pocklington 1993: 19). It may even inspire religiosity:

> It may well be admitted that there is much in the contemplative character of (the angler's) pursuit, and in the quiet scenes of beauty with which it brings him face to face, to soften and elevate, as well as to 'humanize'. The rushing of white water, and the deep greenery of woods and fields, seem incompatible with what is base and sordid. They act like a tonic on the mind and body alike, and the fisherman, solitary with his own thoughts, shut out from the world, 'shut in, left alone' with himself and perfection of scenery, can hardly fail to be penetrated with the spirit that haunts solitude and loveliness. A chord is touched that must find an echo in every heart not utterly dead to gentle influences – awakening what is good, silencing what is bad; directing the thoughts into purer channels, and leading them almost instinctively to 'look through Nature up to Nature's God' (Cholmondeley-Pennell 1870: 15).

As Izaak Walton put it, fishing was a pious practice: 'employment for idle time, then not idly spent' (Walton 1971: 45).

In recent years however, the stereotype of fishing as an innocent rural entertainment has been increasingly challenged by a new breed of animal welfare activists: anti-anglers. These militants wish to change common perceptions and practices. Instead of seeing angling as a socially beneficial sport of no harm to anyone or anything, they regard it as a degrading activity on a par with foxhunting and harecoursing. To them, fishing is not a placid pursuit to be promoted but an uncaring bloodsport to be banned. And they are beginning to get their message across.

The aim of this chapter is to review the basis of anti-anglers' arguments and of anglers' counter-arguments. But first, I give brief histories of angling and anti-angling.

***

The first English references to angling as a sport occur in the fifteenth century in such works as Wynkyn de Worde's *Treatyse of Fysshynge with an Angle*, published in 1496, which details the correct way to use rods, horsehair lines, and artificial flies. At this time most angling was for carp, anglers using a simple baited hook with a float and a line attached to a loop on the top of a long wooden rod. Of course most anglers then were members of the more leisured classes. Angling, viewed as a philosophical, contemplative pastime, was thought particularly suitable for clergymen (Thomas 1983: 1977). Only professionals and the well-to-do had sufficient free time to develop their angling skills for the sole sake of pleasure. Workers could not afford to regard fishing as a form of recreation. To them, it was an instrumental means to a pragmatic end: supplementing and varying the domestic diet. By the end of the sixteenth century angling became sufficiently popular to support a market in handmade rods and hooks. And by the middle of the seventeenth century it already had its greatest writer, Izaak Walton, whose *Compleat Angler. Being a Discourse of Rivers, Fish-ponds, Fish and Fishing* has never gone out of print.

As angling slowly became more commonplace, class divisions in its practice deepened. Over the nineteenth century salmon disappeared from English rivers, mainly because of increasing pollution, and only the more wealthy among English salmon anglers could afford to travel to Wales, Scotland, and Ireland. As demand to fish the English chalk streams favoured by brown trout rose, owners of land adjoining their banks began to charge for the rights to fish from them, so excluding the majority of anglers. In the 1870s the government instituted rod licences for game-angling in order to raise revenue and halt the depletion of English stocks of trout. Also, salmon and trout anglers, partly to increase their sense of class distinctiveness, came to eschew any other kind of bait than a fly, and then came to rank themselves according to the type of fly used (wet, nymph, or dry). Since fly-fishing is much more skilled than coarse fishing, both in the casting of the line and the 'playing' and landing of the fish, fly-fishers learnt to regard their type of angling as not just the most expensive, but as the highest form of the sport as well. The more fluent among them gradually produced a literature to substantiate this claim. By the 1890s these writers has established a flyfishing philosophy about the nature of their feelings and the relationship to the rivers and fish (Voss Bark 1992: 76).

Coarse fishing (where the prey are not eaten but returned to the water) only emerged as a particularly popular form of rural recreation, for the working classes, when large numbers of people moved to towns in search of work in factories. In the newly industrialized towns proletarian groups organized angling trips to the nearby countryside. Public houses and working-men's clubs ran angling competitions, with winners receiving cups, medals and prizes, and participating teams betting on the results. Some of these competitions became so large that hundreds of anglers participated simultaneously, each being allotted a specific position on the riverbank. By the beginning of this century nearly every pub in northern England had its own angling club; in London there were over 600 pub-based clubs.

In 1869 the Angling Association was founded to safeguard coarse anglers' interests. In late Victorian times they successfully urged their Members of Parliament to lobby for a close season, from the middle of March to the middle of June, when fish might spawn in peace. Competitions became so popular that the National Federation of Anglers (NFA), formed in 1903 to protect the sport, took over the management and co-ordination of all annual national and divisional championships. These came to be sponsored by industrial (and, later, fishing-tackle) companies, which offered substantial prize money. Competitions declined during the First World War as did pub-based clubs, which were afterwards replaced by company angling clubs.

Since the Second World War most company-based clubs have been superseded by local clubs who own or lease the rights to fish a particular stretch of water. Competitions have regained popularity. However, since the late 1960s, anglers no longer compete to catch the largest individual fish but the greatest combined weight of fish. At the same time, some anglers have developed an alternative form of competitive fishing: specimen hunting. Their aim is to catch the largest examples of particular species, especially carp, pike, and tench. In recent decades the commercial development of angling has been further stimulated by the stocking of flooded gravel pits and reservoirs. In 1994 the government bowed to pressure from entrepreneurs who wished to exploit their resources throughout the year by abolishing the close season for fishing in still waters. There are at present attempts to abolish the close season for fishing in streams and rivers as well. The majority of members of the National Federation of Anglers are opposed to this attempt.[1]

While there is a long tradition of opposition to the hunting of animals because of the pain suffered by the prey (Spencer 1993), the history of anti-angling is much more patchy, mainly because many people are unsure whether fish have sensation. During the eighteenth century many protested against the crimping of fish, i.e. cutting their live flesh to make it firmer. In 1799 Charles Lamb branded anglers 'patient tyrants, meek inflictors, of pangs intolerable, cool devils' (quoted in Thomas 1983: 177). Benjamin Franklin (1964: 87) considered fishing 'unprovoked murder'. Byron, in a notorious passage, called angling 'that solitary vice', 'the cruelest, the coldest, and the stupidest of pretended sports':

Whatever Izaak Walton sings or says;
The quaint, old, cruel, coxcomb, in his gullet
Should have a hook, and a small trout to pull it.

Don Juan, Canto xiii

But those who specifically spoke out against the practice were relatively very few. For instance, Henry Salt, a turn-of-the-century campaigner for animal rights, only devoted *one phrase* of his book on the topic to fishing (Salt 1892: 77).

The emergence in recent decades of organized anti-angling is a direct by-product of the modern animal rights movement. The initial stimulus was a letter of protest against angling by Bill Maxwell Brody to *The Times* in March 1981, which led to a gathering at the Friends' Meeting House, Euston, London. Ronnie Lee, a co-founder in 1976 of the Animal Liberation Front (ALF), was among the participants. At the meeting it was agreed to establish the Council for the Prevention of Cruelty by Angling (CPCA), to be headed by Maxwell Brody. Repeated bouts of ill-health, however, forced him to resign in mid-1983. His successor, Richard Farhall, directed the organization until 1989 when he became General Secretary of the Vegan Society and editor of *The Vegan*. With his departure the organization almost folded, for lack of actively involved people to run it. However in 1991 it was effectively relaunched when a new group of anti-anglers assumed its leadership.

A major, initial problem for the Council was that of being taken seriously. Many organizations concerned with animal rights would not associate themselves with it in any way because they were scared of looking ridiculous, and they refused to help disseminate its leaflets. In order to overcome this problem, the Council produced a newsletter, *Hookup*, which provided detailed arguments against angling as a cruel practice. To demonstrate the seriousness of its endeavour, it also campaigned against the use of leadshot, livebait and keepnets, and protested about the amount of tackle litter left by anglers. Each edition of *Hookup* included a policy statement that the CPCA did not condone 'non-violent, illegal, direct action in pursuit of animal rights' while also carrying a series of reports about 'direct action': for example, the use of paint-stripper on a fishmonger's van; the release of trout from fish farms; the disturbing of fishing competitions; the painting of anti-angling slogans; the gluing of locks to fishing tackle shops.

In mid-1985 members, considering that the full name of the Council was too clumsy and unspecific, changed it to the Campaign for the Abolition of Angling (CAA). Shortly afterwards, they renamed the newsletter *Pisces*. These changes heralded the initiation of new campaigns. *Pisces* started to carry critical articles on organizations which were believed to be supporting anglers or, at least, not strongly condemning them: for example, Friends of the Earth, the Royal Society for the Protection of Birds, the Royal Society for the Prevention of Cruelty to Animals, the Green Party, the Council for the Protection of Rural England. After criticizing the League against Cruel Sports (the largest animal rights organization in the country), Richard Farhall agreed to meet with a League representative. Given that their ulitmate aims were similar, they resolved that each organization would stop criticizing the other. In the summer of that year the CAA launched its first annual 'letters campaign', in which at the summer opening of the coarse fishing season hundreds of local newspapers were sent letters of protest against angling. The CAA also started to produce a series of information leaflets for its members to distribute. Topics included: basic information on angling; how to persuade councils to restrict angling; a list of trout farms in operation.

The changes in the name of the organization and its newsletter also heralded a hardening of attitudes, as evidenced by its new policy statement, included at the beginning of each issue: 'The CAA neither condones nor condemns the use of illegal action in pursuit of animal rights, but sympathises with the sense of frustration behind such activities.' In 1987, following a proposal by Ronnie Lee, the statement was changed to 'The CAA does not take part in illegal activities but appreciates the effectiveness of direct action and sympathises with those who carry it out.' *Pisces* continued to run reports on ALF activities against angling interests. The issue for January 1986 included an article entitled 'It's More Fun by Post' which pointed out that nuisance could be caused by having junk mail directed to 'anyone you love to hate'. In the issue for October 1988, an ALF activist was quoted as telling the CAA office, catapults 'are really nifty for breaking tackle shop windows'. Menacing calls were made, in the name of the Campaign, to the president of the NFA. At much the same time, the leadership of the CAA began to receive death threats.

Not all of the CAA membership were happy with the hardening of approach. In 1988 *Pisces* started to publish letters opposing violence and 'direct action'. In the issue for April 1988 Ronnie Lee responded to these critics. He argued that since the majority of the British public did not appear to be opposed to angling,

It is difficult to see how angling can be ended, or even very significantly reduced, without the use of direct action. . . A very large amount of damage can be caused in quite a short time by only a fairly small number of people. Those who make or sell equipment for angling are not going to continue to do so if their profits are destroyed by property damage and those who take part in the so-called sport will be discouraged from doing so if they know there is a good chance of their continued participation leading to personal economic loss (quoted in Barker n.d.: 3).

Since the relaunch in 1991 of the CAA, no further letters of protest by members about direct action have been published.

The new leadership of the CAA, which was responsible for its relaunch, is much more organized and effective than that of its predecessors. The original 'letters campaign' at the opening of the fishing season has now been expanded into a National Anti-Angling Week, during which CAA representatives give over fifty interviews to journalists while groups in different parts of the country set up street information stalls, picket tackle shops, and go 'sabbing' (carrying out acts of anti-angling sabotage). Styles of sabotage vary according to circumstance. As one exponent told a journalist:

If we've got a large number, like thirty or forty, then we'll do fishing tournaments, but if there's only a few of us then we'll do individual pleasure anglers.

. . . These blood junkies see us coming along and they can't believe it and their first reaction is just to turn to violence ('Anglers avoid campaigners' net', *The Guardian*, 19 June 1995, p. 6).

In 1992 the CAA commissioned the professional production of a video, *Angling. The Neglected Bloodsport*. Its distribution has boosted enormously the attention the organization has received from newspapers and television companies. Representatives of the CAA travel the country giving talks and their recently produced fact and project sheets for primary and secondary schools are much solicited by pupils and teachers. The CAA value these presentations to schoolchildren highly:

The response from this group is very positive, with many young people choosing to do projects and essays on animal abuse. They seem to be much more aware of all issues of human, animal and environmental abuse than past generations and do not immediately make artifical distinctions between those animals it is acceptable to eat/abuse and those that are favoured species such as pets (Macdonald 1993: 15).[2]

In 1994 the Campaign's newly formed Youth Group began to produce its own magazine. *Pisces* appears more regularly and in a more professional format. It continues to provide reports of 'sabbing activities' as well as news of angling malpractice, and of keepnet and angling bans by local councils. It also supplies the names and the addresses of companies which, the Campaign believes, ought to be boycotted because they sponsor angling matches.

Though the management of the organization and its activities has become much more competent and its aims are taken seriously by a wider section of the population, the CAA remains a small group. In 1986 it had 157 members; nine years later it had 350.[3] Many are strict vegans, avoiding all animal products in their diet, clothing and toiletries. As far as the Campaign's leadership is able to judge many of its members are not on the dole but gainfully employed, and believe in animal welfare rather than animal rights, i.e. they believe in reducing animal suffering rather than allowing all animals to live a natural existence, free from human interference.

The present challenge facing its leadership is how best to expand. One problem is that fish are not as photogenic as mammals. Watching a programme on the catching of roach does not stir the emotions as much as one on the clubbing to death of doe-eyed baby white fur seals. Sabbing may gain the organization attention (especially when a wet-suited anti-angler disturbs a fishing competition at a position on the riverbank where a television camera team has been told to station itself) but that kind of publicity may put off more potential recruits than it might attract.[4] In 1995 in order to broaden its membership the CAA changed its name to Pisces.[5] The leadership decided to make this change because they felt the inclusion of the ultimate aim of the organization – the abolition of angling – in its title sounded too extreme and edged on the cranky. 'Pisces', they thought, would be more acceptable to the general public. The editor of the newsletter itself has decided to concentrate its content on anti-angling in particular rather than animal rights in general. It is hoped this softening of its image without dilution of its message will increase their chances of success.

The original idea of the Council was to work closely with angling groups. Through education, it would stimulate change in the cruellest of angling practices. These early attempts at dialogue did not meet with any degree of success and the Council soon redirected its efforts from reforming anglers to informing the general public. The absence of productive dialogue between the two groups has led to them stereotyping one another in public. In *Pisces* anglers are presented uniformly as uncaring sadists obsessively concerned with satisfying their predatory desires. The only exceptions admitted are disgusted fishermen who provide useful quotes about the barbaric practices of some of the more singleminded anglers. Committed opponents of the anti-anglers publicly typecast their adversaries in a similarly oversimplifying manner, branding them as extremists with terrorist tendencies.

Members of the CAA, however, are prepared to admit that not all anglers are of the same kind. As far as they can ascertain, the majority of participants would classify themselves as pleasure anglers, who get as much enjoyment from 'getting away from it all' and savouring the peace of the countryside, as from the actual process of outwitting and catching a fish. This group ranges from the family party who fish on holiday to the more regular weekend participant. 'From the CAA's experience, they are the people who are most open to compassionate arguments, if they can be convinced that the suffering to fish outweighs the pleasure they get personally' (Macdonald 1993: 8). *Pisces* usually makes no comment about flyfishing because it is thought game-anglers generally treat their prey with more compassion and more skill. Unlike some of their coarse-fishing brethren, they do not try to catch and recatch the same fish purely for the sake of their own pleasure but cast their flies for prey they will dispatch and eat quickly once landed. *Pisces* does criticize sea-angling because it 'seems to attract people with a particularly callous attitude. . .Big game and in particular shark fishing seems to appeal to the very worst "macho" attitudes of proving yourself by catching and killing a large predatory animal in an extremely brutal way' (Macdonald 1993: 9).

Angling representatives dispute some of these statements. They point out that shark-fishermen are increasingly turning to 'catch and release'; the survival rate of returned sharks is said to be 'good'. But as Des Taylor, a columnist for the *Angling Times*, lamented:

Sea-fishing has been abused in this country, and I have witnessed many occasions in the past when hundreds of pounds of dead fish have lain in the bottom of the boat, most ending up in the dustbin.

Some charter-shippers and anglers are pioneering new thoughts on conservation in sea-fishing. . .pity they could not have seen the light twenty years ago! (Taylor 1994a)

The CAA is particularly opposed to match fishing because it attracts anglers who are highly competitive while 'the incentive of cash prizes means that the fish caught are treated with even less consideration than normal. . .These incentives mean that few are open-minded enough to listen to any arguments against their chosen pastime. Greed is a very compelling motive to continue!' (Macdonald 1993: 9). Angling spokesmen contest these comments, and claim that match fishing is good for angling in general: just as motor sports stimulate technical improvements in cars, so matches promote good angling techniques. For instance, the move from barbed to barbless or semi-barbed hooks was spurred by the practice of match-anglers. These spokesmen for the sport also argue that match-fishers, far from treating fish with less consideration than normal, treat them with much more than normal. They have, after all, to keep their prey alive for them to be counted in their catch.

The Campaign is against specimen hunting for similar reasons: the use of fish as pawns by competitive humans attempting to gain fame as record-breakers. A reporter for *The Guardian* neatly illustrated the attitude of one of these 'suburban Hemingways, the domestic equivalent of big-game hunters':

For some, Monday was the culmination of several weeks of planning. Rob, a professional angler and editor of Big Carp magazine, has been coming for six weeks, throwing bait out to the same spot every day, hoping to lull the carp into a false sense of security. 'They love it. It's like someone was leaving Big Macs around for us. You eat them all, every day, and then suddenly one burger hooks you in the gob and jerks you through the ceiling. Brilliant' (Leedham 1992).

***

Anti-anglers argue that their opponents are unfeeling killers of sentient beings whose desire to practise their pastime overrides any avowed concern for the environment. Anglers counter-argue that their sport is a traditionally established practice of benefit to society, the British economy and nature. As far as they are concerned, angling should not be threatened with prohibition but actively promoted by the government and sponsored by British businesses.

The first campaign mounted by the CPCA was against livebaiting, because it was one of the most visually abhorrent of anglers' practices. Livebaiting is the use of living fish as bait to catch predators such as pike or perch. The living fish is impaled on a treble hook and then cast into the water. Once in the water, the hooked livebait remains there until it is eaten by a predator or 'succumbs to the injuries inflicted on it in the course of attachment. It is not unusual during casting for a live bait fish to tear free from the tackle, inevitably increasing the severity of its impalement injuries' (Medway 1980: 31). A live bait fish may also succumb to stress because of the extended prolongation of its natural flee response (Verheijen and Buwalda 1988: 37).

Many anglers are well aware of the very questionable nature of livebaiting and the ethics of the practice has long been the subject of dispute amongst them. *Pisces* frequently quotes the negative comments of anglers on the practice: 'The plain fact of the matter is that livebaiting is cruel and don't let anyone tell you otherwise' (Watson 1990); 'I livebait and I bet you do too. It's barbaric and we shouldn't but we are there to catch pike' (Bailey 1991); 'Livebaiting is a sensitive subject, with the likes of ALF types about – if needed they should be used with discretion' (Anon 1991). The Medway report, which stated that the practice was not essential for the capture of predatory fish since other efficient methods were available, recommended that it be banned (Medway 1980: 31).

Further reasons for the abolition of the use of livebait are worries about the possible risk of spreading disease since the livebait may come from waters other than those in which the anglers fish for pike, and about the introduction of alien coarse fish, such as spore-eating ruffe and poke, to certain local waters, where they endanger rare species, such as the powan in Loch Lomond and the charr and the vendace in Furness and South Cumbria. It seems that popular repugnance of the practice, anti-anglers' campaigns against it, and fears about the transmission of disease and upsetting of the piscatory balance are having an effect. In the last five years an increasing number of local authorities and angling clubs have introduced their own bans on the use of livebait, despite protests by the Pike Anglers Club. Several rivers authorities are at present considering whether to impose bans. Also, an increasing number of anglers now use single, instead of treble, hooks when fishing with livebait.

The CAA has also continued to campaign against the use of keepnets: long mesh nets staked out underwater, used above all by match anglers to keep any fish caught until the weigh-in at the end of the competition. It claims that these nets often cause distress and even death through overcrowding, a build-up of waste products and de-oxygenation of the water; that the outer mucus layer on the surface of fish and even their scales are sometimes damaged; that disease can be transferred from fish to fish. In 1991 the NFA, aware of the ambivalence of many of its members towards the practice and wishing to fend off any criticism by its opponents, commissioned the Institute of Freshwater Ecology to investigate scientifically any changes in the quality of water in keepnets during the confinement of fish. The Institute, whose report was endorsed by the National Rivers Authority, found that the changes in the chemical quality in the water within the keepnets used in their experiments were not at a level which posed any ill threats to the confined fish (NFA 1991). The only consequent recommendations made by the Federation were that nets should be cleaned after each use and that where high catches were expected, for example during matches, it was advisable for anglers to use more than one keepnet.

The CAA questioned the Institute's report on the grounds that it had not been independently commissioned. The Campaign also stated that its findings were counter to the numerous reports it received about anglers' abuse of fish in keepnets. If these reports were unfounded, it argued, why had Germany and several British local authorities banned the use of keepnets? The NFA has since introduced a 'Keepnet Code', a copy of which is now included in every keepnet sold in the country, advising anglers on the best way to stake out their nets, place fish in them and return them to the water. The problem for the Federation here appears to be that while the proper deployment of keepnets has yet to be shown conclusively to be damaging to confined fish, inconsiderate anglers may still use this potentially damaging piece of equipment – if poorly laid out, overfilled, wrongly emptied or inadequately cleaned after each use – without sufficient care for the animals they confine within them. It may also be very difficult for anglers to meet the requirements of the Code in certain settings, for example where the water flows very slowly or where it may be very difficult to stake out the net, such as watersides with particularly steep banks.

The most successful of the anti-anglers' campaigns has been that against the use of leadshot as weights. The CAA, together with other groups concerned about animal welfare, argued that the British swan population was declining, especially in central and southern England, because the birds were poisoning themselves by ingesting leadweights left by anglers. In 1986 in reaction to this sustained campaign the Government's environmental watch-dog, the Nature Conservancy Council, warned anglers that unless they adopted lead substitutes voluntarily, it would have no option but to recommend statutory intervention. The NFA had resisted any form of ban until a substitute as dense and malleable as lead had been found. But on receiving the government warning, the NFA rapidly agreed to ban the use by its members of leadweights between 0·06 and 28·35 grams. But since not all anglers are members of the NFA and since the complaints persisted, the following year the Government introduced legislation – the Control of Pollution (Anglers' Lead Weights) Regulations, which prohibits the supply and import of leadweights between the afore-mentioned parameters. In the subsequent nine years the swan population of Britain has increased dramatically. Some anglers have started to complain that there are now so many in certain favoured habitats, such as stretches of the Avon, that they are stripping the waters of reeds essential for the survival of the fish (*The Times*, 22 April 1995: 5).

Anti-anglers might take a certain degree of pride for their contribution to the successful outcome of this campaign, but to them leadweights are only a specific instance of a more general problem: tackle victims. The CAA has long complained that nylon line is often discarded when it becomes tangled during casting, and that it frequently breaks when hooks became snagged on underwater obstructions or bankside vegetation. Even the most careful, skilful angler cannot avoid some loss of line. Since it is only very slowly biodegradable, the Campaign argues that it is the:

cause of death and injury to millions of animals. Waterfowl are especially vulnerable. They pick up hooks, line and weights while feeding and slowly starve to death. Entanglement in line can sever wings and limbs. Pets and livestock are also frequently affected. It is left to animal organisations to pay for the rescue and rehabilitation of the lucky minority of tackle victims that are found (CAA 1993: 4–5).

There are no overall figures for the number of animals injured by tackle annually. Two examples may give an idea of the scale of the problem: in its 1992 report the Westmorland branch of the RSPCA stated that its inspectors regularly had to attend to swans tangled in fishing line or which had swallowed hooks or other tackle – in Cumbria alone 92 swans had to be rescued, 18 of which had to be put down; during the 1991–92 fishing season the National Animal Rescue Association had to treat 670 waterfowl and other birds, over three-quarters of them maimed by tackle (the number of those found dead on site was not recorded) (*Pisces* January 1993: 5–6, October 1993: 3).

The CAA argues that fishing tackle is only one form of the litter that is left by anglers, all of which endangers wildlife and children, and detracts from the beauty of the countryside. While each issue of *Pisces* usually contains a long series of reports of the latest examples of tackle victims, there has been only one quantitative study of this problem to date. At a lake in Llandrindod Wells, Wales, it was found that although the site was used by visitors other than anglers, 64 percent of the number of litter items (93 percent of the total surface area of litter) were recorded in those parts of the shoreline (18 percent) predominantly used by anglers. An island in the lake, used exclusively by anglers, was particularly affected by litter (Forbes 1986).

Anglers counter-argue that they have learnt to be more tidy. In the early 1990s the NFA introduced a 'Nylon Line and Litter Code' for its members, which angling clubs have tried to enforce strictly. The Federation likes to quote the longitudinal results of the tackle-clearing projects run in 1978, 1982, 1989 and 1994 by the Young Ornithologists' Club, the youth section of the Royal Society for the Protection of Birds. Comparing results over the 17 year period it appears the amount of line left by anglers has declined by 95 percent, the amount of weights by 90 percent, the number of hooks by 76 percent (RSPB 1994). While anti-anglers acknowledge that their opponents might have become somewhat neater in their habits, they dispute the comparative conclusions of the RSPB project, for neither the areas covered nor the methods used for removal of litter were exactly the same each time the survey was carried out. (Angling representatives reply that if the same area was covered each time the amount of litter removed on each occasion would be even less.) Anti-anglers also argue that even if the results of the project could be accepted uncritically, the number of anglers taking their litter home is still woefully insufficient, as the continuing work done by animal welfare organizations tragically demonstrates.

Anglers often claim they are conservationists, deeply concerned about the state of waterway environments, and that without them there would be few fish today in British rivers.[6] The CAA admits that some anglers do good work monitoring waterways, pressing fisheries to clean up and taking polluters to court. But it argues that, on closer examination, anglers' claims to be committed aquatic environmentalists ring very hollow. Besides the tackle they discard and the litter they leave, anglers, by their very presence, threaten the habitats of otters.[7] (Anglers counter that they tend to keep away from these areas, because they know they will have fewer fish.) Fish-eating birds are at even greater risk: since 1993 the Government, under pressure from angling bodies, has granted licences for the shooting of cormorants, a previously protected marine species driven inland by commercial overfishing of the North Sea; Tweed fishermen recently campaigned successfully for licences to shoot goosander, another previously protected species, because it was thought they harm salmon stocks.

The CAA also protests against the damaging consequences of specimen hunting.[8] These anglers' desire to catch exceptionally large fish has led commercial fisheries to import carp though health checks are, as anglers admit, inadequate (Green 1994). At the same time it seems many carp are being brought into this country illegally. The result of all these imports is that a killer carp disease, Spring Vireamia, is now spreading through British waters. Fisheries are also importing other kinds of huge fish, including alien species, which may upset the delicate balance in a fishery. For instance, channel catfish, a recent import, grow remarkably quickly and are notorious for the voracity of their appetite. As Des Taylor (1994a) complained, 'Some fishery owners are so greedy, they have risked all by bringing in foreign fish, which could lead to the greatest ever disaster in angling history.'

Angling bodies might try to defend their sport by saying that they issue detailed codes of practice which they do their best to enforce. At the same time, they would admit that they are unable to police all anglers all the time because it remains an essentially solitary sport and because many anglers are not members of any association, nor even pay the government's annual rod licence. However some anglers contend that the ethos of the sport is changing fundamentally and that codes of practice have only been instituted in an attempt to halt a decline in standards:

Rule and law breaking are prevalent in angling. It is openly boasted about, even published on occasions. It seems to be okay if you can get away with it.

Tackle stealing and the illegal removal of fish seems to be on the increase, as are selfish and antisocial attitudes commonly found by river and lake, much of which stems from that fish-at-any-cost way of life so many anglers now possess (Pocklington 1993: 12).

As far as the CAA is concerned, all this evidence demonstrates that anglers are only concerned with conservation to the extent that it serves their own interests, and in order to be able to catch the fish they want when they want how they want, they are prepared to change and even damage the environment and do their fellows down in the process.

***

Even if every single angler in Britain stopped using livebait, threw away their keepnets and lead weights, and always took home all their tackle and every scrap of litter, anti-anglers would still be deeply dissatisfied.

They might be pleased that anglers had learnt to give up some of their more unattractive habits, but they would continue to campaign strongly for the total abolition of angling. For they believe – and this is the crux of the matter – that fish are capable of experiencing pain and that in a society with any pretensions to civility people should not be allowed, for the sake of their own pleasure, to inflict pain habitually on other sentient beings. Committed supporters of angling as a pastime dispute strongly these claims about the supposed capacity of fish. Of course, the central problem in this acrimonious debate is how to ascertain definitely whether or not fish feel pain.

The first hurdle to overcome is that of anthropomorphism. All too often people readily project their emotions and intentions onto some animals, and just as readily refuse to project them onto others. But this uncritical projection of human feelings and experiences, or the witholding of such empathy, can lead easily to a misreading of an animal's suffering. The subjective experiences of an animal, if it has any, may be totally different from our own, reflecting the different way of life and the different ways in which its body works (Bateson 1992: 30). To many Britons, pets are to be loved and almost all mammals to be treated considerately. Fish they tend to regard as cold, slimy, voiceless inhabitants of an alien, unknowable environment, incapable of stimulating emotion in humans. Many people who eschew meat but eat fish still call themselves 'vegetarian'.

Anglers who do anthropomorphize fish usually do so in self-interested ways:

> I do not believe that salmon or any other fish feel very acutely, a reassuring theory for the tender-hearted fisherman. . .The desperate struggle of the fish confirms the same view. Not all the instinct of self-preservation would induce a man to put a strain of even a pound on a fishing-rod if the hook was attached to some tender part of his flesh (Gathorne-Hardy 1898: 22).

> Fish do not feel very much from the hook. . . There is no way that fish would leap about so energetically if it hurt (Milner 1993: 7).

> I will never be convinced that a fish feels pain from a hook in the lips. . .Fortunately for anglers, fish have small brains, little intellect and short memories (Pocklington 1993: 20).

In response to such comments, the CAA argues that 'fish fight vigorously when hooked because they are unable to make the connection between the hook and the angler. Frenzied struggle is the result of fear of the unknown (or for those who remember being caught, fear of being dragged out of the water) and their inherent will to survive' (CAA 1993: 3). Yet the Campaign does not provide any scientific evidence to back these almost equally anthropomorphizing claims. Spokesmen for angling bodies claim that hooked fish do not fight out of fear, but simply because they are restrained.

Some anglers argue that since it has been known for fish to be caught twice in the same day angling cannot be an unpleasant experience for the fish. The CAA counter-argues that:

anglers go to great lengths to disguise hooks with maggots, fake flies, etc. to trick the fish into *biting*. Many anglers will admit that it requires unusual skill to entice a fish which has been repeatedly caught to take a baited hook. Although the fish may become wary if the same type of bait is used, it does have to feed to survive (CAA 1993: 3).

Here, both anglers' argument and anti-anglers' counter-argument rely on angling lore, for there has been no scientific study made of the subsequent feeding behaviour of fish which have once been hooked and released.

An associated argument deployed by anglers is a quasi-biological one, based on the comparatively primitive position of fish in the vertebrate evolutionary scale, e.g. 'fishes are low in the order of living things so they do not feel fear and pain as higher creatures do' (Arnold 1969: 104). One commentator on human affairs, the distinguished newsjournalist (and avid angler) Jeremy Paxman, has stated that 'the fisherman's quarry is a stupid, cold-blooded creature, so far down the evolutionary scale that his pursuit seems an absurd waste of the talents of *homo sapiens*' (Paxman 1994: xii). Yet simply because fish occupy a relatively lowly rung among vertebrates on the evolutionary ladder does not necessarily imply that they do not experience pain in a manner analogous to that of humans. It is very revealing that though many anglers will deny that fish feel pain, many angling practices are intended to minimize any pain a caught fish might possibly suffer.[9]

In this context of badly-argued controversy between pitted opponents where anthropomorphism and a superficial neo-Darwinism are deployed as modes of debate, the most appropriate and least emotive approach is to review what scientists themselves consider relevant neural homologies and justifiable behavioural analogies.[10] The physiologist Patrick Bateson, Professor of Ethology at Cambridge and member of the Insitute of Medical Ethics working party on animal experiments, argues that no single criterion provides an all-or-none test for the existence of a subjective sense of pain. This means that in order to build up a useful picture of a particular animal's capabilites all the relevant evidence needs to be considered as a whole. For Bateson, the best that scientists can do is provide criteria that are based on measurements of an animal's behaviour and analyses of the way its nervous system works. His committee compiled a list of seven criteria, all of which are associated with the experience of pain in humans. It is then simply a question of passing down the evolutionary scale and noting how many criteria each type of animal fulfills. One immediate consequence of this use of multiple criteria is that the boundary between pain and its absence is not clear-cut but very fuzzy. As Bateson confesses, it is more or less arbitrary at which point on the scale we decide that animals are fulfilling insufficient criteria for us to be able to say that they are capable of experiencing pain (Bateson ibid.)

Fish are a particularly contentious case for they meet three of the criteria while it is still unproven whether they fulfil the remaining four. Firstly, fish have brain structures analagous to the human cerebral cortex; secondly, they associate neutral stimuli with noxious ones; and thirdly, they have opoid-type receptors. (Opoid substances are implicated in the control of pain.) It is unknown whether fish have noiceptive systems. (Noiceptors are the distinct neuronal receptors found in humans which are responsible for the perception of pain. As yet they are morphologically indistinguishable from other unspecialized thermo- or mechano-receptors.) Consequently it is unknown whether fish, like humans, have noiceptors connected to the higher brain structures. Also, it remains to be demonstrated conclusively whether the responses of fish are modified by analgesics, and whether their responses to noxious stimuli persist (ibid.)

***

Until further scientific work is done, we are unable to state conclusively whether fish do, or do not, feel pain. Anti-anglers may take the evidence so far available as sufficient for them to be able to argue that angling must be abolished, and the sooner the better. In turn their angling opponents may argue that the jury is still out, and that in Britain plantiffs are innocent until proven guilty. Given our present level of ignorance about what exactly fish experience, the only conclusion we may draw is that the question about angling will remain, for the time being, a primarily moral one: is it right to hook, play and keep fish in nets if we are unsure whether they suffer in the process?

Anti-anglers are getting their message across and are no longer universally trivialized as 'cranks'. As one fisherman recently lamented:

> Forget the tweedy wisdom of Mr Crabtree, casting for chub in cartoon idylls. Angling now demands an attitude . . .It is no longer politically correct to seek tranquility with rod and line. Fish have feelings and it would be as well to know – or, at least, to have an opinion – whether or not their cerebral cortex registers pain when the hook goes in (Oakes 1995).

But was angling ever so innocent? Izaak Walton intended his portrayal of fishing as a source of peace and promoter of simple virtue to be a personal protest at the depradations of the Civil War. The well-to-do and aspirants to that level used forms of fishing to reinforce class distinctions. Today, the sexism of much angling serves to underline outdated gender stereotypes while big-game fishing allows its practitioners to demonstrate their support for a strong-armed *machista* ideology. It could thus be argued that angling has never been an innocuous pastime rather, that has been part of its ideological representation. Anti-anglers threaten to undermine that ideology by exposing publicly the values which underpin it. No wonder that angling spokesmen contest their words and actions so much.

Notes

1. Much of this potted history relies on Billett 1994: 185-202
2. In reaction to this strategy of the anti-anglers, angling bodies have also started to take their message into schools. And they have a supporter in the Royal Family. Page Two of the 2 November issue of *Angling Times* was headlined: 'Charlie is our darling! Fight antis with education says Prince.'
3. Unlike most angling associations, whose female membership is about 10 percent, the membership of the CAA is divided almost equally between men and women.
   Angling in Britain is a very male-oriented sport, e.g. 'If you fancy

fishing in a country where it's pure "boy's own fun" then Sweden is the place for you!' (Taylor 1994b). It is often a sexist one as well (e.g., see Mills 1985: 75). In Paterson and Behan (1990) Peter Behan, a professor of pharmacology, argues that the only explanation for the otherwise 'extraordinary' fact that women hold most of the British salmon fishing records is the fishes' attraction to the pheromones produced by female anglers. During October and November 1994, *Angling Times*, one of the two bestselling angling papers in the country, ran a weekly bingo competition. All instalments of the contest included a photograph of a young blonde with banknotes stuffed between her body and her clothes. As the competition progressed she was portrayed wearing less and less. The back page of the 16 November issue was headlined, 'Next week. Bingo. Debbie reveals all – and YOU could be a winner.'

4. In February 1993 the angling press took pleasure in reporting that three of the CAA's 'National Officers' had been imprisoned on a charge of criminal damage to a meat-processing factory by fire. The charges were dropped several months later.

Most sabbing methods were legal until 1994 when the Criminal Justice Act came into force. The Act specifically outlaws the disruption of angling; it states that all waterways are private land and makes an offence of 'aggravated trespass'. Even before the introduction of the Act, arrests were often made for a variety of public order offences. According to the National Secretary of the Campaign,

'It seems likely that the popularity of angling in the police force was a strong motivator in the high humber of arrests that took place' (Macdonald 1993: 16).

5. In this article I usually refer to the CPCA/CAA/Pisces as the CAA because that is the name under which it has operated during most of the period I am discussing.

6. Some anglers have very particular interpretations of the 'nature' they claim to protect. As John Parkman, consultant to the British Field Sports Society, told a reporter, 'All this nonsense about lead in swans and tackle maiming birds and all that rubbish, of course it happens, but then in nature these things happen all the time' ('Anglers avoid campaigners' net', *The Guardian*, 19 June 1995, p. 6).

7 Izaak Walton's fisherman states, 'I am, Sir, a brother of the Angle, and therefore an enemy to the Otter: for you are to note, that we Anglers all love one another, and therefore do I hate the Otter both for my own and for their sakes who are of my brotherhood' (Walton 1971: 4).

8. The commercial interests involved in specimen hunting are now so great that rustling big fish has become a growth industry (Leedham 1992).
9. One lifelong fisherman told a reporter, 'I will say that when I've caught a salmon that's run all the way up the river and you've fought it for perhaps half an hour, there's always a moment of regret when you bang it on the head, but that's forgotten when you have a nice smoked salmon sandwich' ('Anglers avoid campaigners' net', *The Guardian*, 19 June 1995, p. 6).
10. It is revealing that copies of one of the rare experimentally based articles on the behaviour of fish when subjected to noxious stimuli (Verheijen and Buwalda 1988), whose interpretation relies heavily on the use by analogy of models of pain perception developed by researchers in human psychology, were given to me by *both* anti-anglers and their angling opponents. The 'conclusion' they reach is that hooked carp (the fish used in their experiments), when caught by skilled anglers who do not play the animal for an unduly prolonged period, experience 'mild to moderate discomfort'. To anti-anglers this level of pain is unacceptable; to their angling opponents it is both acceptable and a good example for their argument that all anglers should be properly trained.

Bibliography

Anon (1991), Letter, *Angling Times*. 11 December

Arnold, R. (1969), *The book of angling*. London: Arthur Baker

Bailey, John (1991), Letter, *Coarse Fisherman*. May

Barker, Keith (n.d.), *A Brief History of the Development of the Campaign for the Abolition of Angling*. Specialist Anglers Conservation Group. Cyclostyled pamphlet

Bateson, Patrick (1992), 'Do animals feel pain?', *New Scientist*, 25 April, pp. 30–33

Billett, Michael (1994), *A History of English Country Sports*. London: Robert Hale

Campaign for the Abolition of Angling (1993), *Angling – The Facts*. Cyclostyled pamphlet

Cholmondeley-Pennell, H. (1870), *The Modern Practical Angler. London: Routledge*

Cox, Nicholas (1674), *The Gentleman's Recreation*. London

Forbes, I. J. (1986), 'The quantity of lead shot, nylon fishing line and other litter discarded at a coarse fishing lake', *Biological Conservation*, vol. 38, pp. 21–34

Franklin, Benjamin (1964), *The Autobiography of Benjamin Franklin*. L. W. Labaree, R. L. Ketcham, H. Boatfield and H. Finneman (eds) New Haven: Yale University Press

Gathorne-Hardy, A. E. (1898), *The Salmon*. London: Longmans

Green, Kevin (1994), 'Beware dodgy imports', *Angling Times*, 23 November, p. 15

Leedham, Robert (1992), 'Hooked on a fishing line', *The Guardian*, Weekend Supplement, 20 June, p. 16

Macdonald, Marianne (1993), *Angling. An activist's view of this bloodsport*. Paper given at the Institute of Social Anthropology, Oxford University

Medway, Lord (ed.) (1980), *Report of the panel of enquiry into shooting and angling*. London: Royal Society for the Prevention of Cruelty to Animals

Mills, Derek (1985), *The Fishing here is great! A light-hearted discourse on the social history of angling as depicted on old postcards*. London: Wilson

Milner, Judith (1993), *The Woman's Guide to Angling*. Stoke Abbott: Harmonsworth

National Federation of Anglers (1991), *Changes in water quality within anglers' keepnets during the confinement of fish*. Cyclostyled pamphlet

Oakes, Philip (1995), 'Angling with attitude', *The Guardian*, Weekend Supplement, 5 August, p. 47

O'Gorman, James (1845), *The Practice of Angling, particularly as regards Ireland*. Dublin: William Curry Jnr.

Patterson, Wilma and Peter Behan (1990), *Salmon and Women: The Feminine Angle*. London: Witherby

Paxman, Jeremy (1994) *Fish, Fishing and the Meaning of Life*. London: Michael Joseph

Pocklington, Bruce (1993), *The Pleasures of Coarse Fishing. An Angler's Pitch*. Tunbridge Wells: Spellmount

Royal Society for the Protection of Birds (1994), *Tackle tackle: A young people's survey of discarded fishing tackle*. Cyclostyled pamphlet

Salt, Henry S. (1892), *Animals' Rights considered in relation to Social Progress*. London: Bell

Spencer, Colin (1993), *The Heretic's Feast. A History of Vegetarianism*. London: Fourth Estate

Taylor, Des (1994a), 'Angling, or a load of carp?', *Angling Times*, 16 November, p. 9

— (1994b), 'Trip to remember', *Angling Times*, 30 November, p. 11

Thomas, Keith (1983), *Man and the Natural World. Changing Attitudes in England 1500–1800*. London: Allen Lane

Verheijen, F. J. and R. J. A. Buwalda (1988), *Do pain and fear make a hooked carp in play suffer?* Utrecht University

Voss Bark, Conrad (1992), *A History of Flyfishing*. Ludlow: Merlin Unwin

Walton, Izaak (1971 (1653)), *The Compleat Angler. Being a Discourse of Rivers, Fish-ponds, Fish and Fishing*. London (Facsimile of the fifth ed., pub. 1676) London: Scolar Press

Watson, John (1990), Letter, *Coarse Fishing*. November

Acknowledgements

I am grateful to Keith Barker, David Bird, Richard Farhall and especially Marianne Macdonald for assistance.

7

The Venice Regatta:
From Ritual to Sport

Lidia D. Sciama

Introduction

Ritual and sport, generally associated with festive occasions, are both prominent features in Venetian regattas. Like the popular *festas* and rituals described in Boissevain (1992), regattas have recently enjoyed an active revival, itself largely due to a search for a local identity. In the Venetian context competitions between oarsmen from different localities, ranging from neighbourhoods and islands in the lagoon to a variety of different groupings, and often associated with important festivities, generally culminate in affirmations of a distinctive common identity in the main September regatta, which ideally involves the whole city and is considered the high point of a yearly cycle of races.

As my discussion will show, while a distinction between ritual and sport is posited for the purpose of analysis, I do not consider them as discrete and mutually exclusive categories, since they often overlap, and in some instances almost coincide. Thanks to their formalized and repetitive conventions, sports present sequences and structures which are in themselves closer to ritual than to practical actions. Especially in their most competitive manifestations, they mobilize local, regional and national loyalties and feelings of belonging, since individual sportsmen and teams are viewed as representatives of their communities. What is more, while successful sportsmen certainly win rewards that might suggest that their activities should be categorized as practical and economic, these aspects of sport are usually made out to be secondary, in the name of an ideology that places greater value on their nature as games: the aim is not only to win, but to play (Archetti 1994: 7–10).

In Venetian boat races, however, there is an inherent distinction in their traditional form, since they generally consist of two main parts, comparable to two acts in a drama: the first is a highly repetitive celebration of the city and of its past, the second a race between boats; ritual and sport are present in each part in different measures (Leach 1954: 10–14; Dei et al 1992: 9). What is more, historical analysis shows that with changes in the city's social and political structure either ritual or sport may gain greater prominence. Venetians themselves often make a distinction between the celebratory first part of the Regatta and its 'sportive' second part. However, my conclusion, based on analysis of the way boat races are conducted and of the discourses that constitute them, is that no clear-cut distinction can be made, since in the context of Venice's environmental problems not only regattas but boating in general has become a ritual statement about a collective identity defined in terms of a basic relation between people and territory.[1]

Environment, Sport and Identity

As my informants repeatedly tell me, 'Regattas express the very essence of "Venetianness" (*Venezianità*),' i.e. of a 'spirit' which, they explain, is a compound of qualities of character, moral attitudes, ambitions, skills and above all ways of adjusting to their given environment. Such assured and forceful statements and claims about a Venetian identity, however, are frequently contradicted by expressions of uncertainty and concern about the city's future. Indeed, Venetians have long been speaking and writing of a loss of confidence and a 'crisis of identity'. This paper is an attempt to locate that crisis, describe some of its features, and explore ways in which it has affected the organization, and become part of the discourses which constitute that most Venetian of sports, boat racing.[2]

Often when we speak of social identities, we speak either of minorities, or of different groups engaged in dialogical or oppositional relations. By contrast Venice, or more specifically its historic centre, is often described as an urban microcosm, but one that is unique among cities. Both its history and its unusual environment make it so different and individual among cities that uncertainties about identity may appear to be quite uncalled for. In particular insular Venice presents features of cohesion and intimacy, while physical separation from the mainland in some ways defines it as a world apart.

However, in addition to an insular city centre surrounded by numerous peripheral islands, the Venetian municipality comprises extensive inland areas on the internal coast at Mestre and Marghera, where residential settlements, related to the foundation of chemical industries, were first developed in the 1920s and '30s and greatly expanded since the 1950s. These are mainly populated by former inhabitants of insular Venice and, to a larger extent, by peasants who migrated from neighbouring rural areas to work in the factories. The haphazard and surprisingly large-scale expansion of Mestre and Marghera has been one of the factors that led inhabitants of insular Venice to become keenly aware of environmental problems and to reflect upon their collective identity.

Some people at present speak of 'two Venices' – a terrestial and a maritime one, sometimes mutually antagonistic and sometimes held together by their common history and economic interests. A city identity is then often contrasted and compared with a provincial or regional one, while a predominantly maritime and lagunar image of Venice is opposed to a more inclusive one in which inland, formerly agricultural now industrialized, areas are viewed as complementary to the coastal and eminently urban historic city. Over the last 40 years or so both Venice and Mestre have gone through separatist moves, because union of such disparate places actually makes administration difficult. But repeated referendums have shown that most people in the end prefer to keep Mestre and Venice together. Separation of insular Venice would, it is feared, turn it into an increasingly backward-looking museum city, while the very problems of Mestre and its industrial areas keep the historical centre in contact with the contemporary world.

Inhabitants of Mestre are themselves divided: some identify strongly with a maritime culture, while others say that they consider themselves *terrafermieri* creatures of the dry land. It is of interest that while some of the latter told me that they 'have got the lagoon out of their system,' and have abandoned boats in favour of cars, motor-sports and football, some of the former do take part in rowing competitions. In the drive to reconstitute a regional identity and reaffirm, or fashion, a common culture wider than a narrowly insular one, some inhabitants of the mainland too have sought to rediscover a 'maritime', or at least a 'riverain' and 'water-bound' past; they too have organized boating clubs and regattas in the gulf's internal waterways, where in late Roman and mediaeval times Venetians first developed their skills as boat-builders, navigators and merchants.[3]

A need on the part of the inhabitants of the historic centre and lagoon islands to re-define their identity is also related to their keen awareness of the city's social and environmental problems. A shortage of adequate housing, as well as a lack of primary productive activities, have led a considerable number of families, especially the young and the working class, to move to the hinterland, and have turned the city into one mainly of professionals, shopkeepers, waiters and street vendors. At the same time a frightening increase in the number of tourists, especially since the 1970s, makes circulation uncomfortable, increases human pollution, and aggravates the housing problem. Finally – and this is directly relevant to the present work – from the point of view of those working on boats and gondolas an increase in the number and speed of motor boats ruins their craft by creating strong waves, and thus makes their work difficult and even dangerous.

Here, then, we see that for inhabitants of insular Venice a sense of identity begins to emerge through a number of oppositions, or contrasts, such as those between: land/sea; past/present; modern/ancient; industrial/ preindustrial; productive activity/tourism as consumption and destruction of wealth rather than its transformation; and so on. I hesitate to call these oppositions, for fear of imposing too rigid a structural scheme, but in fact these terms are constantly opposed in everyday conversations and in political discourse.

All I have written so far, however, leaves out the most important element of the Venetian landscape, the great mediator between sea and land, the lagoon. Accounts of its natural rhythms, reconstructions of its history, and alarming reports on its present state may help explain some of the reasons why a renewed appreciation of boating and waterways is held up as the most significant expression of a Venetian identity. Indeed, over and above all Venice's problems are fears that the lagoon's waters may have been irremediably polluted, its soil damaged by inconsiderate extraction of water for industrial use, its channels dug too deep to resist violent flooding from the sea, and its function as an element of unity rather than separation between islands greatly diminished. The lagoon and its navigation thus provide the dominant themes and rich imagery in Venetians' conceptualizations of a sense of identity and in their frequent comparisons between past and present.[4] As is often pointed out, while in the past the lagoon was regarded as a kind of defensive wall and protective buffer for the city, its waters are now perceived as a hindrance to modern living, and are feared as a threat to its architectural fabric.

Such fears may best be explained if we consider that relations between land and water in the Venetian environment always were problematic, from the city's beginnings. As is probably well known, Venice's historical centre is entirely built on a system of islands on an old river delta. The original riverbeds are now covered with salt water, but they can sometimes be seen when the tide is very low, and their presence still determines the distribution of sandbanks and navigable channels, as well as the direction of the tides. Confronted with damage caused by industrial works at Marghera, and stimulated since the 1960s by a general rise in interest in environmental issues, experts now emphasize that the lagoon is by its own nature in a state of uncertain balance, and has very little protection against the opposed actions of the sea and the rivers. For, while on the one hand the rivers carry wastes that tend to cause silting and make the lagoon less navigable and sometimes swampy and malarial, on the other hand the sea tends to flood the city and raise the water above tolerable levels. To maintain the lagoon's equilibrium, therefore, both forces must be kept in check and neither allowed to become dominant (Bellavitis and Romanelli 1985:3).

Comparisons with the past are often invoked to give greater relief to negative judgments of the present. Thus writers often recall the long history of Venetian hydraulic engineering, and of different attempts to contain or redirect the courses of rivers in order to solve the intractable and contrary problems of flooding and silting. Indeed, as was learnt by experience, the construction of dams in the fifteenth century brought only negative consequences, since it caused severe inundations in the hinterland, which inevitably gave rise to strong enmities between the city and the mainland farmers and land-owners. A different policy, mainly developed since the sixteenth century, was to re-direct the courses of rivers away from St. Mark's basin. That too required that mainland cities, especially Padua and Treviso, be kept strictly under Venetian control since, predictably, such plans were opposed by landowners. Some of the conflicts that followed clearly foreshadow those which, under greatly changed conditions, are still present in what is today discussed as 'the problem of Venice', since the old antagonism between insular Venice and its nearby inland cities is echoed in the recurrent differences between the municipal and regional governments, and in the continual charges of Venetians against inland manufacturers and farmers, whom they hold responsible for the pollution of rivers that, issuing into the lagoon, cause it irreparable damage.

Before industrialization, as Venice's environmentalists point out, to prevent the lagunar environment from evolving towards permanent conditions of land or of sea, the contrasting pressures of sea and rivers were kept in a state of equilibrium; silting was largely overcome by the channelling of rivers away from Venice, while seawater was allowed to enter freely and cleanse the lagoon's basin. To avoid too impetuous an inrush of tides, the port openings were left rather shallow.

However, the complex hydraulics of the lagoon were not understood, or not adequately taken account of, by those who, viewing Venice as a backward city, aimed to modernize and industrialize it. Transformations carried out over the last two hundred years, first by the French, then by the Austrians, and finally by the Italian government after unification in 1866, are now viewed as extremely misguided.[5] Since their aim was to use the lagoon as a port which could receive ships with increasingly large draughts, they dredged down its main channels from a depth of four to ten metres. The Lido port was widened by joining together two of its three openings and its depth changed from one and a half to over ten metres. At the same time, a greed for land led to reclamations and so to a considerable reduction in the size of the lagoon's basin. As a result, tides were allowed to rush in violently, while a reduction in the total area of the lagoon did not leave sufficient room for the waters to spread out. The combination of these factors, then, inevitably led to a greater frequency of high tides than had occurred previously, and to slipping of materials, which in turn led to silting of canals and erosion of the soil of the lagoon.

Critics of industrialization point out how the partisans of development no longer regarded the lagoon as a protective container for the city, but as a marsh which it was necessary to reclaim. A point much emphasized by those who, idealizing the past, would like to see Venice regain its lost harmony is that throughout the Renaissance its magistrates and engineers conceptualized the lagoon as a living organism. The system of canals was likened to human circulation, and the ebb and flow of tides to breathing, while its marshes, crossed by a multitude of rivulets and meandering waterways, allowed the tidal waters to spread and seep into the open banks, unimpeded by quays and docks, just as liquid is absorbed into a sponge, or air enters our lungs. But the transformations made by developers gravely disturbed its harmonious functions.

Organic analogies, according to some of Venice's inhabitants, also apply to its past social and economic life. For example, when communication took place mainly by water, the city was at the centre of a star-like system radiating in different directions. But with the building of a modern causeway leading directly to the mainland, the traffic has been channelled on a straight southeast/northwest axis, excluding areas on the south and the north of the lagoon. Internal communication and exchanges have decreased, and the outlying islands, in particular Pellestrina and Burano, have remained almost entirely cut off. While such images of lost harmony may be more imaginary than real, there certainly is a widespread feeling that the lagoon is no longer treated as a unifying element and that Venetians have become alienated from their natural environment.

The Regatta's Historical Background

In their attempts to bring some light upon the earliest origins of Venetian regattas, historians and folklorists often offer functional explanations side by side with narratives of mythical events. One common hypothesis is that the first competitions may have taken place in conjunction with military exercises, or may have occurred spontaneously among the estuary's market gardeners and fishermen, eager to bring their products to the Rialto market in the early morning. It is often argued that, due to a 'natural instinct' in those who row side by side to overtake one another, the origin of regattas may go back to the earliest invention of boats. Eventually, as historians suggest, competitive rowing, an exercise 'dear to the people', would have been put to good use in the training of soldiers and sailors, as large boats specially appointed to take men to the Lido for archery practice would have spontaneously competed to get there first, and subsequently would have been encouraged by the institution of government prizes (Michiel 1829: xix). The original aim of boat racing, then, would have been essentially a practical one.

As well as offering such simple functional explanations, however, historians generally associate Venice's early regattas with an ancient feast, the *Festa dei Matrimoni*, or *Festa delle Marie*, instituted to celebrate an important victory in 948. According to a legend, often retold by later writers, every year, on the anniversary of the translation of St Mark's body from Alexandria to Venice on 31 January 827 (a day that may also coincide with that of some ancient *Ludi Mariani*) Venetians used to celebrate collectively numerous marriages in the Bishopric of San Pietro di Castello.[6] According to Michiel, one of the *festa's* most nostalgic nineteenth-century historians, Venice's legislators saw that the government should be a party to all rituals, so that also those of a personal and family nature were richly celebrated, since devotion and pomp always went together (ibid.: xv). In particular, marriage, as the best means to bring about amity and peace among people and to constitute 'the great social family', was always celebrated in public with great solemnity and was almost a national festival (ibid.: 91).

Twelve young women of great beauty and good character would every year be granted a dowry by the state and taken to the altar by the Doge himself. According to the legend, in 948, on the evening before the ceremony, while the brides, dressed in their most precious clothes and each carrying her dowry box, gathered on the consecrated ground before the Church to wait for their bridegrooms, Slav pirates, taking the congregation by surprise, kidnapped the brides, and took them and their boxes to a secure spot, in the vicinity of Caorle, north-east of Venice.[7] There they were rapidly overtaken by the Doge near a river port (now named the Port of the Damsels) and both the brides and their boxes were quickly recovered.

The legend was reported in detail in the Guild Statute of the Makers of Wedding Boxes, where it also was claimed that the craftsmen had played a large part in the victorious battle against the pirates. It was then decreed that to commemorate the recovery of the brides, a procession on water, followed by a regatta, should be held every year. Four boats, each carrying three girls would start from the Church of San Pietro di Castello and enter the Grand Canal accompanied by singing and dancing on barges and in the streets. Clearly the main themes of the legend are the Venetians' pride in their superiority over the sailors from the Istrian and Dalmatian coasts, as well as confidence that they had at last established their control over the gulf and ensured the safety of its navigation. As with most Venetian celebrations, the *Festa delle Marie* brings together religious and secular elements, but their fusion is particularly striking in this instance, thanks to its eminently popular character.

By the end of the thirteenth century the Feast had become increasingly sumptuous, since the girls were dressed and endowed by their parishes, in mutual competition. The government ordered that they should be substituted with wooden statues, but the change was not at all welcome to the people, who pelted the boats with turnips.[8] Eventually, since even the wooden Maries continued to be very expensively dressed and adorned, the Feast was abolished altogether in 1379, after the War of Chioggia.

After the suppression of the 'Marie', the main city ritual came to be the *Festa della Sensa*, celebrated in early May on Ascension day. That festival also essentially affirmed the dominion of Venice over the Dalmatian coasts and the Adriatic gulf. Its origin was related to the legendary departure of Doge Orseolo II in 999, to help some of the coastal cities of Dalmatia against Croatian pirates who, sailing down the river Narenta from the east, were a constant threat to their security and peace. As in the *Festa delle Marie* and especially in its later elaboration, the symbolic core of the *Sensa* was that of marriage.[9] In a ritual which some historians derive from an ancient cult of Poseidon, the Doge would ride out to the port in his sumptuous state barge, followed by a grand

'The Wedding of the Doge to the sea after mass at San Nicolo, Gabriele Bella, eighteenth century (Fundazione Querini Stampalia)'

procession of gaily decorated boats. When he reached the liminal area where the sea meets the lagoon, first the Patriarch would lower a bucket full of holy water into the sea with a blessing, then the Doge would throw a gold ring into the waves, pronouncing the formula *'Desponsamus te, mare, in signum veri perpetuique dominii.'* After this 'wedding' the Doge would attend mass at the church of San Niccoló, patron saint of sailors.

The *festa* derived its political significance partly from the fact that, according to legend, the first ring for the wedding had been given to Doge Ziani by Pope Alexander III. Like a sacred investiture, therefore, that marriage granted Venice a legitimate claim over the gulf, a claim it felt entitled to defend against possible rivals, for example Ancona (Lane 1973: 57, 73–5). The main feature of the Ascension feast was a grand display of power and wealth in the lengthy procession of state barges and ordinary peoples' boats that followed the ducal barge, *Bucintoro*. Thus, although some regattas would also take place, these were by no means as prominent as those in the *Festa delle Marie*. The *Sensa*, however, gradually became the foremost politico-religious festival, and in the fifteenth and sixteenth centuries the legend of the Papal grant was given increasing prominence and construed as historical truth by the Republic's official historians.

A comparison between the two feasts leads one to conclude that a reason for the suppression of the *Festa delle Marie* may have been the fact that, encouraging fierce competition between different quarters of the city, it kept internal rivalries and divisions alive in a boisterous and potentially turbulent population.[10] On the other hand the *Sensa*, glorifying the godliness and magnificence of the city, emphasized unity because it was inspired by universalistic themes overriding merely sectional partisan loyalties, and indeed it continued to be celebrated until the very end of the Republic (Muir 1981: 149; Bloch 989: 13–18). Regattas too, although no longer related to the *Festa delle Marie* but variously rearranged throughout the city's yearly festive cycle, continued without interruption. They always included ceremonial barges as well as the light boats especially crafted for racing, and they reflected the political realities and the fashions and styles of different periods.

Although, as we have seen, in its early days competitive rowing may have been associated with the world of work and military service, in the late fifteenth and sixteenth centuries its organization was left to companies of noblemen, who sometimes introduced eccentricities, like a race between heavy work boats made even heavier by a ballast of water and one, in 1502, in which the rowers were totally naked. In the seventeenth-century regattas were again staged by the state, and magistrates would put patrician families or craftsmen's guilds in charge of their design and organization. The decoration of boats and the dress of rowers in the historical procession always followed the art styles of the period and reflected interesting cultural facts. For example, a taste for exotic costume led to 'Chinese', 'African' or 'New World' boats.

Throughout the eighteenth century numerous races were organized to welcome foreign ambassadors or visitors to the state. Even Napoleon, whose conquest had put an end to Venetian independence, was welcomed to the city with a spectacular regatta, which started from under a specially-built triumphal arch. Hopes that he might bring about social reforms were soon dashed and, when the French gave Venice over to Austrian rule, the arrival of the Emperor Ferdinand I, in 1838, was similarly greeted with a grand cortege and run of boats. But although the Austrians had at first been welcomed as liberators delivering Venice from the French, their presence also soon became oppressive (Urban 1992: 130).

Local historians maintain that during the Austrian occupation and the Italian wars of independence (1815–1866) the city's gondoliers were among the first to develop a strong sense of collective identity. Like the boat builders in the Arsenal (Venice's state shipyard), they declared their commitment to insurgence against Austria and their support of Italian unity. In the same period the most politically conscious and articulate among the gondoliers began to see themselves as representatives of a social category, and one called upon to defend its interests as a prominent section of the city's working population. After the unification of Venice with Italy in 1866, the gondoliers wrote a long memorandum to the new government asking the municipality to return to the 'old rules', i.e. those of pre-revolutionary Venice, and to allow their own leaders to select their champions, choose their boat-builders, and generally organize the competitions, for only then would they be able to regain their honour and dignity after years of foreign oppression (Crovato and Crovato 1982: 31–3).

During the years of Austrian occupation both official races and ceremonial displays had dwindled. But in 1899 the Regatta was again revived, in the grand manner, to coincide with the opening of the International Exhibition of Modern Art, which, as its organizers intended, was to bring new life to the city's culture and to accentuate its cosmopolitanism. And it is since that time that the Regatta has been designated as *La Storica*.

Regattas Today

The recent active revival of boat-racing, and of rowing as exercise and entertainment, is partly due to Venetians' experience of a collective identity crisis. The revival began because of a protest about industrial pollution and urban decay. In 1975, following the example of peace marchers, a group of citizens, mainly members of the Green party, invited all those who owned or had access to a boat to join a long, non-competitive procession on the lagoon to be called the *Vogalonga*. This was quite a spectacular event; it has taken place every year since, and although it may have lost some of its initial support – and is not formally considered as one of the 'canonical' regattas sponsored by the commune – it certainly contributed to reviving a general interest in rowing and an awareness of environmental issues.

When I did my research in the historic centre of Venice, I counted 27 societies for rowing Venetian style, eight canoeing societies and 22 rowing associations and clubs, in a variety of firms and unions of workers, for instance those of the city policemen and of the gas and insurance companies. Rowing instruction, especially for young people, has also been made available by some Neighbourhood Councils. The Municipality of Venice itself owns 120 boats: these are specially constructed in various sizes and shapes to take part in regattas, and are available for all those who are accepted to enter. In 1981 the number of regattas reached a record of 180 and it has now settled down at about 140.

The regatta known as *La Storica* is only one within a cycle of races that take place every year between May and October. The cycle is not permanently fixed: inclusion or exclusion of races reflects local politics and relations between parts of the city. One of the organizers of regattas made it clear to me that only six are 'truly traditional', while those of St. Erasmo, Mestre and the Ascension Feast (or *Sensa*) are extemporaneous creations, which the Municipality will not support or publicize. According to the inhabitants of those areas, however, such races have taken place in their island-villages since time immemorial, while some events now described as 'traditional' are very recent creations.

Where, as in the island of St. Erasmo, people are vine growers, boat races are linked with the grape harvest. The regattas of Pellestrina and Burano, originally held on the days of the villages' *festas*, have become part of the official calendar only since the 1920s, when the two islands were joined to the Venice commune. That is not to say that inhabitants of those islands did not participate in the great city regattas, for, on the contrary, they were always among its main protagonists. But, while each village was represented by a large boat decorated with its typical products, costumes and tools, when their inhabitants took part in competitive races, provenance was certainly not the sole or main criterion in the formation of crews. Individual oarsmen could be recognized as coming from some particular locality only by the most expert and dedicated spectators as well as, of course, by their families and neighbours, who took great pride in their victories.

I need not describe here the six races at present recognized as 'official' by the municipality, except to explain that those of Burano and Murano are reserved strictly for champions, since they are meant to give a chance to those who suffered a defeat at the *Storica* to redress the balance and recover their honour. Thus, while the *Storica* represents Venice's grand official image of itself, both for itself and for its visitors, the later regattas, at Murano and Burano, are eminently local occasions, as alien to most of Venice's tourists as they are gripping to the city's in-groups of passionate fans.

An Event. The Spectators

A *Regata Storica* can be watched in different ways and with different degrees of participation: people whose homes have a good view over the Grand Canal invite their friends to tea; the occasion offers a good opportunity to reciprocate hospitality and a chance for those invited to stay off the streets, usually crowded with tourists. Casual visitors and passers-by may find inexpensive positions on barges moored at the sides of the Grand Canal. But the most sought after vantage-point is a specially constructed floating dais, with banked rows of seats, like those of a theatre, temporarily placed at the finishing post on the Grand Canal. Its centre is generally occupied by the Mayor, visiting politicians, city councillors, notables and their guests, while some seats may be sold at very high prices. It is usual for Italy's Prime Minister or other senior politicians to put in an appearance, and the occasion is televised.

Many Venetians, though not personally engaged in the race, follow the competitors on boats, or moor their boats at the sides of the Grand Canal to get a close view and a sense of sharing with their favourite heroes. When, during my first fieldwork in the '80s, I lived with a family of market gardeners from the island of Sant'Erasmo, watching with them was an entirely different experience from previous occasions when, observing from some high palace window, the Regatta had looked a rather remote, if spectacular event. As with bicycle or horse races, one can only see the boats passing, while to follow the whole event in detail and grasp the turning points of the competition, one would need to watch it on television. But my hosts assured me that they much preferred being there.

Two members of the family were participating in the race, and so to have the best possible view, it was important to get quickly into a good position, as near as possible to the finishing post on the Grand Canal. The barge was prepared for the trip with remarkable speed and efficiency. First it was rapidly scrubbed, dried, and furnished with pieces of carpet, cushions and a few chairs; then a large box containing a pot of beans and pasta, soused fish, oysters and clams in a cooler, biscuits and fruit, was placed in the prow.

The grandmother was settled in a chair under an umbrella, then the whole extended family rapidly embarked. By about 2.00 p.m., i.e. over three hours before the main race was due to start, the boat was moored almost directly opposite the Grand Jury. Once settled among a crowd of barges and boats jostling for position, the family started to consume their meal, without any formal rule or sequence, exchanging jokes and pleasantries, and sometimes a few hostile comments on the people or rowers of other islands. Once peaceful relations with neighbouring boats had been established, wine would be freely offered to anyone within reach and recommended as a genuine island product.

While waiting, the men would talk of previous regattas, pass appreciative comments on the champions, play cards, discuss current affairs or sleep, while the children would start getting troublesome and put themselves in some danger by jumping from boat to boat. The historical parade was watched with little interest, but as the racing boats approached comments were hushed and one could mainly hear the names of the rowers, called out loudly with cheers and encouraging cries.

The first part, as I explained above, is a sumptuous procession, headed by the Ducal barge *Bucintoro* (actually a reproduction, since Venice's state boat was destroyed by the French in 1797) followed by many colourfully decorated barges, representing magistrates or noble families, as well as purely decorative or allegorical ones. Other boats represent rowing societies, firms, and associations of workers. The friars of various orders (especially of San Francesco del Deserto) used sometimes to put in an appearance. But recently, they say that they have not had suitable brothers.

The ceremonial parade begins to give way to the competition when boats, decorated with the fruit and vegetables they produce or the fish they catch, start to appear from the outlying islands. Some of these may be purely representative, but they are usually the standard-bearers of the first competition. This is between large coloured boats with six oarsmen, called *Caorline*. Each represents a neighbourhood (the city's old *sestieri*) or a peripheral island. Mestre also participates, thanks to a crew of river boatmen. This part of the race is comparable with the Siena *Palio* in as far as it is a competition between neighbourhoods, but it certainly does not seem to arouse quite the same fierce and passionate commitment as the Sienese event. Indeed, as my informants explained, the crews are not always restricted to rowing in the boats that represent their birthplaces, but are redistributed to achieve maximum efficiency.

The real competition, however, the one my friends from Sant'Erasmo had been waiting for, is that between champions on light two-man gondolas.

The Rowers

The Venetian style par excellence is one-man rowing. That, as one of its champions explained to me, 'is the university-level of rowing.' The rower must simultaneously propel and steer the boat with a steady rhythmic movement, without losing direction as he gains speed. He must stand as far back as possible, in order to be able to take long strokes and accelerate rapidly, especially at the moment of take-off.

The energy needed to row gondolas, at a low speed, is actually very small, since a rower can transport him- or herself, and three additional passengers, using the same amount of energy required to walk on flat land. But at higher speeds the energy cost is greater than with other types of boats. Good rowing, however, is a matter of style as much as strength, since it depends on a delicate balance of movements. It is very important for each man to feel completely at ease and in harmony with his boat and above all with the oar-lock, which is the pivot of the relation between his body, the boat itself, and the water. A mistaken position can render the whole effort useless. Rowers must rely on talent and practice, since the forces involved are too volatile for it to be worth following any strict detailed rules of rowing practice (Donatelli 1990: 149–52).

The final preparation of the boat is left to each contestant. On the Friday before the race, after the last practice, the boat is beached and cleaned, then turned over and stood on trestles. The bottom and sides are carefully scrubbed, and left to dry. Any mark or scratch will be filled to achieve the greatest possible smoothness. On the Sunday the keel is rubbed with sandpaper, then greased. The boat is placed on cloth, then gently lowered into the water and towed to the starting point.

The route and the formalities of the Regatta have remained largely unaltered for centuries. The boats are taken in advance to the starting point, in Costello's Motta di Sant'Antonio, where they are lined up behind a string. When the string is broken at the sound of a cannon, they race away to the other end of Venice, then they turn around a pole dug into the bottom of the canal, and go back to the finishing post in the centre of the Grand Canal. The first four are solemnly presented with coloured silk flags, white or red for the first, green for the second, blue for the third and yellow for the fourth. But while the first, second and third also receive a sum of money, the fourth must be content with the gift of a suckling pig.

Races are preceded by avoidance of heavy drink and food and by a period of sexual abstinence – a matter that gives rise to much ribald joking in anticipation of the impending end of abstention. In the past, on the days before the races rowers would worship the Virgin in a particularly devout manner. On the day before the contest the champions would go to the Church of the Madonna della Salute taking oil and candles as propitiatory offerings. Some of the winners would eventually place their flag on the Virgin's altar as a sign of dedication and respect. Though worship of the Virgin is not as widespread and intense as it was and winners now often use their flags to decorate their homes, one custom that is still practised is the blessing of the boats by the parish priests.

In the past, the dressing of a champion (which has been compared to that of toreros) was done with some solemnity. Relatives and friends gathered in his home and, while his mother or wife helped him wrap his coloured silk band round his waist, she reminded him to cross himself when he passed the Church of the Salute, even if that meant missing an oar stroke, and then solemnly handed him an oar. His father would give him a few last-minute instructions on the treacherous currents and shallows of St. Mark's basin, and on ways of standing up firmly for himself in case of unfair competition (Michiel 1829: 189 ff.; Tamassia 1980: 55). One tradition that has been maintained is that of champions' meals, often described as 'family suppers', which are held before and after each regatta. They are attended by the competitors, the sponsors and judges, the Mayor and city authorities, one or two newspapermen, and some older champions.

Starting positions are assigned by drawing lots, and are apparently quite decisive, since those who claim to know the waters inch by inch say that conditions and currents can vary at very small distances. The first rule is not to get in the way of other competitors. Crews must be about a metre away from others, and must not touch another's stern. In order to overtake they must steer wide of others and not touch their oars. Usually such rules are not observed to the letter, and although umpires follow the competing boats, much happens under the water that cannot be seen. Transgressions give rise to fierce disputes, and regattas are very often followed by lasting feuds and acrimonious court cases.

Individuals[11]

Rowers in Venice's regattas are usually referred to as gondoliers, boatmen, and fishermen from the peripheral islands. This general description, however, does little justice to their differences and hierarchies, and above all to the strong emphasis placed on individuality. So great and so severe are the demands of training to win that personal achievement and dedication are given full and public recognition. A man who eventually became one of the city's most prominent champions told me how terrified and intimidated he was, when at seventeen, he found himself, the son of a poor fisherman from Burano, competing against the top oarsmen of his day.[12] What was at stake, he explained, was not only his pride and his natural desire to win but also his prospects of future employment and his chance of making a living. For instance, in the past, success at the races was a sure way of qualifying for secure and remunerative employment as a gondolier in the service of some rich employer, or as a regular at one of the *traghettos* across the Grand Canal.

A position as gondolier was in fact regarded as a privilege; it was often inherited or achieved by rising from the humbler position of boat-servant. For inhabitants of the peripheral islands, who were traditionally regarded with disdain and condescension by the Venetian working class, it was particularly difficult to penetrate the closed ranks of the city's boatmen. As well as advancing his economic prospects, a solid record of victories would greatly raise a man's prestige in his peer group. Achievement of championship standards, 'an honour and a distinction before the whole city', would qualify him as a leader and a representative of his own community. An interesting testimony to the champions' social prominence is a fine collection of their portraits, some of which are now displayed in Venice's naval museum.[13]

Despite their initial difficulties, inhabitants of the outlying islands always figure in relatively large numbers among the main rowing champions. In an attempt to make an approximate survey, I found that out of 70 oarsmen born roughly between 1850 and 1950, 15 were

Sergio Tagliapietra, *Ciaci*, born in Burano in 1935, has collected over 200 red flags. He won the Murano competition 18 consecutive times, came first 13 times in the *Regata Storica*, and 19 times in Burano. He also won canoeing competitions in the Olympic games in Melbourne (1956) and Tokyo (1964). At present he is responsible for the upkeep of boats in the commune's boatyard, and for the training of future generations of rowers

(Portrait by Andrea Pagnacco; Crovato and Crovato 1982: 91).

Venetians from the historical centre; ten were from Murano, while the largest relative numbers were from Pellestrina and Burano. It also emerged that a tendency to row with brothers and establish dynasties of successful champions was strongest in the islands,[14] as was a tendency to challenge rivals, and to develop long-standing enmities, or short-lived and opportunistic alliances.

Unions, separation and changes in the composition of two-man crews are now often referred to as marriages, divorces and courtships, and are followed with intense interest by members of the rowing community. Clamorous fights between champions have always occurred, and are long remembered and talked about with great glee by their enemies. But recently, when a prominent champion, who failed to win the race because he was overtaken – as he claims, unfairly – by his brother, appealed to the jury to revise their decision, it was generally thought that his *egoismo* had really got out of control. The character of sport as a disinterested and playful activity, it was felt, should never entirely be lost through too great a craving for victory, and indeed an incapacity to accept defeat can become as risible as a tendency to enter competitions one has no real chance of winning. Challenges are part of the fun and of the folklore of boat-racing. As we have seen, races in Burano and Murano give those who have been defeated in the *Storica* a chance to redress the balance and restore their reputation – a personal need that is very deeply engrained in a society where honour is of great importance. Challenges are at the same time motivated by ambition and by a strong desire for equality, and they are often issued against those whom success makes too boastful and presumptuous.

An exemplary story is recorded in a recent collection of memories of old champions or gondoliers, some of whom, according to its writer, still remember an episode that occurred about a hundred years ago. A champion, called Nane, or Giovanni, 'a stern rower of Apollonian features' and repeated winner of the *Storica*, was taken into the service of an English countess, wife of a Prime Minister. She soon fell desperately in love with him and took him back to England. He got so grand that, before returning, he telegraphed a noted boat-builder and ordered a brand new, richly decorated gondola. At his arrival at the station a crowd of fans cheered him 'for his amatory as well as his sporting triumphs', and he found the new boat waiting for him at his door. His pride and vainglory, however, became intolerable, and a few years later he challenged another popular champion, Giobatta Graziussi, nicknamed Titcle. He won but, just as he was returning home with his new silk trophy, the fans of his rival ignominiously taunted him and pushed him

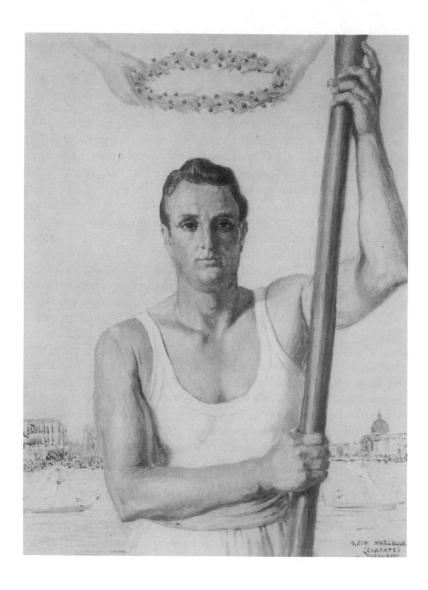

Marcello Bon, *Ciapate*, portrayed by Giuseppe Cherubini, was born in 1918. He too started his life as a fisherman in Burano, and later worked in Venice as a gondolier. He won the *Storica* six consecutive times, and was one of *Ciaci's* numerous rowing partners (Crovato and Crovato 1982: 83).

'The Women's Regatta in the Grand Canal,
Gabriele Bella, eighteenth century (Fundazione Querini Stampalia)'

into a canal. According to the story, this so humiliated and embittered him that he gave up racing altogether (Crovato and Crovato 1982: 57).

While egalitarianism is an important value, rowing is by no means exclusively a young man's sport, since men go on competing well into their 40s, and sometimes their 50s. They usually contrive to retire after a victory and are very critical of the young. It is generally believed that dedication to competitive rowing and a successful sporting career do not depend on physical strength alone. On the contrary, they require gifts of character and mind, which practice of the sport in turn will develop. A natural outcome is a transition in later life to a position of responsibility. Those with firm characters become *padrini*, i.e. instructors and judges. They continue to take part in the traditional dinners before and after the races, and they generally regard themselves as important father-figures, placing very strong emphasis on control, discipline and obedience. They often take an interest in the problems of their neighbourhoods, and they expect to be acknowledged and greeted with respect by the city's politicians.

Women

As is recorded in numerous writings and in visual representations of Venetian *feste* in the past, womens' competitions were often included in Great Regattas. According to extant records, the first race between women was introduced in 1493 to amuse two noblewomen, Beatrice of Este and her mother-in-law, who had come to Venice on a diplomatic mission. But in the eighteenth century women's races went out of favour. At present, women are active participants in most regattas. Some of them, like their male counterparts, have achieved championship standards and take part in the Olympics. But the women complain all the same that they have never had the recognition they deserve from their male colleagues or responsible city councillors (Testa 1983: 53–5). For example, until recently, they were never offered the traditional suppers that are a prominent feature of the social life of male sportsmen, since conviviality outside the home is, on the whole, still not considered desirable or appropriate for women.[15]

While the women maintain that men's rowing is no different from theirs, the men observe that women do not have the necessary strength or 'deep roots' in rowing traditions that they have. Therefore, the women feel that they are definitely placed in the ceremonial rather than the *truly sporting* parts of regattas, and that their efforts are viewed not as sport

Albino Dei Rossi, *Strigheta*, like *Ciaci*, started his life as a fisherman in Burano, and eventually became one of the city's most popular gondoliers. As Crovato and Crovato write, he was well-known for his voluble character, his elegant and forceful oar-strokes and his intimate knowledge of the lagoon. He achieved an unprecedented record with his fourteen victories at the *Regata Storica*. The family's reputation is now upheld by his two sons, Bruno and Franco. His portait is by Marco Novati (Crovato and Crovato 1982: 91).

but merely as folklore and spectacle. Rowing is thus very strongly marked as a masculine pursuit. Emphasis on masculinity, however, is not derived solely from machismo, since it is usually related to Venice's political and cultural history – one in which gender distinctions have always been strongly demarcated, as has the division of labour, linked to the city's maritime environment and its naval and fishing traditions (Sciama 1992: 122–3). It may be relevant that Venice, since its political and economic decadence, has been increasingly represented as symbolically feminine, and often as a not-very-good woman, sometimes metaphorically as a harlot (Ruskin 1858), sometimes as an invalid (a swampy breeding ground of infection), or, as we have seen in my initial oppositions, as a spoilt wastrel (see e.g. Tanner 1992).

Thus it is not surprising that some still view the participation of women in competitive races as transgressive. However, the fact that many perceive rowing as a mainly male activity need not be construed solely as an assertion of domination: it may be better understood as an expression of a male desire for harmony in a difficult environment, and of a will to affirm a vital sense of identity – not, I think, quite a certainty of what the city *is*, rather of what it aspires to be.

Conclusion

Recent writings on Venetian rowing emphasize its nature as a 'real sport':

> For the untrained eye of the public. . .the Historical Regatta used to take on the contours of folklore. After 1975 and the *Vogalonga* such error is not possible any more. . . rowing is a true mass pheno-menon. . . it has exploded unexpectedly and is not going to stop. . . It now appears for what it really is. . . *a sport*, in the fullest sense of that term, indeed, in the lagoon's environment, a prince among sports (Cecconi and Stumento 1983: 3. My italics).

Several informants, themselves active participants in the main rowing contests, firmly opposed a view of the *Regata* as a historical pageant, and they proudly stressed its high standing as a national sports event – proved to their satisfaction by the recognition of the media. As they argued, what real sportsmen, other than those who had long lost their power, or had always been weak, would go about wearing some ridiculous costume?

Thus sport and ritual are often contra sted. That distinction, however, soon fades as we realize that evocations of the past and competitive races are similarly linked with a strong need for identity, both that of the city as a whole and that of the different localities which constitute it. While in that respect the recent revival of festive regattas is comparable to the modern revitalization of rituals analyzed in Boissevain (1992), it is important to note that in the Venetian case revivals of the city's rituals have taken place repeatedly, in particular at times of uncertainty or triumphant success, when the need to affirm a local identity was heightened.

When, at the turn of the first millennium, Venice was establishing its dominance over the gulf, the ritual was gradually elaborated – not without incorporating and syncretically reviving elements of earlier, prechristian, celebrations. About eight centuries later, when Venice was to make the transition from political independence to membership of the recently formed Italian State, which would place it on a par with any other Italian city, the change was felt by many as a 'Fall'. As the allegorical marriage of the Doge to the sea (in which domination was strongly symbolized) had long lost all political significance, that part of the Regatta which celebrated the city's history became predominantly audience-oriented: the gilt and decorated boats, manned by people wearing 'historical costumes', had no function other than to remind participants and spectators alike of the city's past opulence and power. A distinction between historical pageant and sporting display thus became increasingly marked.

However it is also the case, especially during the last twenty years or so, that the competitive part of historical regattas, in light boats manned by rowers wearing the traditional but spare gondoliers' outfits, both emphasizes the agonistic side of rowing, and affirms the primordial relation of Venice's people with their environment, clearly transcending historical circumstance. Furthermore, in the context of Venice's environmental problems, at the same time as regattas express social relations, their participants creatively keep alive and renew skills and traditions which they consider essential to its threatened continuity. Thus the sporting and ritual aspects of the Regatta, though rhetorically separated by some, are united by the common desire for identity, one with historical depth and an environmental dimension.

Appendix

Table 1. Population resident in the Historic Centre,
Estuary, and Terrafirma

	Historic Centre and Giudecca	Estuary	Terrafirma	Of no Fixed Abode	Commune
1950	184,447	42,627	94,488		321,562
1955	167,089	46,615	115,777		329,561
1960	145,402	49,025	152,575		347,002
1965	123,773	51,279	188,907		363,919
1970	111,550	50,729	205,249		367,528
1975	104,206	49,670	210,674		364,550
1980	95,222	49,240	207,811		352,453
1985	86,072	48,584	200,084		334,932
1990	79,487	47,480	193,894	129	320,990

The total population of the commune reached a maximum of 367,528 in 1970, with a 14 percent rise since 1950. After 1973, following a general national tendency, it has taken a downward trend; in 1990 it was down by 12 percent.

Comparing figures for Venice's different areas, we see that the population of the terrafirma increased by 123 percent between 1950 and 1975, and then began to decline. The population of the estuary increased by 20 percent between 1950 and 1965; in the following 25 years it has declined by 7.5 percent, and in the islands of Burano and Murano, where the condition of housing was particularly poor, it has declined by even more. In contrast, the population of Ca'Vio, in the peninsula of Cavallino, where new housing has been built, has noticeably increased.

Between 1950 and 1990, the historical centre lost over 54 percent of its population. It may, however, be pointed out that the figure for the years 1945 to 1950, which was approximately 150,000, was artificially high since, between 1943 and 1945, large numbers of people who, having been committed Fascists, feared the impending arrival of the Allies to Rome and moved temporarily to Venice. There they were joined by others who felt confident that the city would not be bombed.

Notes

1. This paper is based mainly on fieldwork conducted in 1993.
2. A concern with identity and a keen perception of a crisis may partly have entered a   Venetian discourse from the media, so that it is difficult to see clearly in what measure they may derive from a widespread intellectual fashion. Notions of identity and ethnicity are often invoked by informants, to make sense of circumstances they regard as problematic, just as they are applied by anthropologists in ordering ethnographic materials. However, distinctions should be made between the interpretative frameworks of anthropologists and those of the people they study. While problems of collective (or individual) identity are often related to changes that are difficult to grasp or describe coherently, the factors Venetians most often refer to are: an increasing emphasis on individualism, and an intensification of nationalist or regionalist movements, related to changes in political structure, environment and population over the last 200 years.
3. Despite a traditionally strong opposition between country- and city-dwellers (in this case homologous with maritime and rustic life-styles), both are aware of a common past and a common regional or provincial culture. But the 'modern' environment of Mestre, with its high-rise apartment blocks and busy main streets still used as motorways into Venice, is generally seen as extremely uncomfortable. Those who moved to Mestre or Marghera from the country miss the fresh air, open spaces and contact with nature. On the other hand those insular Venetians who moved because of the scarcity and obsolescence of housing, and many of whom commute to work in the historical centre, often lament the loss of aesthetic pleasure, educational and entertainment opportunities, and of the safety and peace due to the absence of cars.
4. As Poppi observes, 'the very fact that they constantly talk about, compare and contrast *chis egn* (those years, the past) with *inchecondi* (nowadays, the present) in dichotomous terms indicates the degree of closeness – if not identity – with the past that shapes the actors' own perception of themselves' (1992: 119).
5. Napoleon's army entered Venice in 1797; under the treaty of Campoformio, the Veneto Region was handed over to Austria in exchange for the Low Countries. Except for a brief period as a revolutionary republic in 1848–9, Venice remained under firm Austrian domination from 1815 till 1866, when it was joined to Italy.
6. The legend was not actually recorded by chroniclers, but has been passed down by writers, like Lorenzo de' Monaci and Marin Sanudo,

who may have collected it from oral sources (Molmenti 1880: 194).

7. In some versions the pirates are described as Triestin or Istrian, and their leader is called Gaiolo.

8. 'Wooden Maria', *Maria de tola*, is used to describe stiff, flat-chested women.

9. Both festivals would require a far more extended study than space allows in this paper. For a clear historical analysis of ritual in the Renaissance period see Muir 1981.

10. In later centuries, other Venetian games, such as the battles between the city's two main factions, Nicolotti and Castellani, which often proved violent and dangerous, and the runs with bears and bulls through the streets and *Campi* (especially Campo San Stefano) were also discouraged and then expressly forbidden.

11. I call this section 'Individuals' because, as can be deduced from the way regattas were organized and the winners rewarded, each person felt engaged in a direct and unique relationship with the whole, i.e. the Republican State. This is understandable where relations were ruled by 'contract' rather than 'status' and were conducive to a greater degree of individualism than was the case in predominantly agricultural areas of Italy.

12. James Fenimore Cooper tells a similar episode in his novel *The Bravo* (1859)

13. In the nineteenth-century the portraiture of champions, a tradition that goes back to the seventeenth-century (when rowers were mostly employed by aristocratic families), had entirely given way to photography. Since 1982, however, portraits by well-known artists have been commissioned by the *Associazione Settemari*, a club with a strong interest in local culture and environmental issues (Crovato and Crovato 1982: 91).

14. Especially Sant'Erasmo, Burano and Giudecca, although Murano also has a group of no less than five brothers.

15. In Venetian such dinners are designated by the same word as 'brotherhood', or company of men', *fragia* from Latin *frater*.

Bibliography

Archetti, Eduardo P. (1994), 'The Moralities of Argentinian Football'. Paper presented at *European Association of Social Anthropologists Conference, Oslo*

Bellavitis, G. and G. Romanelli (1985), *Venezia*. Bari

Bloch, Maurice (1989), *Ritual, History and Power.* London: Athlone Press

Boissevain, Jeremy (ed.) (1992), *Revitalizing European Rituals*. London: Routledge

Cecconi, M. and L. Strumento (1983), *La Voga Alla Veneta*. Venezia

Crovato, G. and M. Crovato (1982), *Regate e Regatanti*. Venezia

Dei, F., P. Apolito, G. Dore, P. De Sanctis, V. Cannada-Bartoli, V. Esposito, and P. Clemente (1992), *Il Calcio: Una Prospettiva Antropologica*. Siena: Ossimori. vol. 1, pp. 7–31

Donatelli, C. (1990), *La Gondola*. Venezia

Lane, F. (1973), *Venice, A Maritime Republic*. Baltimore

Leach, Edmund (1954), *Political Systems of Highland Burma: A Study of Katchin Social Structure*. London: Athlone Press

Michiel, R. G. (1829), *Origine delle Feste Veneziane*. Milano

Molmenti, L. P. (1880), *Storia di Venezia nella Vita Privata*. Torino

Muir, E. (1981), *Civic Ritual in Renaisssance Venice*. Princeton

Poppi, Cesare (1992), 'Building Difference: the political economy of tradition in the Ladin Carnival of the Val di Fassa,' in Boissevain (1992)

Ruskin, John (1858), *The Stones of Venice*. London

Sciama, Lidia (1992), 'Lacemaking in Venetian Culture', in Ruth Barnes and J. B. Eicher (eds), *Dress and Gender. Making and Meaning*. Oxford: Berg

Tamassia Mazzarotto, B. (1980 (1961)), *Le Feste Veneziane. I Giochi Populari, Le Cerimonie Religiose e di Governo*. Firenze

Tanner, A. (1992) *Venice Desired*. Cambridge

Testa, S. (1983), *La Voga alla Veneta*. Venezia

Urban, L. (1992), *Venezia e le Feste Sull'Acqua.* Venezia

Acknowledgements

I am greatly indebted to those rowing champions and their families whose enthusiasm, humour and generosity made my research both challenging and pleasant. Historical research was conducted mainly on secondary sources.

9

Players, Workers, Protestors: Social Change and Soccer in Colonial Zimbabwe

Ossie Stuart

Until quite recently historians of Southern Africa tended to ignore popular culture in general and soccer in particular. Instead they were mainly preoccupied with social division in relation to what is known as the mode of production.[1] The significance or otherwise of soccer in the development of Africa has rarely been elevated above the status of a curio.

There has been only a very small number of writers who have studied soccer in Africa. Three of them have chosen to attempt to assess its significance in the context of social and political development of African states. Clignet and Stark (1974) in their study of soccer in Cameroon sought, among other things, to discover how football helped to shape patterns of modernization in that country. They pointed to the salience of ethnic difference in the game. This, in their opinion, placed soccer at the centre of the dominant political and social structures in Cameroon. The game influences and is in turn influenced by these structures. Though their study was conducted almost twenty years ago it is clear that they pointed to the game as a crucial tool in the making of Cameroon urban identity.

However, in 1974 it was not easy to justify research on the construction of ethnic identities. Clignet and Stark hinted at the problem their discipline — anthropology — had with writing about 'ethnicity'. Postcolonial revisionism was at its zenith in the early 1970s. Pre-revisionist writers were accused of writing about African tribalism in paternalist terms. For their pains they were condemned as apologists for colonialism. To get ahead in 1974 it was certainly not de rigueur to talk about ethnicity or tribalism, or anything which was thought to confirm African backwardness.

Unfortunately a latent fear of paternalism still remains where research on popular culture in Africa is concerned. So, subsequent studies have ignored the central point of Clignet and Stark's pioneering work. Terence Mornington, in his analysis of the politics of Black African sport (1985), saw it merely as an arena for inter-ethnic rivalry. He did so to bolster his argument that, far from being an aid to the modernizing process, ethnicity in African soccer has been a bar.

Likewise West, in his study of the African middle class in Colonial Zimbabwe (from now on I will refer to it as Southern Rhodesia), implies that soccer is an obstacle to modernization. He describes inter-ethnic soccer rivalry in Bulawayo during the 1940s and '50s as 'political jockeying, personal disputes and petty squabbling within and between the associations, including accusations of misappropriation of funds, regionalism, and, especially in Bulawayo with its ethnically heterogeneous population, tribalism' (West 1990).

It should be remembered that West's study is concerned with the rise of the African middle class in Southern Rhodesia. His interest in this period stems from it being a time of dramatic political action. In 1945 and 1948 two massive strikes by African workers took place in Bulawayo. The first involved Bulawayo's railway workers, galvanizing political and trade union activity among Africans in the city. From that time, trade and political organizations proliferated throughout Bulawayo. Not a week went by without at least a major association meeting or a wildcat strike in demand of better wages (Stuart 1989).The second strike was a general one, involving the majority of labourers throughout the city.

This political confrontation has been understood within the context of the development of an urban proletariat in Southern Rhodesia (Phimister 1985). Consequently, that West conflates those who played soccer into one almost homogeneous group is entirely consistent with the way in which these events in Bulawayo have been understood by scholars. For him, the only significant difference between participants in sport was social class. Soccer was played by the African elite, while boxing, the other major popular sport played in Bulawayo at this time, was the sport of the proletariat. Like the political and trade union organizations he studied, West regards soccer as merely another vehicle for elite expression.

West came to this conclusion after studying a two-year boycott of African-played soccer, which began in 1947, by all the players, clubs and supporters in Bulawayo. To him the boycott was just part of the 'political jockeying, personal disputes and petty squabbling' between African elites, which not only characterized sport but also the political and employment associations which quarrelled over the right to speak for Bulawayo's African population. Contrary to West's narrow perspective, I wish to argue that the boycott was at the centre of the making of urban African identity in Bulawayo at a time of dramatic change in that city. What was at stake was not just elite status and class positions, for at that time individuals (including football players) were competing to assert and impose their rival interpretations of what it meant to be an African citizen in Bulawayo.

I too will look at that boycott but will draw a different conclusion to the one offered by West about its significance. Endeavouring to follow the lead given by Clignet and Stark, I will argue that soccer plays a central role in imagined ethnicity in Africa. It is part of the lived cultural identity of tens of thousands of urban inhabitants across Africa. As such, it has played, and continues to play, a central role in the social and political development of the continent. However, this does not mean that I do not acknowledge the structural factors, and give due weight to the macro-structural and economic conditions that shape the context within which African creativity takes place. Indeed, Bulawayo at this time was at the heart of the considerable economic and social change taking place in Southern Rhodesia. Thousands of Africans were entering the city in search of work; inflation was rising and wages levels falling. The African expressive cultures of this time, of which soccer was a part, were able to communicate a sense of the existing structural constraints, and, as importantly, of the opportunities that were then available. The priority of this chapter is not to dwell on the political and economic constraints which confronted Africans in Bulawayo in the '40s but on their attempts to maximize the opportunities for alternative and oppositional agencies (which will exist even in the most restricted circumstances).

After a brief description of the sports boycott, I shall go back to the beginning and describe how soccer came to Africa and why it became a central feature of life in the urban areas in general and Bulawayo in particular. Finally, I will seek to place the Bulawayo soccer boycott in this wider context. The purpose is to show that soccer, like other contemporary sport and cultural movements, was not a brake on African modernization but was at its fulcrum.[2]

The Boycott

At the end of the 1930s in Southern Rhodesia the white-run liberal voluntary organization, the African Welfare Society (AWS), established and ran all officially sanctioned soccer played by Africans in the country. At the beginning of the Second World War, AWS soccer was played in all the major centres of the land; annually teams competed for the national trophy, the Osborn Cup (Bulawayo, Annual Report 1941). Of all the African Welfare Societies, the Matabeleland branch in Bulawayo was by far the most successful. It also ran the largest and most popular African soccer league.

By the middle of the decade, the Welfare Society's resources were unable to keep pace with the activities the Society was obliged to undertake. Bulawayo was a migrant town, and few Africans, unlike its small white population, had the permanent right of abode in the city. The vast majority of Africans who did work in the city either commuted daily from outside the municipal boundary or lived in illegal urban squats. The few officially sanctioned urban African locations in Bulawayo were overcrowded and crime-ridden. Despite the absence of suitable accommodation, the number of Africans seeking employment and accommodation in Bulawayo increased dramatically from 1935 onward as the world economy moved out of recession. Bulawayo's population was estimated to have grown from 15,000 in 1935 to 35,000 in 1945 (Census of Population of Southern Rhodesia 1946) to over 85,000 by 1953. This tremendous growth affected the AWS detrimentally. Its recreational activities spanned many fields and became more extensive and sophisticated: by the early 1940s it ran regular cinema shows, maintained the local library, and oversaw sport ranging from boxing and soccer to cycle racing and basketball; it also ran the only health clinic available for Africans in Bulawayo (Ashton 1957). The successful organization of all the social and recreational facilities for all Africans in Bulawayo was jeopardized by the increasing numbers. Very soon the Society was obliged to turn to the City Council to take over the running of many of its former activities.

The boycott began when the local authority, in the form of the Bulawayo Council, agreed to take over the financing and organization of all African football in the town. With the agreement of the AWS, the Council had been steadily taking responsibility for the majority of the services to Africans previously provided by the Society. This was part of the 1946 Native (Urban Areas) Accommodation and Registration Act, a policy which, for the first time, obliged local authorities throughout

Southern Rhodesia to take some responsibility for a settled, yet temporary, African urban population in what was still perceived to be part of European territory, the city (Native Administration Committee 1943).

This agreement between the Council and the AWS was fiercely opposed by the soccer players and their supporters. As has already been mentioned, strikes and protests had become part and parcel of daily life for many Africans. Furthermore, the increasing poverty of the burgeoning population, and the City Council's apparent indifference or perceived culpability contributed to increased tension in the city. The African teams, rather than come under Council control, wanted to run and finance their own game. More importantly, perhaps, the clubs feared that Council-run soccer would mean an end to the considerable freedom they had enjoyed under AWS patronage. The AWS-run league was almost totally dominated by the clubs themselves. They merely had to report back to the AWS executive committee on a regular basis. For these reasons, the footballers were hostile to increased Council involvement, fearing it would erode their independence and influence.

The Council response to these protests was simply contempt. The white-run Council had little comprehension of the importance of soccer to the newly settled population in Bulawayo. Furthermore, they appeared to relish the prospect of a confrontation with the African population. The new policy of local responsibility for the African population had been imposed upon the Bulawayo Council against its will by Central Government (Committee to Investigate Conditions of Africans Employed in Urban Areas 1944). Any demonstration indicating that this policy would be costly to implement would strengthen the argument that the 1946 Urban Areas Act was a mistake.

In response to the Council's insistence on total control, the soccer players threatened a total boycott of the first season of Council-run soccer, which was due to begin with the 1947 season. This act of disobedience suited the Council in its argument with central government. However, the Council believed that such a challenge would be short-lived, crushed in the old fashioned way, by the offer of privileges to a few and the 'stick' to the majority. The Native Welfare Officer believed that 'inducements' would soon break the strike and was given permission to offer individual teams substantial material and financial bribes, such as new kit and balls as well as generous prize money, if they agreed to join the new Council-run league. Yet, on the beginning of the new season, no African teams turned up to play. This remained the case for the rest of the season and the boycott began to spread to teams in other urban centres. The 1948 season began with the Council offering even to share with African soccer clubs the revenue raised from gate takings if they would only join the Council League. But no team obliged.

The Council had to accept defeat. Their exploitation of the boycott had completely backfired. The unity demonstrated by the soccer clubs had taken the authorities by surprise. Such was the strength of the soccer players' resolve, the Council began to fear their growing power and influence. From the Council's point of view, the sole purpose of African soccer was social control. To achieve a degree of this, they were now forced to accede reluctantly to the demands of footballers. The settlement the two camps agreed was that the Municipality and the football association should combine and use the Barbour Fields without any definite lease being granted by the Municipality; that two trustees be appointed – one by the Municipality and the other by the African Football League; that the League be allowed to charge gate money on the understanding that it would be entirely self-supporting, purchasing its own equipment and clothing (Native Administration Committee 1949).

In 1953 the central government recognized the Association (Ashton 1957). Was this unprecedented victory by Africans in a highly oppressive environment merely, as West claimed, political manoeuvring by the African elite to gain a victory and resources? Or was it something far more significant? To answer this we have understand how and why soccer became a significant form of popular culture in Southern Rhodesia.

Introduction of Soccer in Africa[3]

Soccer is highly adaptive culturally:

> No other sport lent itself so easily and cheaply to the varying conditions of urban life. It was simple to play, easy to grasp and could be played on any surface under any conditions, by an indeterminate number of men. It needed no equipment but a ball, and could last from dawn to dusk. Football could be played by anyone, regardless of size, skill and strength (Walvin, 1975: 9).

Soccer was brought to Africa by European settlers. Working class settlers played the game amongst themselves wherever they went. Africans were introduced to it through a number of sources: at schools, colleges and the missions. They also came across it while working as ancillary labour for the colonial armed services.

For Africans across the continent, school was one of the primary routes to soccer. In Cameroon, for example, the École Supérieure of Yaoundé provided many of the players for the Canon, Unisport, Dragon and Tonnerre teams. Nigerian and Ghanaian teams obtained their players in a similar fashion. The same occurred in South Africa (the other great soccer territory in the continent): Zonnebloem and Adams College in Natal and schools such as Lovedale, Healdtown, and St Mathews in South Africa introduced soccer to most of those who were to become Africa's educated elite. For instance, it was students from these colleges who, in the 1910s, took the sport to Southern Rhodesia.

African labourers discovered soccer via the British Colonial Army. For instance, the siege of Ladysmith during the Anglo-Boer War helped to spread the game among migrant labourers trapped in that city. In turn, they passed it on to other migrants throughout Natal and the Transvaal, including Johannesburg. Names of the earliest teams (e.g. 'Ladysmith' and the 'Invincibles' in Natal) are indicative of this military influence. The Royals of Pietermaritzburg, another early turn of the century team, probably took their name from the Royal Engineers based in that region.

Missions in South Africa were quick to recognize the value of soccer and encouraged it among their congregations. In the 1890s, Adams College – then known as Amanzimtoti Institute – had a senior team, the Shooting Stars, and a junior one, the Flying Stars. In 1907 players from these teams and local town teams formed the first soccer association, the Durban & District Football Association.

During this time, other teams were established in Durban, based upon workplace or a part of town. The Natal Government Railways' team was called 'NGR', and the Mzinyati mission one the 'Willows'. Other similarly based teams were the Vultures, the Wanderers, and the Native Swallows. The Condors played in New Scotland, the Natal Cannons in Inanda, while both the Corinthians and Jumpers played in Verlum. Though the majority of these Natal teams consisted of migrant workers they were not distant from the elite-based colleges and schools. Adams College regularly played against the worker teams. Couzens (1983) suggests that it was this close relationship between all the clubs which enabled them to create the Durban & District Football Association.

Football began a little later on the Johannesburg Reef. For example, Witwatersrand District Football Association was formed in the 1910s. Given the colonial economy, most of the teams were based on mining employment. Communities such as Sophiatown, Eastern Native Township, Western Native Township and Pimville played each other on a regular basis. Different yards (workers' residences) formed their own teams and challenged each other. Furthermore, individuals who learnt the game in employment or army service took it back with them when they returned to their country of origin.

This set the pattern for the growth of soccer in South Africa as the municipalities, mines and other employers began throughout the 1930s to provide grounds and resources for the game. For example, by 1937 the Johannesburg Bantu Football Association had registered 435 senior and junior clubs. All this is beyond the scope of this paper. All I wished to establish was the important influence of South African soccer on the territories to the north, including Southern Rhodesia.

Soccer in Southern Rhodesia

During the 1910s and '20s many thousands of migrant workers from what are now Zambia, Malawi, Mozambique and Zimbabwe travelled south to South Africa where the highest wages in the region were to be found. Some went south for the sake of their education, attending such institutions as Zonnebloem, Adams and Lovedale Colleges. Couzens points out that Charles Lobengula, the son of the king of the Ndebele people, was the Zonnebloem College centre-half between 1905 and 1907 and later its club secretary (Couzens 1983). Benjamin Burombo, who became a political activist in his home country, perfected his football while in Johannesburg during the 1930s. He played for the Johannesburg Mashonaland Club. On his return to Southern Rhodesia, Burombo set up and coached a team on a pitch next to his home in Selukwe (Bhebe 1989).

Though missions and schools in the country also played an important role in the introduction of soccer, as occurred in South Africa, the main introducers of soccer to Africans in Southern Rhodesia were members of the armed services stationed there during the 1900s and '10s. The wars in South Africa and East Africa during World War One brought thousands of British soldiers to the region. Africans from Southern Rhodesia fought alongside these troops. Along with influenza, these Southern Rhodesians picked up soccer.

The game was played in Salisbury, Umtali, Bulawayo and in any village where a pitch could be built. Ironically, it was not until the authorities moved to control the leisure time of the growing number of people living in the urban centres that the future of the game was secured. The authorities provided the necessary resources, such as kits, equipment and the pitches, and created the infrastructure from which both the great regional and national clubs sprang, and from which the first African sporting heroes were to emerge. This all began when the AWS was established, specifically to provide a diversion for African youngsters away from what the authorities regarded as dangerous activities such as vice, gambling and, worst of all in the minds of colonial government, strikes and other forms of protest (Stuart 1989).

The takeover of soccer was a complete success, as best described by a contemporary observer, Sergeant Masotsha Ndlovu, a key labour activist in the establishment of the Industrial Commercial Union (ICU) in Bulawayo:

M. Ndlovu: We mobilized until 1934 when the Europeans collected money in Parliament after Mr Fletcher and other Ministers in Parliament said 'The ICU is civilized, do not say it is not civilized because it knows what it is doing. Very soon all the people will join it and we will be forced to pay Africans more money. The best thing to do is to weaken it. Let us collect money.' They donated money in Parliament, £50. . . and so on until there was enough money. They asked the Rev. Ibbotson of the Methodist Church to leave Church duties and start a new organization, Native Welfare. The new organization promoted sporting and recreational activities with various prizes to be won. If one played football and won, he was given a pair of football boots and a uniform, if you competed in a bicycle race and won, you were given a new bicycle. People then began not to attend meetings. They were fascinated by the new entertainment provided by the Welfare. That weakened the ICU as I used to wait under the tree without any people coming.

Mark Ncube: Did you also participate in these games?

M. Ndlovu: A! What? Football! No. I used to go and watch at a distance, I detested that seriously. I knew that was killing us (Ncube 1981).

Ndlovu was right that something was indeed dying. It was the old identity and cultural ties that had sprung up around Bulawayo during the first three decades of this century. In its place were evolving new identities constructed within the emerging structural context of Southern Rhodesia. Soccer, far from killing Africans, was part of the new expressive culture of Africans in Bulawayo. The life of one of Bulawayo's first sporting superheroes is a case in point.

Called Just Rize, but popularly known as the 'Kontrola', this player was described in 1953 as 'one of the most brilliant football players in Southern Rhodesia'. Yet his fame depended solely upon the political and economic structural context of the time, and, specifically, the reorganization of soccer by the colonial authorities. Born in 1921 in Northern Rhodesia, Just Rize learnt his football skills in the great industrial region known as the Copper Belt. He was later employed in the Northern Province of that colony as a Sports Organizer where he played for the region's team. In 1944 he left for Shabani (Zvishavane) mine in Southern Rhodesia, but soon moved on to Bulawayo. There Just Rize joined the Northern Rhodesia Football Club. After playing a few local matches he caught the eye of the Selection Committee who promptly selected him for the City Team. Between 1944 and 1953 he played for the 'Red Army' and was considered to be the best centre-half in the colony. He was extremely popular among ordinary people throughout Bulawayo (Bulawayo African Home News 1953).

Quite apart from what he achieved in soccer circles, Just Rize symbolized the dramatic change in identity individuals experienced when they migrated to the city. Soccer transformed this individual from a little-known person on the Copper Belt to a widely-known star in a city hundreds of miles from his place of birth.

Soccer in Bulawayo

By 1939, football in Bulawayo, though overseen by the AWS, was almost completely African-controlled. It was run as an autonomous organization responsible only to the Management Committee of the AWS. In 1938 the junior African football clubs in Bulawayo, organized by the Welfare Officer and the Location Superintendent, were absorbed into the Bulawayo African Football Association. Though it came under the direction of the AWS Welfare Officer, the Association had its own constitution, bank account and African officials (Ashton 1957).

By 1941 the football season, which lasted for nine months, consisted of sixteen teams (e.g. the Matabeleland Highlanders, the Mashonaland Club, the Northern Rhodesia Club, the United Africans Club and the Home Sweepers Club of Western Commonage) competing each weekend in a local league and regularly playing teams from Johannesburg, Bechuanaland, Mashonaland and the Belgian Congo (Nehwati 1970). Even relatively small towns like Umtali (Mutare) had organised their own teams. In 1933 the secretary of the Umtali District Native Football Association felt sufficiently strongly about the failure to invite teams represented by his organization to participate in the Governor's Cup competition, which was sponsored by the Mashonaland AWS, that he sent a letter of protest to the British Prime Minister (West 1990). The organization of football – around the Governor's Cup in Salisbury and, nationally, around the Osborn Cup (donated by the Governor in 1937) – was the AWS's most significant achievement.

Popularity

So far I have indicated how soccer has introduced to people living in the great towns of South Africa and Southern Rhodesia, and how it played an important role in the development of urban life in the overcrowded, squalid townships of the region. What I have yet to do is to explain why soccer was (and still is) such a popular African sport.

Ranger suggests that European-introduced sport became an African possession, games they were prepared to fight for, because they could be given new meanings and functions in their new African contexts. This was an exercise of adaptive creativity by Africans (Ranger 1987). In other words, African sports became a symbolic arena for the making of African identity.

At this time, the great African cities were extremely hostile, fast-changing and overcrowded urban centres. They had poor facilities and no health care. Job security was limited. The death rate was high in these environments. The city was a completely different context to those from which male and female migrant workers originally came. To make real their new experience as inhabitants living cheek-by-jowl with others from southern Africa, these people were obliged to remake their identity. As a result, 'traditional' symbols were mobilized in new ways to make sense of the new urban African experience. African popular culture quickly became an affirmation of their cultural reality – a soccer club was something to belong to, somewhere to seek solace, support and advice, and also maintain links with the country of origin and even to obtain a decent burial.[4]

Soccer played a key role in providing one of the few avenues available anywhere in colonial Africa to social mobility and high status. It should thus be unsurprising that there was no boundary between political action and sport. Some of the principal actors in the demonstrations and strikes in Bulawayo that mark this period were also significant figures in soccer in Bulawayo. Benjamin Burombo, the founder of the British African National Voice Association in Bulawayo, maintained his interest in soccer and was involved with the Mashonaland Club in Bulawayo (Bhebe 1989). Sipambaniso Manyoba, one of the most significant political figures of the time (he was the Organizing Secretary of both the

Federation of African Trades Unions and the Matabele Home Society), was also the team captain of both the Matabele Highlanders Soccer Club and the Red Army (Welfare Society's Sports Committee 1942). Both Manyoba and Burombo were deeply involved with the protests of this period, including the boycott of soccer in 1947.

Conclusion

The soccer boycott was not just about elite manoeuvres, as West implied. The sport had become part of the cultural reality of Bulawayo's urban inhabitants. For the myriad of different peoples, communities and generations squashed into Bulawayo in the post-Second World War period sport provided cohesion and unity. This period was a time of extreme poverty, starvation, overcrowding and drought in the countryside. It was also a period of intense onslaughts, led by Bulawayo's Municipality, on African wages and rations. The attempt to take over the running of soccer – in all but name controlled by the soccer teams – was an attack on one of the principal havens for African men and women in the city. The victory Africans won represented an important step on the way to modern Zimbabwe.

Notes

1. Notable exceptions are Baker and Mangan (1987) and Bozzoli (1983).
2. This study is gender specific. I am looking at African men playing soccer. However, this is a study of how one cultural symbol – soccer – is used to construct identity in an urban African town. Other symbols have played a similar role in the making urban ethnic identity, some of which either involved or were mobilized by women. This study is, therefore, merely a metaphor for construction of urban identity in Bulawayo. The absence of the female image is not to imply that they played no part in this process.
3. The information in this section comes mainly from Couzens (1983).
4. Kapuscinski, in a vibrant portrayal of African popular culture, demonstrates how the urban bar played the role of a cultural symbol through which people in the former Belgian Congo were able to make sense of their changed circumstances as urban workers:

   A white informer will not go to a bar because a white person stands out. So you can talk about everything. The bar is always full of words. The bar deliberates, argues and pontificates. The bar will take up any subject, argue about, dwell on it to try to get at the truth. Everybody will come round and put in their two cents' worth. The subject does not matter. The important thing is to participate. An African bar, the Roman Forum, the main square. . . Robespierre's Parisian Wine Cellar. Reputations, adulatory or annihilating are born here. Here you are lifted onto a pedestal or tumbled with a crash to the pavement. If you delight the bar you will have a great career; if the bar laughs at you, you might as well go back to the jungle. In the fumes of foaming beer, in the pungent scent of the girls, in the incomprehensible rolling of the tom-toms, names, dates, opinions, judgements are exchanged. They weigh a problem, ponder it, bring forth the pros and cons. Somebody is gesticulating, a woman is nursing a baby, laughter explodes around someone's table. Gossip, fever, crowding. Here they are settling the price for a night together, there they are putting together a revolutionary programme, at the next table somebody is recommending a good witch-doctor, and further on somebody is saying that there is going to be a strike. A bar like this is everything you could want: a club a pawn shop, a board-walk and a church porch, a theatre and a school, a dive and a rally, a bordello and a party cell (Kapuscinski, 1990: 52–3).

Bibliography

Primary Sources

Ashton, E.H. (1957), 'African Administration in Bulawayo'. Historic Reference Collection Library of Bulawayo.
Bulawayo African Home News, 12 September 1953 Historic Reference Collection Library of Bulawayo
Bulawayo, Annual Report (1941); Minutes of the Mayor Of Bulawayo, S/BU 257. National Archive of Zimbabwe (NAZ)
Census of Population of Southern Rhodesia (1946), Report of the Census of Population of Southern Rhodesia held on the 7th May. Part VII, Natives in Employment, Table III. Historic Reference Collection Library of Bulawayo
Conditions of Africans Employed in Urban Areas (1944), Evidence by Councillor D. Macintyre to the Committee to Investigate the Economic, Social and Health Conditions of Africans Employed in Urban Areas. S1906, NAZ
Native Administration Committee, (1943), Minutes of Special Meeting of Native Administration Committee - Held in the Committee Room, Municipal Buildings, on Tuesday the 27th April. Council Archive, Bulawayo Municipal Building

Native Administration Committee (1949), Minutes of meeting of the Native Administration Committee: Held in the Committee Room, Municipal Buildings, on Wednesday the 9th March. Council Archive, Bulawayo Municipal Building

Native Welfare Society's Sports Committee (1942), Minutes, 26 October, RH16/1/2/1, NAZ

Ncube, M (1981), Interview with Sergeant Masotsha Ndlovu on 8th October, 1981. A.O.H./1, NAZ, Bulawayo Branch

Secondary Sources

Baker, W. J. and J. A. Mangan (eds.) (1987), *Sport in Africa: Essays in Social History*. New York: African Publishing Company

Bozzoli, Belinda (ed.) (1983), *Town and Countryside in the Transvaal.* Johannesburg: Raven Press

Bhebe, N. (1989), *B. Burombo: African Politics in Zimbabwe.* Harare: College Press

Clignet, Remi and Maureen Stark (1974), 'Modernisation and Football in Cameroon', *Journal of African Studies*, vol. 12, no. 3, pp. 409–421

Couzens, Tim (1983), 'An introduction to the History of Football in South Africa' in Bozzoli (1983), pp. 198–214

Kapuscinski, Ryszard (1990), *The Soccer War*. London: Granta

Mornington, Terence (1985), 'The Politics of Black African Sport' in Lincoln Allison (ed.), *The Politics of Sport*. Manchester: Manchester University Press

Nehwati, F. (1970), 'The Social and Communal Background to "Zhii". The African riots in Bulawayo, Southern Rhodesia in 1960.' *African Affairs*, vol. 69, no. 276, July.

Palmer, R. and N. Parsons (1983), *The Roots of Rural Poverty in Central Southern Africa*. London: Heinemann

Phimister, I. R. (1983), 'Zimbabwe: the path to capitalist development', in D. Birmingham and P. M. Martin (eds), *History of Central Africa*, vol. 2. London: Longman

Ranger, Terence O. (1987), '"Pugilism and Pathology": African Boxing and the Black Urban Experience in Southern Rhodesia' in Baker & Mangan (1987)

Stuart, Ossie (1989), *'Good Boys', Footballers and Strikers: African social change in Bulawayo, 1933-1953*. Unpublished doctoral thesis, School of Oriental and African Studies, London

Walvin, J. (1975), *'The People's Game': The Social History of British Football*. Newton Abbot: David and Charles

West, Michael Oliver (1990), *African Middle-class Formation in Colonial Zimbabwe, 1890–1965*. Unpublished doctoral thesis, Harvard University

10

Nationalism at Play: The Basques of Vizcaya and Athletic Club de Bilbao

Jeremy MacClancy

A culture is not a static entity but a continuing construction of its members. Even the marked sense of culture upheld by politicized ethnonationalists is not a rigid selection of past and present ways but an everchanging collection of beliefs and practices which evolve according to contemporary circumstances, their upholders' conception of those circumstances and their aims for the future. For instance, over the last hundred years those aspects of the Basque past and Basque culture lauded by members of the Basque Nationalist Party and its breakaway groups have altered greatly: present promoters of this nationalist ideology no longer praise the distinctiveness of Basque physiology and genetics but enthuse over the uniqueness of their language (the only non-Indo European tongue still spoken in Western Europe); pioneer nationalist ideologues denigrated all art while their modern successors have placed a usefully vague conception of 'Basque art' at the very centre of their economic strategy for the revitalization of their depressed region (MacClancy 1993a; n.d.) Today Herri Batasuna, the revolutionary socialist radical separatist Basque party associated with the terrorist organization ETA, simultaneously lauds certain splendid moments of Basque history *and* the development of distinctively Basque variants of modern Western culture, such as *el rock radical vasco* ('radical Basque rock and roll'). While *batasuneros* wish some of the glories of the past to reflect back on them, they do not want to be constrained by an obsessive fidelity to the past. They wish to create a culture broad and supple enough to include both bereted farmers and urban skinheads (MacClancy 1988, 1993b).

Urla makes a related point in her work on current Basque ethnonationalist culture: that many nationalists wish to be seen as both the heirs of a laudable history and also as 'up-to-date' as those of their contemporaries in other lands interested in both the renovation and the recuperation of their way of life. Peering backward does not mean that nationalists cannot also be as 'advanced' as some of their neighbours. They want their way of life to be seen not merely as different, but as simultaneously different and the same, as culturally distinct in certain time-honoured ways and as culturally common in others – modern others. Thus they are as much involved in the 'invention of modernity' as in the invention of tradition (Urla 1993).

In this essay I wish to illustrate this Janus-like character of Western ethnonationalism, its continual concern to create an ever-evolving, distinctive cultural mix of the antique and the contemporary, by discussing the remarkably close and evolving relations between one nationalistic community, the people of the Basque province of Vizcaya, and its most famous football team, Athletic de Bilbao.

Identity

It was the British who first brought the game to the Basqueland. In the early 1890s, in the environs of Bilbao, sailors whose ships imported coal to the United Kingdom and engineers working for local coal-mineowners and shipbuilders would occasionally play football wherever they could find a flat piece of free ground. To most residents of Bilbao these games were their first sight of football, though many had already read about it in the newspapers, or heard of it from those sons of the local bourgeoisie who had been educated in British Catholic public schools. Interest rapidly grew, and the first 'friendly' match between British and Basque teams was played on 3 May 1894. The expatriates won 6–0.[1]

As the popularity of the game continued to increase, locals and expatriates started to form their own joint clubs. Athletic Club Bilbao, formed in 1901, gained renown two years later by winning the first-ever Championship of Spain, held in Madrid. This was merely the very first of an illustrious record which the club has been able to maintain up to recent times: besides gaining a host of other trophies, it has won the national championship twenty-three times, has been top of the league eight times, has participated in all the main European championships, and has never been relegated to the second division – a distinction it shares with only two other clubs in the country, Barcelona and Real

Madrid. 62 of its footballers have played for Spain, one of them (the goalkeeper Jose Angel Iribar) holding the record for number of games (49) played in the national team. When Athletic won the league in both 1983 and 1984 it is estimated that, on each occasion, crowds of over one million came to greet the ceremonial arrival of the victors into the city. To put that figure into perspective, when in May 1994 Manchester United both came top of the league and won the F.A. Cup (and thus became only the fourth British club this century to do so), the crowd that greeted their ritual tour through their home-suburb failed to number more than several thousand.

Local support of the team, however, is based not just on its sporting achievements, deeply impressive though they may be, but on what it represents, for Athletic is seen as *the* team of the Vizcayans (the province whose capital is Bilbao), and, in national contests, as *the* team of the Basques. When trying to account for the degree of identification between the team and its supporters, one fact locals often emphasize is the financial basis of Athletic Club itself. For Athletic, unlike most Spanish teams, is not a limited company but a club jointly owned by its members (*socios*, present numbering some 32,000). Further income is raised not by allowing a wealthy person with spare cash to invest to take it over, but by increasing the annual subscription. Of course this policy severely limits the amount of money Athletic can raise in any one year. Members, however, would rather have it that way, and so feel in some sense that the club 'belongs' to a broad section of the community, than allow it to fall into the hands of a single person, who might have designs on his new possession.

Another characteristic of the club which dissociates it from almost all other Spanish clubs is its rule that only those born in the region can play in it. In the first years of Athletic a significant minority of its players were resident Englishmen: Alfred Mills, an engineer, was one of its thirty-three founders, and noteworthy players of its first decade include Langford, Dyer, Evans and Cockram. But by 1919 the team had become exclusively Basque, and in that year the Junta Directiva of the club decided that it would remain so as a matter of principle.

An important financial consequence of this rule is that Athletic, unlike most other clubs, does not spend a sizeable part of its income on purchasing stars from other teams. It may take on promising players from lesser local clubs, but the amount paid for these transfers is very much less than that paid by other major teams which buy in established players from its competitors. Thus Athletic has on the whole spent its money by investing it in the youth of its region: in the Bilbao suburb of Lezama the club has set up what has become a virtual academy of football, where teams of adolescents receive intensive training in the finer points of the game from ex-players. This policy of cultivating local talent rather than purchasing already proved players is known as '*la cantera*' ('the quarry'), and is one major reason why people of the area have been able to identify so easily with the club. For it means not only that many supporters at a home match know they are witnessing the efforts of their fellows, but that if local boys display ability they may dream of being seriously considered by the selectors.

The players, however, are no longer exclusively Basque. In the 1950s the rules were somewhat relaxed to allow those born in the Basqueland, whatever their parentage, to be considered for the club. Thus local-born sons of immigrants, like their Basque friends, could start to dream of making it to Athletic's first eleven. But even this relaxation of the rule could still lead to unfortunate occurrences. Manolo Sarabia, who went on to become a great player for the team in the 1970s, recalled what had happened in the mid-1960s to his brother, a promising forward who was twelve years older:

> They called him to come sign up, but on his filling in the form, they realized that he had not been born here, but in Torres, in the province of Jaen, where my family comes from. . .
>
> My brother returned home very upset, almost crying, because, of course, his dream, like that of all the lads round here, was to play in Athletic. I was just a kid then, but seeing him so unhappy, I went up to him and said, 'Don't worry, Lazarus: I'll play in Athletic, because I was born here, and they won't be able to say no to me.' For that reason, getting to play for Athletic was for me like a sacred commitment, something that I had to achieve, whatever it took (quoted in Unzueta 1986: 120).

In the 1970s the club relaxed its rule further, allowing those who had not been born in the Basque provinces but had been brought up there from an early age to be considered for Athletic. This broadening of the club's pool of potential players coincided with the extended definition of Basqueness that radical nationalists had started to propound at that time; to these activists 'a Basque' was not someone who fulfilled the conventional ethnic criteria, but someone who lived and sold their labour in the Basque Country. As one member of Athletic's management put it to me, '*Lo importante no es donde se nace sino donde se pace*' ('What is important is not where one is born but where one grazes.') He admitted that the club's definition of 'the Basque Country' would include the three historic Basque provinces of southwestern France; it was merely that 'we have not yet gone there to look for players'.

In the first decades of the club all its players were amateurs, albeit dedicated ones, who only received payment for the expenses they incurred in away matches. In the words of Jose Maria Erice, who played for the team from 1917 to 1926, 'We were like true brothers. The same with the directors. Our way of doing things was based purely on love, on playing and sacrificing oneself for the colours of the city and the team' (quoted in Athletic Club 1986, vol. 1: 27). In the mid- to late 1920s, however, Athletic imitated the recent example of other teams by progressively placing its players on a professional footing. Supporters of Athletic took pride in the fact that members of its first team received relatively little. Even that minimal income, however, could be very important in times of general hardship. Panizo, a great player of that period, remembers:

I don't know if today this will be well understood but in the 1940s, after the war, with the misery that there was and everything else, for us, to play in Athletic, to play in international games, to be able to bring up a family, that you were paid for doing something that you liked doing over and above everything else, was like a blessing from heaven (quoted in Unzueta 1982).

Generally, members of the team were not meant to be playing primarily for the money, but for the pride that came in representing the premier Basque side, and representing it well. This supposed and proclaimed relative lack of pecuniary interest in playing for Athletic was a further reason for supporters' ability to identify with the players. For, as relatively lowly-paid 'workers', they could be seen by many of their followers as, in some sense, their equals, if there was not much money to be earned by kicking a ball around for the first half of their lives. They could be regarded, not as avaricious individuals whose only end was to exploit their talent in order to accumulate capital, but as ordinary Basques making the most of their particular physical gifts for the pleasure it gave them and the renown it might win them and their community.

Of course, as the fame of Athletic grew, the indirect financial advantages of playing for the club became more and more apparent. Becoming a highly respected figure in the local community brought benefits, as Venancio, a member of the first eleven in the late 1940s and early '50s, admitted:

For me, Athletic solved my life. In my business dealings, it opened lots and lots of important doors. I was Venancio, he of Athletic, and people received me in a different way. What I could dream of once I had joined Athletic! It was like a miracle (quoted in Athletic Club 1986, vol.2: 187).

Within a few years of the club establishing its commanding presence in Spanish football, players for the team began to displace famous bullfighters as popular idols. Unlike these trained killers, however, who were often associated in the popular imagination with sexual excess, the players of Athletic were represented as 'eleven villagers', as men who, off the pitch, were as sober as their fellow Basques, and as religious as them. Whenever Athletic comes top of the league or wins a trophy, the team and the club's directors attend a special mass given by the Bishop of Bilbao at the church of San Anton, where their victory is offered up to the Virgin of Begoña, the patron saint of the city (Terrachet 1969: 6). Until the 1970s the team would also spend a week at the end of the season cloistered in the Jesuit university of Bilbao, performing spiritual exercises. Senior priests in the local hierarchy are keen to laud the players as symbols of fraternity and honesty, and as role-models for the male youth of the region; even Pope Pius XII, who granted the players a special audience in 1956, called them 'a model team from the moral and religious point of view' (Terrachet 1970: 145; Uriarte 1986).

During the years of Franco's regime the club's twin policies of the *cantera* and of not allowing its players to become rich, together with its string of successes, won Athletic great popularity throughout the country. In provinces as distant from Bilbao as Granada and Murcia, non-Basque fans of Athletic spontaneously set up their own supporters' clubs (*peñas*), where they assiduously followed the fortunes of the team, known as one of 'eleven villagers', and debated the finer points of their game. Panizo remembers them well:

There were *peñas* everywhere, in even the most unexpected villages. They would come to see us in our hotel, would chat with us, identify themselves with us, because they saw that we were ordinary people, that we did not think ourselves different, that we had not gone there to act like great persons. How were we going to go there and act like great persons if everyone already knew that, if it weren't for football, we'd be wearing overalls in a factory or digging up potatoes in the fields! (quoted in Unzueta 1982).

Basque followers of Athletic, as several pointed out to me, also take pride in the fact that support for the team, unlike that for most British clubs, cuts across conventional class divides. It is true that in its first years Athletic was primarily a team of *señoritos* ('young gentlemen', or in its more pejorative sense 'young upper-class parasites'). Many early players did come from the ranks of the bourgeoisie: indeed, the centre-forward who led the team to victory in the inaugural national championship was a marquis, while Jose Antonio de Aguirre, a lawyer from a well-to-do background who in 1936 became the first President of the Basque Government, played centre-half for Athletic throughout the 1920s. (It is most probably the example of his career which led to the adage that in order to get to be anyone in Basque politics one had to have studied at the local jesuit university or to have been a footballer (Unzueta 1983)). But as the game became generally more popular and as footballing became a full-time profession, the proportion of young men from affluent families in the team decreased while the following of the successful club extended further and further across the social spectrum. One sign of the continuing cross-class nature of Athletic membership is that its president is usually a member of the established local bourgeoisie rather than a self-made businessman. In Britain football might be regarded as primarily the reserve of the urban proletariat, but in the Basqueland it is lauded as a common interest for members of all social classes. Another indicator of the breadth of the team's following is the fact that an informal talk, given in April 1994 at the Bilbao campus of the Universidad del Pais Vasco by Jose Clemente, a famous but controversial trainer of its first eleven in the early 1980s, attracted a far larger audience of students than would a discussion held there led by a world-famous academic. Also, some senior ecclesiastics, such as Monsignor Enrique Tarancon and Juan Arrupe, respectively Primate of Spain and General of the Company of Jesus in the 1960s, were and are quite open about their support for the club (Terrachet 1970: 146–7).

One journalist characterized the variegated social nature of the club's support by saying 'Intellectuals, film directors, rockers: all can be supporters, there's no incompatibility' (Cerrato 1986: 216). Another tried to put across the same point in an even more striking manner:

Perhaps it would be better to say that here (in the stadium) concur a crucible of diverse and differentiated attitudes, feelings, and thoughts. Here coincide a comedian, a theologist of liberation, a cobbler, a musician, a shopkeeper, a quick-change artist and a woman of loose morals who vibrates with the goals of Athletic more than with her next client (Rodrigalvarez 1986).

One consequence of the close identification between the team and its supporters is the statement by numerous fans that they, the loyal football-going public, contribute in an important manner to the success of Athletic. As one historian of the club put it, if the first eleven are the shocktroops, its followers are 'the faithful infantry', 'the back-up brigade' (Athletic Club 1986, vol.3: 3). One fan has confessed the ideas he and his kind have about their role:

> In our innermost being lies the belief that Athletic wins its matches because we urge them on. . . We have stimulated and urged the team on, and they have won; therefore we ourselves have won, and for that reason we are a part of Athletic (Merino 1986).

One fan, Gabriel Ortiz, became locally famous in the 1950s and 1960s for his ability to time his very loud cries of 'Atleeeeetic!' so well that he could stimulate thousands into shouting the customary response, 'Eup!' (Unzueta 1983b). Felix Marcaida, a great player of the 1950s, has admitted the powerful influence of the club's following: 'When San Mames (the Athletic stadium) urged us on, we flew. But when the public screamed at me, everything would go wrong for me. The public is of great importance for a player' (Athletic Club 1986, vol. 3: 126).

Perhaps local sports journalists should be regarded as part of Athletic's public as well, for several commentators (Alonso 1986; Bacigalupe 1986; Frade 1986: 35–7) have referred to the traditionally close alliance between the team and the Basque press, to the affectionate and relaxed relations between players and regional reporters. All the main Bilbao newspapers maintain one journalist who specializes in Athletic. Every day each of them devotes one or two pages to the activities of the club, and on the days following matches, three pages. As one of these journalists complained to me, it is permissible for him and his colleagues to criticize particular players, or the way the whole team is playing, but it would be 'very difficult' for them to make fundamental criticisms about the nature of the club and its support, for that would be seen as tantamount to criticizing Basque society itself.

One effect of all the different factors which facilitate a sense of identity between the players and their fans is that Athletic has frequently been called *una gran familia rojiblanca* ('a great red and white family', after the team's colours). This metaphorical manner of portraying an ethnically-bounded football-loving collection of people in terms of generic kinship has potential meaning because the links between the directors, the players, and their public are meant to be as close, as affectionate and lacking in instrumentality as those between members of a family. Athletic has, perhaps even more frequently, been described as 'something more than a club', though just what that 'something more' might be is often left unstated. One local journalist (Estevez 1986) called it 'a feeling', another (Roca 1986) referred to 'those who carry Athletic inside themselves', while one historian of the club has described it as 'something very intimate, very much its own' (Terrachet 1969: 147). Perhaps the most articulate on this topic has been the local-born novelist Luis de Castresana, who was a child-exile during the war,

> Athletic is for me something more a football team; it is part of the emotional landscape of my Bilbao, my Vizcaya. . .
>
> I suppose that, at root, we Vizcayans love Athletic because we intuit that it has something which belongs to us, because we intuit that within it is a piece of ourselves.
>
> I remember how much we, Basque children evacuated overseas during the war, were animated, shored up, and unified by having a red and white T-shirt and by calling our team 'Athletic de Bilbao'. I believe that what we did then in Brussels was to discover for ourselves, from the nostalgia of a long absence, one of the characteristics which best and most deeply defines the Bilbao team: that is, its identity as an umbilical cord linking men to the land, its geographico-emotional capacity
>
> Athletic is like the river, the *ochotes*, the blast furnaces, the *sirimiri* (a local wind) or the Arenal (a small park in the centre of Bilbao): something which, in a way, is already consubstantial with our urban psychology (Castresana 1968).[2]

Just how strong and warm the links between the club and the community it represents can be was demonstrated by the reception given to the league champions when they returned ceremonially to Bilbao in May 1984. In the words, once again, of Castresana,

> Bilbao yesterday was something more than a mass frenzy and something more than a fiesta. It was an experience. It was the communion of a people with its team and, at root, the communion of a people with itself. . . Athletic is ourselves (*El Correo Español*, 7 May 1984).

Durkheim could not have put it better.

Style

On 1 September 1920 Spain played against Sweden in the semi-final of the Olympic Games. By the end of the first half Sweden was leading 1–0. Then, halfway through the second half, the Spaniards were awarded a free kick. As the Athletic player Sabino Bilbao ran to take the kick, his fellow Athletic player Belauste rushed up the pitch shouting, 'Sabino, kick the ball to me, I'll overwhelm them!' He caught the ball and, running towards the opposition goal chased by three Swedes, kicked it into the net. Shortly afterwards the outside-left scored another goal, the last of the match. In the legendary history of Spanish football this incident is crucial, for it marks the birth of '*la furia española*' (Unzueta 1983a). And, as every knowledgeable Athletic supporter knows, since the majority of the national team played for the club, *la furia española* was in reality *la furia vasca*, the characteristic style of Athletic.

The most lauded components of this simple, effective but distinctive style were fieriness and long passes. It was unpretentious, direct, and aggressive, with a profusion of centres at the same level as the centre-forward (Shaw 1987: 21). It was a very quick, strong, hard, physical style, one of vigorous players who, it was proclaimed, would not give up but would relentlessly pursue the ball until the final whistle (Delgado 1986). Their momentum was such that they were expected to overwhelm or crush their opponents, and they often did so. Players were seen as so courageous and furious, ready to give their all for the 90 minutes of a game, that they were called 'lions', and were meant to be as admired and as feared as the big cats. 'It is said that Athletic fattened itself on rivals who kneeled before them', and that unfortunate opponent teams were 'thrashed, pounded down, and squashed by the weight of the goals won against them' (Belarmo 1986). This fury, however, was expected to be a measured, calculated one; footballers who played like 'blind hurricanes' might have impressed some spectators but would have ended up losing their team matches (Escartin 1986).

This style of strength, speed and total commitment was regarded as very Basque, since it exemplified the customarily prized attributes of male force and determination. As Sabino Arana (1910), pioneer ideologue of Basque nationalism and founder-president of the Basque National Party (PNV), wrote in an article on the game, 'The Basque race is, through the conviction of its positive physical superiority, one of the most saturated with that healthy spirit of battle, of competition, summed up by Saxons in the word "struggle"'. Similarily, the professional football of other regions was said to represent their respective local ways of life:

that of Catalonia was thought to be 'colder' and 'more technical', that of Andalusia 'more reckless and pyrotechnical' (Mandiola 1969).

At the same time as being regarded as Basque, however, Athletic's playing style was also seen – as Arana's comment suggests – as very English (Mingolarra 1990). According to supporters, it was partly thanks to the British and Anglophiles who had introduced the game, and to the series of British trainers hired by Athletic, that the club had come to adopt and perfect this particular form of play. The best-remembered of these imported instructors was Pentland, a former inside-left for Blackburn Rovers and English international, who was employed by the club for several seasons during the 1920s and early 1930s. It is said that he used constantly to repeat his maxim 'The most difficult game is that of the Sunday coming'. This association of the club with the homeland of the game was seen not as detracting from its 'Basqueness' but as a source of additional prestige, since the most successful British teams were still then regarded as among the very best in the world.

Politics

As a representative and integral part of modern Basqueland, Athletic has frequently reflected the contemporary political concerns of many Basques. During the Republic it clearly supported the popular campaign for Basque autonomy (Shaw 1987: 21). At the beginning of the Civil War in 1936 most of its players tried to enlist in Basque militias, but many were soon required to join a freshly-created Basque 'national' team which toured internationally, with great success, for propaganda and fund-raising purposes. After the tour, which included games in France, Czechoslovakia, Poland, the USSR and Mexico, all but two players decided to remain abroad rather than return to their defeated homeland, where they risked imprisonment.

The ideologues of the new totalitarian order imposed on the country lauded sport as a moral activity which expressed and reinforced the 'two magnificent virtues' of patriotism and discipline. Even spectatorship had its ethical worth and propaganda value, for it was thought that a sporting spectacle could win over the thousands of stimulated young spectators. But first, the teams had to present themselves in the appropriate manner, and the games take place within the appropriate frame. Thus, in an effort to 'Castillianize' Basque football, perpetrators of the regime forced the club to change its name to 'Atlético de Bilbao', and regional championships, seen as 'no more than an egoistical desire to cultivate an autonomy through sporting separatism', were prohibited.[3]

This Franquist policy did not always work as its proponents had intended. For though the Junta Directiva of Atlético was mainly composed of place-men prepared to play their new masters' game, any success enjoyed by the team was generally regarded by locals as reflecting well not on the present regime but on the Basques themselves: 'That Athletic, of the years of rationing and the black market, was the "other food" of the people of Bilbao. And an *"irrintzi"* (Basque, 'cry, shout') by the Basque people, thrown to the four winds' (Athletic Club 1986, vol.2: 200). Since almost all forms of potentially nationalistic activity were banned, football, which Franco personally liked, became one of the very few legal ways by which Basques could demonstrate who they were and what they were made of (Shaw 1987: 183). And since Franco allowed football to become by far the most popular of all sports played in the country, the achievements of Atlético during this period had that much greater resonance. The team effectively dominated Spanish football during the 1940s, coming top of the league in the 1942–3 season and winning the national championship in the three consecutive years 1943–1945. Victories against Real Madrid, which was seen as particularly Franquist (Franco saw the triumphs of the team as somehow his own (Preston 1993: 700)), were much appreciated by Atlético's fans, especially if the dictator himself had come to watch the game. Supporters of the team also cherished their memory of the Atlético captain, Agustin Gainza, who, in 1958, on receiving the national championship trophy from the hands of Franco at the end of the match, still had the presence of mind to say, 'See you next year.'

In the last years of the regime, as a politically organized nationalism re-arose and its armed movement, ETA, came to be regarded as part of the vanguard of the anti-Franquist opposition, the publicity given by sports journalists to matches played at Atlético's home ground was considered too good an opportunity not to be exploited by politicos in the crowd and on the pitch. From the late 1960s onwards spectators on the stands would ostentatiously wave large *ikurriñas*, the then-banned Basque flag, knowing full well that, by the time policemen had managed to fight their way through the crowd, the banner would long have disappeared (Cerrato 1986). On 8 August 1977 the recently-elected president of the club solemnly raised the *ikurriña*, to the massed cheers of the crowd, before the beginning of the game; Basque dances were then performed to the sound of traditional Basque instruments, and the players ran on to the pitch down a 'tunnel of honour' formed by dancers and spinners in regional costume. The president later stated that raising the banner, though technically illegal, was 'almost a popular petition' (Athletic Club 1986, vol. 5: 47). During the transition to democracy, Athletic (as it quickly renamed itself) openly defended the campaigns for Basque autonomy and an amnesty of political prisoners; many players also began to learn *euskera*, the Basque language whose public use had been prohibited by the regime (Shaw 1987: 192, 226, 231).

During this period, the single most prominent and active nationalist in the team was its goalkeeper, Iribar. When, on 27 September 1975, two members of ETA and three members of FRAP (an armed revolutionary organization) were executed, Iribar persuaded his fellow members of the team to wear black armbands during the next game. Iribar tried to protect himself and his team-mates by saying that their gesture was to commemorate the first anniversary of the death of Luis Albert, an ex-player and director of the club. During the same season Iribar, though invited, chose not to play for the Spanish team for what would have been his fiftieth time. It was widely rumoured that he had declined the invitation because the political wing of the Basque gunmen had told him not to do so. Consequently, when he kept goal for his team in away matches in Madrid and Andalusia, he was greeted not with the cheers he usually received, but with loud boos. In December the following year just before a match (a cup final played at Atocha, the main stadium of Madrid) with Real Sociedad de San Sebastian, the second most prominent Basque team, he persuaded the rival captain to agree that both sides would run on together carrying the still-banned *ikurriña*; one Madrid paper headlined its article on the incident, 'Separatist orgy at Atocha' (Athletic Club 1986, vol. 5: 28). In May 1977, at the final of the European Cup, against Juventus of Turin, Iribar, who headed the home team, came onto the pitch carrying an *ikurriña* while thousands in the crowd also waved the flag, shouting rhythmically 'Presoak kalera!' (Basque, 'Prisoners to the street', i.e. 'Let them go') (Shaw ibid: 193, 232–3). When in 1980 Athletic held a game in homage to their retiring goalie, he gave the share of the gate such an outgoing player usually receives towards the production costs of a technical dictionary in *euskera*, although his own private business (a potato storage company) was not going well at the time (Unzueta 1986; Del Valle 1988: 117, n. 2).

Although most Athletic supporters see the team in nationalist terms, and although all its players are thought to be nationalist unless they show otherwise, many fans do not wish the club to be exclusively associated with one particular political party. Since the death of Franco, the Basque Nationalist Party (PNV) has tried to control its presidency, which is regarded as an important position in Bilbao society. Indeed, the first post-Franquist incumbent, Beti Dunabeitia, went on to become the successful PNV candidate for the mayorship of the city. But in the 1990 elections to replace his successor, who had also been a member of PNV, most members of the club voted in a candidate supported by an alternative nationalist party because (as it was said at the time) they did not want a single political group controlling Athletic.

Herri Batasuna, the political wing of the gunmen, has at times tried to control the direction of Athletic, but has insufficient supporters at the managerial and directorial levels of the club. Instead, it has sought to exploit the team's popularity for its own political ends by getting players sympathetic to the cause, such as Iribar, to speak for it on the hustings. These political divisions within the membership of the club are expressed territorially in its stadium: supporters of PNV tend to stand at either end while *batasuneros* congregate along the two main sides down by the wire fence, where they shout slogans and hoist banners for whatever happens to be the radical nationalist issue of the moment. One advantage of this position is that TV cameras stationed on the sides cannot but help include sight of the banners within the image they capture.

While these different parties have tussled for dominance within the club, none has won a permanently commanding position; and this, it appears, is the way most members want it to be. For Athletic, like the Virgin of Begoña, the patron saint of Vizcaya, is meant to be above factional politics. It is supposed to represent all Vizcayans, and at times all Basques, not just a fraction of them. As one member of the club's management put it to me, the club is meant to fulfill the same unifying function in Vizcaya as the monarchy is meant to do in England.

Present Policies

The two consecutive seasons from 1982 to 1984, when Athletic twice came top of the league and once won the national championship, can now be seen as the latest high point in the club's history. Since then it has entered a prolonged period of crisis, from which it has yet to emerge. It now tends to come towards the bottom rather than the top of the first division, and has changed its top trainer more than eleven times in the last decade.

The fundamental reason for this reversal in its fortunes is money. Some other clubs in the Spanish league, especially 'super-clubs' such as Barcelona, now have so much money invested in them that they are able both to buy for large amounts, outstanding players from other teams in

Spain and abroad, and also to pay their own teams large salaries. This effect of the rising standard of rival teams was compounded by the transfer of Athletic players to non-Basque clubs. Such a move would have been almost unthinkable during the years of Franquism, since Athletic players were supposedly committed to their club. But the offers made to them became, in their minds, too good to refuse. In the early 1980s members of the team were among the worst-paid footballers in all the First Division, earning only about a quarter as much as their opposite numbers in other clubs. There are now over fifty Basque players in non-Basque teams, six of them in the Barcelona squad alone.

To stem this loss of talent, the directors of Athletic decided to end the long-established tradition of 'good neighbourliness' (*buena vecindad*) with the fellow Basque teams of Real Sociedad de San Sebastian, based in that town, and Osasuna, based in Pamplona, by poaching footballers from them. When players from Athletic saw how much was being paid for these imports, they began to ask for higher salaries. The club's directors, by agreeing to these demands, ended Athletic's even longer-established tradition of an 'economy of austerity'. The combined effect of these financially-grounded changes is that the statement 'Athletic is something more than a club' is somewhat less true than it was until relatively recently, and its supporters know it. In a telephone survey of 1,000 *socios* carried out in February 1992 for the newspaper *El Mundo*, the most commonly cited cause of the club's crisis (29 percent of the sample) was that its present players did not give their all: 65 percent of them said they were too mild, their game was no longer one of force or strength, they lacked the desire to struggle, they had become a bunch of *señoritos*. As one put it to me, because the members of the first team now played for money as much as for love, they were not prepared to 'die on the field' and so were letting down their club's glorious traditions.

Yet the majority of Athletic's *socios* are not prepared to see the club's cherished traditions change any more, even if that means that their beloved team becomes unable to repeat its former string of victories. In a subsequent survey of 394 *socios* carried out in September 1992 (*Egin* 21 September 1992), 53 percent said that they were against the transformation of Athletic into a limited company (22 percent of the sample said they did not know), while an overwhelming majority (83 percent) said they were opposed, or very opposed, to the club's buying players from abroad: they did not want a 'foreign legion' in their front line. *Socios* are well aware of the possible consequences of these attitudes: in the *El Mundo* survey 76 percent of them said that they would rather see Athletic relegated to the Second Division than allow the club to give up the tradition of the *cantera*. 33 percent of the sample accepted the present swings of the team betweens highs and lows as practically inevitable, given the policy of the *cantera*, which means that only once in every so many years does the club produce a squad capable of winning titles. Jose Clemente, then re-appointed as its trainer, was clear on this point when asked about it in an interview:

> There is no doubt that, above all in the league, we start out in a position of inferiority, but that way things have more valour. The championship is perhaps more feasible. Nowadays, moreover, Basque football has also to cope with the consequences of the Common Market norm of the free circulation of European players. But I believe that Athletic will continue with its football of the *cantera* unless the *socios* say otherwise. For me, particularly, I would not like to see foreigners entering (quoted in Ortuzar and Rodrigalvarez 1987).

The idea of a *cantera* might be very attractive and highly important to most *socios*, but it demands a high price, for Athletic spends about 200 million pesetas a year on cultivating local talent, although this policy only produces on average one or two players a year for the first team. Thus although buying already proved players from poorer countries, such as Croatia or Serbia, would be much cheaper than maintaining the *cantera*, the traditional policy is kept up because that is what the *socios* want. In 1991 the directors of Real Sociedad de San Sebastian, wishing to improve its performance by hiring foreigners, only managed to abolish its own exclusive policy of the *cantera* by claiming that it had commissioned a mass survey showing that most *socios* would not mind.

The only concession to changing circumstances that a majority of the Athletic *socios* (78 percent of the *Egin* sample) were prepared to contemplate was the introduction of publicity on players' shirts. Yet even here, the change will not be as great as it has been for other teams, as most *socios* insist that if the colours of their team's shirt have to be 'stained' by commercialism, the company to be granted this privilege must be a Basque one.

***

When the British first brought football to Bilbao, the game was seen as something very strange and very new. Playing on a muddy pitch in the rain in daring short trousers which exposed the knees almost scandalized those Catholic *bilbainos* brought up on *pelota*, the Basque ball game played against a hard two-sided court. To them the novel British practice was 'a kind of madness', 'a form of audacity' (Mugica 1982: 11–2), a sporting challenge to which they slowly rose.

By adopting this fashionable import from a prestigious country and developing their own style of playing it, the *bilbainos* were being both very Basque and very modern. Some might single out the Basques as one of the 'most ancient peoples' of Europe, but on this interpretation they were also among the most open to the up-to-date.

Though Athletic's play was originally seen as something very modern, it has since gone on to become one of the most popularly rooted traditions of the Basque Country. It is possible to go a little further, for one might say it has become a 'traditional' part of Basque modernity, a customary component of its twentieth-century nationalism.

Notes

1. Much of this historical section relies on Mugica 1982 and Athletic Club Bilbao 1986.
2. In his novel *El orto árbol de Guernica*, which in 1967 was awarded the Primero Nacional de Literatura, Castresana describes the moment when a football team of Basque children exiled in Brussels share the one Athletic T-shirt they own and so come to feel identified with 'the best team which symbolized and incarnated the whole province' (1966, ch. 12).
3. Information about Falangist attitudes to sport, and the quotations from their writings, come from London 1995.

Bibliography

Alonso, Patxi (1986), 'Un tiempo muy especial', in Athletic Club 1986, vol. 3, pp. 176–177

Arana, Sabino (1910), 'Campeonato de Foot-ball', *Bizkaitarra*, 26 March

Athletic Club Bilbao (1986), *Historia del Athletic Club Bilbao*. 6 vols. Bilbao: Athletic Club

Bacigalupe, Antonio (1986), 'De la critica constructiva', in Athletic Club 1986, vol. 1, pp. 136–137

Belarmo, E. (1986), 'Al Athletic de le quiere por lo que es', in Athletic Club 1986, vol. 1, pp. 156–157

Castresana, Luis de (1966), *El otro árbol de Guernica*, Madrid

— (1968), 'Aliron', *Elogios, asperezas y nostalgias del País Vasco*, Bilbao

Cerrato, J. (1986), 'Historia en paginas de oro', in Athletic Club Bilbao 1986, vol. 2, pp. 216–217

Delgado, Manolo (1986), 'Cuando los sueños se hacen realidad', in Athletic Club 1986, vol. 3, pp. 206–7

Del Valle, Teresa (1988), *Korrika. Rituales de la lengua en el espacio*. Barcelona: Anthropos

Escartin, P. (1986), 'Athletic de Bilbao, Un estilo de juego y una linea de conducta', in Athletic Club 1986, vol. 2, pp. 156–157

Estevez, A. (1986), 'El Athletic, un sentimiento', in Athletic Club 1986, vol. 2, pp. 116–117

Frade, K-tono (1986), *La salsa de San Mames*. Colección 'temas vizcainos', No. 162. Bilbao: Caja de Ahorros Vizcaina

London, John (1995), 'Competing Together in Fascist Europe: Sport in Early Francoism', in Gunter Berghaus (ed.), *Fascist Theatre. Comparative Studies on the Politics and Aesthetics of Performance*. Oxford: Berg

MacClancy, Jeremy (1988), 'The Culture of Radical Basque Nationalism', *Anthropology Today*, October, pp. 34–38

— (1993a), 'Biological Basques, Sociologically Speaking', in Malcolm K. Chapman (ed.), *Social and Biological Aspects of Ethnicity*. Oxford: Oxford University Press, pp. 92–129

— (1993b), 'At play with identity in the Basque arena', in Sharon Macdonald (ed.), *Inside European Identities. Ethnography in Western Europe*. Oxford: Berg, pp. 84–97

— (n.d.), 'The politics and pluralities of "Basque art"', in Jeremy MacClancy (ed.), *Art and Contested Identities*. (Forthcoming)

Mandiola, Ramon (1969), 'Prólogo a la segunda edición', in Terrachet 1969, pp. 7–8

Merino, Juan Luis (1986), 'Pasado y presente de una hincha rojiblanca', in Athletic Club 1986, vol. 3, pp. 116–7

Mingolarra, Jose Antonio (1990), 'Deporte e identidad cultural: el caso vasco'. Paper given in May 1990 at 'Le foot ball et l'Europe', conference, European University Institute, Florence.

Mugica, Jose Maria (1982), 'El Athletic: un club de leyenda', in La Caja de Ahorros de Bilbao (ed.) *Un siglo de fútbol, pelota y remo en Vizcaya*. Bilbao: La Caja de Ahorros de Bilbao

Ortuzar, E. and E. Rodrigalvarez (1987), 'Será dificil que el fútbol vasco vuelva tan arriba', *Deia. X aniversario 1977/1987*. 7 June

Preston, Paul (1993), *Franco: A Biography*. London: Fontana

Roca, A. (1986), 'Carismatico Athletic', in Athletic Club 1986, vol. 2, pp. 196–197

Rodrigalvarez, E. (1986), 'Carta rojiblanca a la Cibeles', in Athletic Club, vol. 3, pp. 96–97

Shaw, Duncan (1987), *Futbol y Franquismo*. Madrid: Alianza

Terrachet, Enrique (1969), *Historia del Athletic de Bilbao. 'Caso único en el*

fútbol mundial'. Bilbao: La Gran Enciclopedia Vasca
— (1970), *Historia del Athletic de Bilbao. 'Caso único en el fútbol mundial'*. Edición Popular. Bilbao: La Gran Enciclopedia Vasca
Unzueta, Patxo (1982), 'Panizo', *El País*, 12 June
— (1983a), 'A mi el peloton', *El País*, 24 January
— (1983b), 'Rompecascos', *El País*, 4 May
— (1986), *A mi el peloton*. San Sebastian: Baroja
Uriarte, Juan Maria (1986) 'Un equipo para un pueblo', in Athletic Club 1986, vol. 5, pp. 196–197
Urla, Jacqueline (1993) 'Contesting modernities. Language standardization and the production of an ancient/modern Basque culture', *Critique of Anthropology*, vol. 13, pp. 101–118

Acknowledgements

I am grateful to the Dirección General de Deportes of the Ministerio de Cultura for funding a research visit to Vizcaya. I am also grateful to Joseba Aguirreazkuenaga, Ruiz Olabuenaga, Oscar Alonso, Patxo Unzueta and Borja Bilbao for help while I was researching this topic. All translations are my own.

Index